APPROACHING THE KINGDOM

AN ANTHOLOGY

APPROACHING THE KINGDOM

AN ANTHOLOGY

JAMES THOMAS ANGELIDIS

Approaching the Kingdom:
An Anthology

James Thomas Angelidis

www.jtangelidis.com

Copyright © 2017 by James Thomas Angelidis.

All rights reserved.

Reprinted with no revisions to literature (except on pages 11 and 12). Included with this reprint, at the end, is the chapter "Evaluations."
Reprinted 2024.

Cover Design:
Layout by James Thomas Angelidis.

Cover Image:
Inside Saint Gerasimos Church in Kefalonia, Greece.
Photograph by Rosalyn Angelidis Shehati.

Author Image:
(On back cover) Photograph by Eddie Manso.

"every scribe who has been trained for the kingdom of heaven is like a householder who brings out of his treasure what is new and what is old."

- Jesus Christ (Matthew 13:52, RSV)

CONTENTS

PREFACE
... 11
THE AUTHOR
- Bio... 19
- About... 21

FROM WWW.JTANGELIDIS.COM BLOG
- My Website... 25
- My Children's Book... 25
- My Second Book... 25
- A Decade in the Making... ... 26
- On Education... 26
- Local Public Library... 29
- Over 50 Images... 30
- The Rock... 30
- Book Club Selection!... 30
- Bob Marley and God... 31
- My New Web Page: Letters... 32
- Quote (5) ... 32

BOOKS
- *And the Lamb Spoke: Lessons from the Gospels*... 35
- *Young Ezekiel: A Life of Loves*... 87
- *Writings*... 233
    - A Theological Memoir... 239
    - Dante's *Divine Comedy*... 271
    - Hierarchy of Truths... 313

- *In the Name of Salvation: Three Theological Treatises*... 343
    - The Supreme Transformation - Water into Wine... 349
    - Agape into Eternity... 383
    - The Messiah Jesus... 423

LETTERS
- God's Supreme Love... 475
- God's Mother - The Theotokos... 477
- O, Saint Augustine... 479
- The Act of Creating... 481
- For Little Leiby... 483
- The Child's Soul... 485

DRAWINGS
- Budding... 491
- A Maddening Birth... 493
- In the Eye of the Storm... 495
- Anno Domini... 497
- The Good Shepherd King... 499

PHOTOGRAPHS
- Author Photo... 503
- First Book Signing... 505

EVALUATIONS
- *In the Name of Salvation* - "In the Spirit of Truth: Identifying My Three Theological Treatises in Church Tradition" ... 509
- *In the Name of Salvation* - Works Cited... 515
- Drawing - *Anno Domini*... 519
- Drawing - *The Good Shepherd King*... 525
- Detail from *The Good Shepherd King*... 531

PREFACE

If there is any one James Thomas Angelidis book to buy for yourself, this is it. In *Approaching the Kingdom: An Anthology*, the reader will find all my works in one place. This [---] volume is the result of a 15 year journey. This process began after college when I was 22 with my search for truth in the so called "real world." And, it includes my more recent letters and drawings. It is a comprehensive representation of my written efforts to save souls.

With this anthology, I have tried to make my books and other works as accessible as possible. It illustrates my vision and presents the way and order my books are meant to be read. My books are in target audience age order - the way I foresee my youngest fans growing up with my work. My plan has always been to raise generations of children, so they can ultimately become adults who are one with God, to save their souls, so they can attain eternal life. And, once they are saved, they can then also save others. This is my way of training young warriors for God.

This volume is also particularly valuable for those adults who do not want to buy my children's book, which is not just for children and is a work they will prize for themselves. Though I drew the illustrations for children, the lessons are for all ages, including adults.

The editing process truly never ends and it can easily drive one mad. There is always room for improvement. As an artist, I long for the perfection of my creation; however, I also know, as an artist, perfection does not exist. An artist must be honest and honesty always translates into truth. There comes a time when an artist has done his best and must leave the interpretive conclusion in the hands of God. It then becomes a part of God's master plan and I - as an artist, writer and theologian - will be seen for what I am in the test of time. Imperfection is human and there is no way of escaping it.

One issue I struggled with was in *Young Ezekiel* in the story of the "plum battle." This is an authentic personal memory that took place in my life with my friends. In the book, Ezekiel, Mike and Gabe are accompanied by their friend Alex. One of my dearest childhood friends was Alex Taranto. He died young - at the age of 18 - from a heart attack due to an undiagnosed enlarged heart. He was a part of the real plum battle at our friend's house and my first instinct in recreating this event in written form was to include and honor him, so I did. The struggle was that I would have liked to have named that fourth person Raph. This way, in naming Ezekiel's closest friends, I would have [named] the archangels - Michael (Mike), Gabriel (Gabe) and Raphael (Raph). I needed to pay tribute to my friend and in doing so, I like to imagine that he is with God in the company of the archangels at this moment. Alex Taranto - may his memory be eternal.

Another issue I struggled with was in *And the Lamb Spoke*. I got the idea for the book's agenda to teach and its structure from Khalil Gibran's *The Prophet*. I initially quoted Gibran in the earlier draft of my book. Near the end of the draft, the Lamb says to Basil, just before they part ways, "I must go. But, if our hands should meet in another dream we shall build a tower in the sky that will lead us to the heart of God," which is a reference to Gibran's prophet's final words to the crowd. However, my editor thought it might not be a proper place for it and that it might be distracting for the children. I agreed with her and took it out to keep it simple for my target audience, 7-9 year olds. At least, now, in this anthology's preface, I can pay tribute to Gibran's *The Prophet*, which was a major influence for *And the Lamb Spoke*.

In my treatise *Agape into Eternity*, I caught an important theological error I made about Jesus's crucifixion. My initial reflection reflected the humanity in me and I wrote that crucifixion was "a torture reserved for criminals, not God's sinless Son." I corrected it with "a torture reserved for criminals, not something we would imagine for the Sinless One." This correction is proper theology that I rightly mention in other places in the treatise. We human beings would like to imagine that Jesus did not have to die the way he did; however, it was a necessary part of God's divine plan to save us from our sins and it shows humankind the awesome depth of God and

Jesus's agape love for us. God - in His Most High Wisdom - put Jesus through that Passion (Suffering), so we would never doubt or forget how much He and Jesus both love us. Jesus's Passion (Suffering) defines divine agape love. I caught the error and made the correction in time before I published my book *Young Ezekiel* where I incorporate the same sentence.

In my treatise *The Messiah Jesus*, I added King David's Psalm 16 prophecy that the Messiah would not remain dead and therefore would resurrect.

One aesthetic error that bothers me in *Young Ezekiel* is that I added one too many *Romeo and Juliet* quotes - just one too many, which I feel disrupted the flow and intimacy of an important scene - the first kiss. I eliminate the one reference during the first kiss scene in the edited draft in this anthology, which gives the scene a better flow.

Now that I have the opportunity here to include some thoughts on my works, I am compelled to mention the importance of Charles Augustus Briggs's *Messianic Prophecy*. I discovered the book sitting on the shelf of a used-books store in New York City and purchased it because I was attracted to the title and so I could have something to read on my subway-ride home. I did not realize how significantly it would further my understanding of the prophecies about Jesus Christ. It was an invaluable resource that I treasure and helped me construct my treatise *The Messiah Jesus*. As the saying goes, I have been able to see as far as I have because I have stood on the shoulders of giants. I thankfully stood on the shoulders of Briggs - specifically, his scholarship in *Messianic Prophecy*.

There are also other places in my books where I make corrections, including spelling and punctuation, such as capitalizing the "C" when referring to Jesus's Cross.

Because of the perfectionist in me, these struggles as an author may sound negative. However, this book is a celebration of all the work I created for God. The reader must not believe that I am not satisfied with the results of my works. I believe in and am proud of them. This anthology is simply my last chance to make things right and is me celebrating a 15 year journey. At the end of almost every night of my adult life, I have recited the following prayer, which is as relevant for a day's end as it is for the end of a life's journey: "Into thy hands, O Lord, I commend my soul and my body. Do thou thyself bless me, have mercy upon me, and grant me life eternal. Amen." In this anthology - *Approaching the Kingdom* - I have laid out the most important things that have helped me reach Salvation and this is my method of helping others attain Salvation. So, enjoy and may God bless you as he did with me when I created these works.

Your servant of God and disciple of Jesus the Christ,
James Thomas Angelidis

THE AUTHOR

BIO

Raised next to New York City in Fort Lee, NJ, James Thomas Angelidis graduated from Boston University with a B.S. in Communication and a minor in Philosophy, from Montclair State University with a B.A. in Religious Studies and from Seton Hall University's Seminary with an M.A. in Theology. During his academic career, he merited awards, honors and the highest grades. After his first bachelor's degree, at the age of 24, he backpacked through Europe for 60 days and visited 28 cities in 11 countries - including France, Luxembourg, Belgium, Netherlands, Germany, Czech Republic, Austria, Switzerland, Italy, Spain and Portugal. For 9 years, he worked at Saint Basil Academy in Garrison, NY where he helped raise children with troubled backgrounds under the guiding light of the Greek Orthodox Christian Church. He spends his time spreading the teachings of his Lord and Savior Jesus Christ with his five books - *And the Lamb Spoke: Lessons from the Gospels* (ages 7-9), *Young Ezekiel: A Life of Loves* (young adults), *Writings* (young adults and adults), *In the Name of Salvation: Three Theological Treatises* (adults), *Approaching the Kingdom: An Anthology* (adults). You can find James's books on Amazon.com and BarnesAndNoble.com. James is online at www.jtangelidis.com, Instagram, Pinterest and LinkedIn.

ABOUT

I believe there is truth in the proverb, "The pen is mightier than the sword."

The damage done by the emperor's sword can be rectified by the writer's pen. Nothing can replace a life lost by the sword, but with the help of the pen, the story of that life can teach, inspire and unveil truth that can save many lives. When the emperor dies, so does his sword, as does his power and his influence on the world; yet, the writer's pen can leave a lasting impression unto the ages. The ideas behind the pen can change the world; something, the emperor tries to do with his sword, but inevitably fails. Certainly, if we dig deeper, we can discover additional meanings within the proverb's words, but it is clear that the pen is powerful. The pen can make a difference in people's lives and with the help of God, I hope to make a difference in people's lives with my pen. I hope to give life.

- James Thomas Angelidis

FROM WWW.JTANGELIDIS.COM BLOG

MY WEBSITE

Greetings family and friends,
Over the years, I have spent much time reading and writing. I studied theology in grad school and my love for it remains in me and probably will forever. The works I have written are about Jesus, who is Salvation. I have created a website to house the works. I would be honored if you checked it out. The address is www.jtangelidis.com. Many thanks, friends. God bless.

MY CHILDREN'S BOOK

One of my works is a children's book called, AND THE LAMB SPOKE. The purpose of it is to expose children to Jesus's teachings found in the Gospels. The book has 15 lessons about topics such as love, giving and forgiveness that are connected with a story about a boy and a lamb. The book is for ages 7 to 9, but adults can enjoy and learn from it, too! You can purchase a hardcover copy on Amazon.com. Half of my profit will go to the children of Saint Basil Academy in Garrison, NY.

MY SECOND BOOK

Greetings family and friends and much love to you,
I've been busy lately. I recently moved into a new

apartment, took on two jobs serving food and just published my second book - IN THE NAME OF SALVATION. This book is for adults and it contains three treatises (or articles) about Jesus, God's Son. It is my way of preparing us for the Kingdom. It would be a great Easter gift for adults and my children's book - AND THE LAMB SPOKE - would be a great Easter gift for the young ones. Both are available on Amazon.com. Take a look. God Bless you! James.

A DECADE IN THE MAKING...

Greetings family and friends and much love to you, I just published my third book - YOUNG EZEKIEL: A LIFE OF LOVES. It is a fiction book and the target group is young adults. It is graduation season and it would be a great gift for high school and college graduates. My goal with my three books - AND THE LAMB SPOKE (for ages 7-9), YOUNG EZEKIEL (for young adults), IN THE NAME OF SALVATION (for adults) - is to raise generations and bring us all closer to Jesus who is the Way to God the Father and eternal life. I published a fourth book, as well, called WRITINGS with the same goal. In the past ten months, I have published four books, but they took a decade to write. You can find them on Amazon.com and BarnesAndNoble.com. Please read and share. God bless you all!

ON EDUCATION

My books are meant to educate and my philosophy on education is influenced by Plato's philosophy on education, which he wrote about in his *The Republic*:

"What about the manner of the style and the speech?" I said. "Don't they follow the disposition of the soul?"
"Of course."
"And the rest follow the style?"
"Yes."
"Hence, good speech, good harmony, good grace, and good rhythm accompany good disposition, not the folly that we endearingly call 'good disposition,' but that understanding truly trained to a good and fair disposition."
"That's entirely certain," he said.
"Mustn't the young pursue them everywhere if they are to do their own work?"
"Indeed they must be pursued."
"Surely painting is full of them, as are all crafts of this sort; weaving is full of them, and so are embroidery, housebuilding, and also all the crafts that produce the other furnishings; so, furthermore, is the nature of bodies and the rest of what grows. In all of them there is grace or gracelessness. And gracelessness, clumsiness, inharmoniousness, are akin to bad speech and bad disposition, while their opposites are akin to, and imitations of, the

opposite—moderate and good disposition."
"Entirely so," he said.

"Must we, then, supervise only the poets and compel them to impress the image of the good disposition on their poems or not to make them among us? Or must we also supervise the other craftsmen and prevent them from impressing this bad disposition, a licentious, illiberal, and graceless one, either on images of animals or on houses or on anything else that their craft produces? And the incapable craftsman we mustn't permit to practice his craft among us, so that our guardians won't be reared on images of vice, as it were on bad grass, every day cropping and grazing on a great deal little by little from many places, and unawares put together some one big bad thing in their soul? <u>Mustn't we, rather, look for those craftsmen whose good natural endowments make them able to track down the nature of what is fine and graceful, so that the young, dwelling as it were in a healthy place, will be benefited by everything; and from that place something of the fine works will strike their vision or their hearing, like a breeze bringing health from good places; and beginning in childhood, it will, without their awareness, with the fair speech lead them to likeness and friendship as well as accord?"</u>

<u>**"In this way," he said, "they'd have by far the finest rearing."**</u>

"So, Glaucon," I said, "isn't this why the rearing in music is most sovereign? Because rhythm and harmony most of all insinuate themselves into the inmost part of the soul and most vigorously lay hold of it in bringing grace with them; and they make a man graceful if he is correctly reared, if not, the opposite. Furthermore, it is sovereign because the man properly reared on rhythm and harmony would have the sharpest sense for what's been left out and what isn't a fine product of craft or what isn't a fine product of nature. And, **due to his having the right kind of dislikes, he would praise the fine things; and, taking pleasure in them and receiving them into his soul, he would be reared on them and become a gentleman. He would blame and hate the ugly in the right way while he's still young, before he's able to grasp reasonable speech. And when reasonable speech comes, the man who's reared in this way would take most delight in it, recognizing it on account of its being akin?"**

"In my opinion, at least," he said, "it's for such reasons that there's rearing in music."

(*The Republic*, Book III, 400d, Translation Allan Bloom, Bold type and underline applied by James Thomas Angelidis)

LOCAL PUBLIC LIBRARY

Very proud to say that my books are highlighted in the Fort Lee Public Library's "Local Authors" section, which is next to the reference department's main desk. Stop by and enjoy.

OVER 50 IMAGES

Happy to announce I have posted over 50 images with quotes from my books on Instagram and Pinterest. If you like what you see please follow and spread the word. God Bless!
www.instagram.com/jamesthomasangelidis/
www.pinterest.com/jtangelidis/

THE ROCK

With the President-elect, there are many unknowns and we now live in a new world. I have tried to stay above politics. I'm all about God. The only certainty in our turbulent and dysfunctional world is God. If you are looking for truth and values, do yourself and your children a favor and read the Bible. Start with the Gospels - the world's foundational rock for thousands of years. As Jesus says, the end times are upon us and "Heaven and earth will pass away, but my words will not pass away" (Matthew 24:1-35). Build your house - your life - on the rock of Jesus's words and not on sand (Matthew 7:24-27).

BOOK CLUB SELECTION!

Greetings All,

My friend Mrs. Evellyn Leontarakis Tsiadis has been supporting me and my children's book - *And the Lamb Spoke: Lessons from the Gospels*. Because of her, the Daughters of Penelope Foundation has endorsed my book in its Book Club for the month of December. It is a wonderful Hellenic women's non-profit organization and I am excited by this distinction. So, if you have not, please purchase copies for the children in your life. It will benefit your children and the children of Saint Basil Academy in Garrison, NY who inspired the book and who will receive half of my profit. Thank you and God bless you! The link - http://dopfoundationinc.com/book-club/month/

BOB MARLEY AND GOD

I have listened to Bob Marley's music on a regular basis for the past 14 years. He and John Coltrane have perennially been my favorite musicians. A keyword to listen for in a Bob Marley song is "Jah," also known as "Yah," which is short for "Yahweh" (the proper name of God in the Hebrew Bible). Bob Marley was not just about marijuana and women. He loved and preached Jah (God) and that sets him apart from all other popular musicians and makes him special.

MY NEW WEB PAGE: LETTERS

A new page on my website for a new year! The page is called LETTERS. My note to Saint Augustine is there. Plus - a homily on God's Mother - a homily on God's Supreme Love - and a letter remembering little Leiby Kletzky who was murdered in NYC in 2011. God bless you and to a holy new year!

QUOTE...
That which comes between you and love is the devil.
- JTA

QUOTE...
Though storge, philia and eros are noble, agape is divine. - JTA, *Agape into Eternity*

QUOTE...
How does a man thank God... - JTA

QUOTE...
Truth is my sword. - JTA

QUOTE...
Pain and struggle add depth to the soul. Recovery is strength. Jesus makes recovery possible. He is Salvation. - JTA, *Young Ezekiel*

BOOKS

And the Lamb Spoke:
Lessons from the Gospels

Story and Art by
James Thomas Angelidis

jtangelidis.com

Copyright 2015 James Thomas Angelidis.
All rights reserved.

Special thanks to...

Craig Cutler whose idea to write a children's book inspired me to write this book based on our children at Saint Basil Academy in Garrison, NY.

Anna Prokos who helped guide me to make the lessons more child friendly.

Christine Papavasiliou who helped me edit the book into final form.

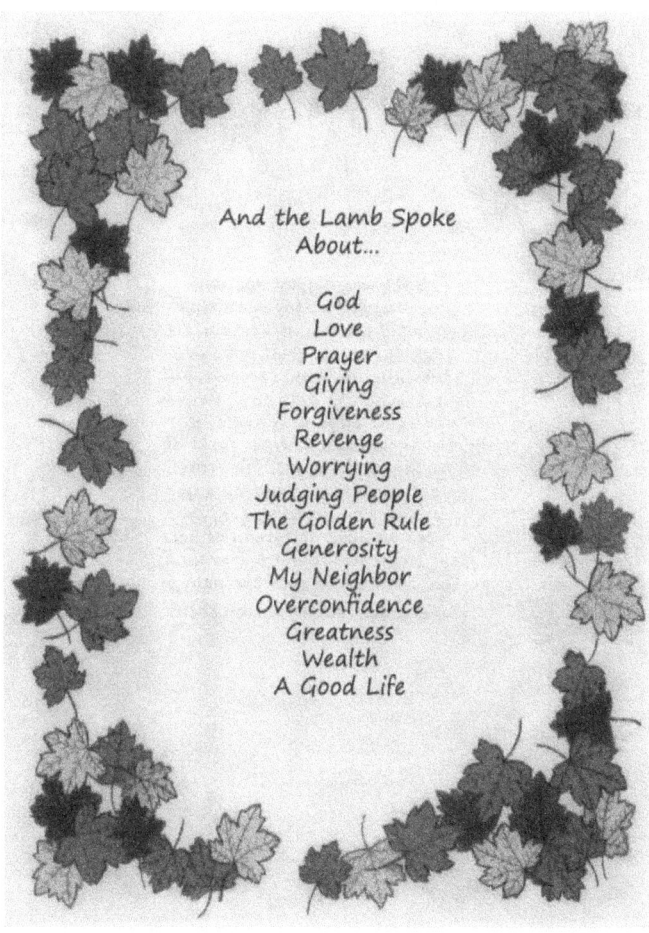

And the Lamb Spoke About...

God
Love
Prayer
Giving
Forgiveness
Revenge
Worrying
Judging People
The Golden Rule
Generosity
My Neighbor
Overconfidence
Greatness
Wealth
A Good Life

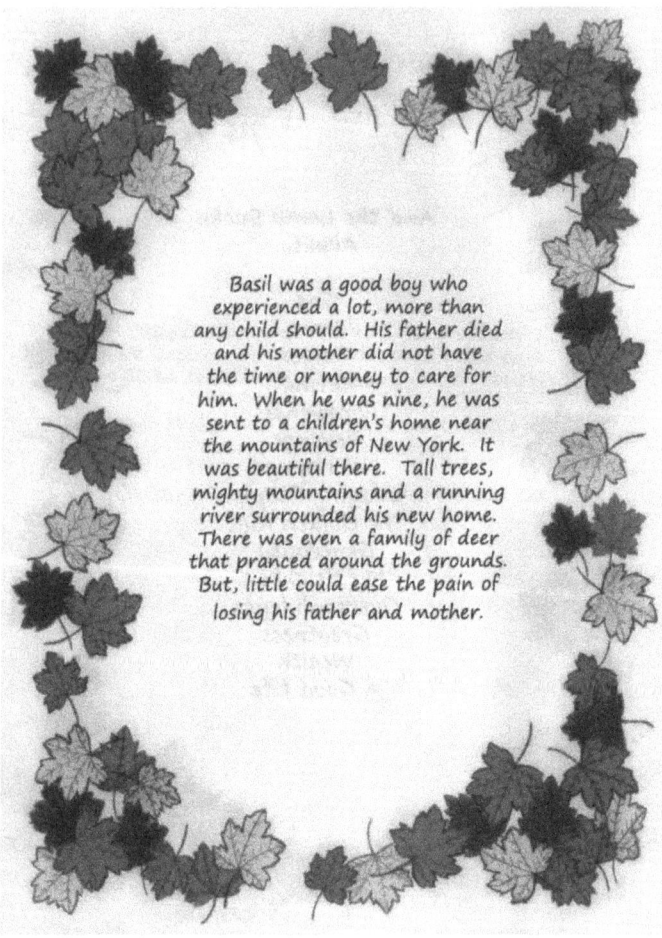

Basil was a good boy who experienced a lot, more than any child should. His father died and his mother did not have the time or money to care for him. When he was nine, he was sent to a children's home near the mountains of New York. It was beautiful there. Tall trees, mighty mountains and a running river surrounded his new home. There was even a family of deer that pranced around the grounds. But, little could ease the pain of losing his father and mother.

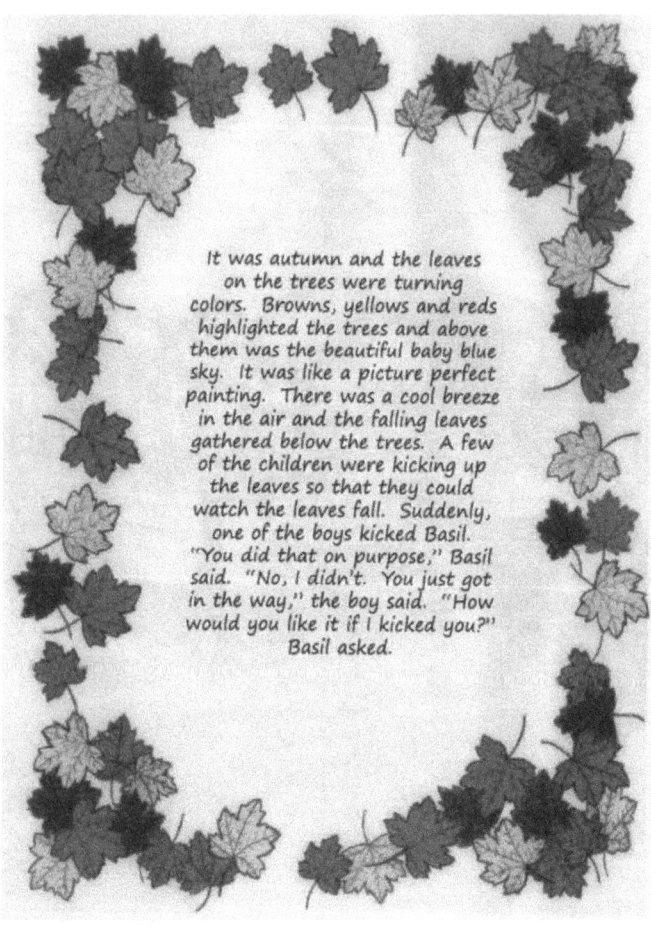

It was autumn and the leaves on the trees were turning colors. Browns, yellows and reds highlighted the trees and above them was the beautiful baby blue sky. It was like a picture perfect painting. There was a cool breeze in the air and the falling leaves gathered below the trees. A few of the children were kicking up the leaves so that they could watch the leaves fall. Suddenly, one of the boys kicked Basil. "You did that on purpose," Basil said. "No, I didn't. You just got in the way," the boy said. "How would you like it if I kicked you?" Basil asked.

APPROACHING THE KINGDOM - JTA

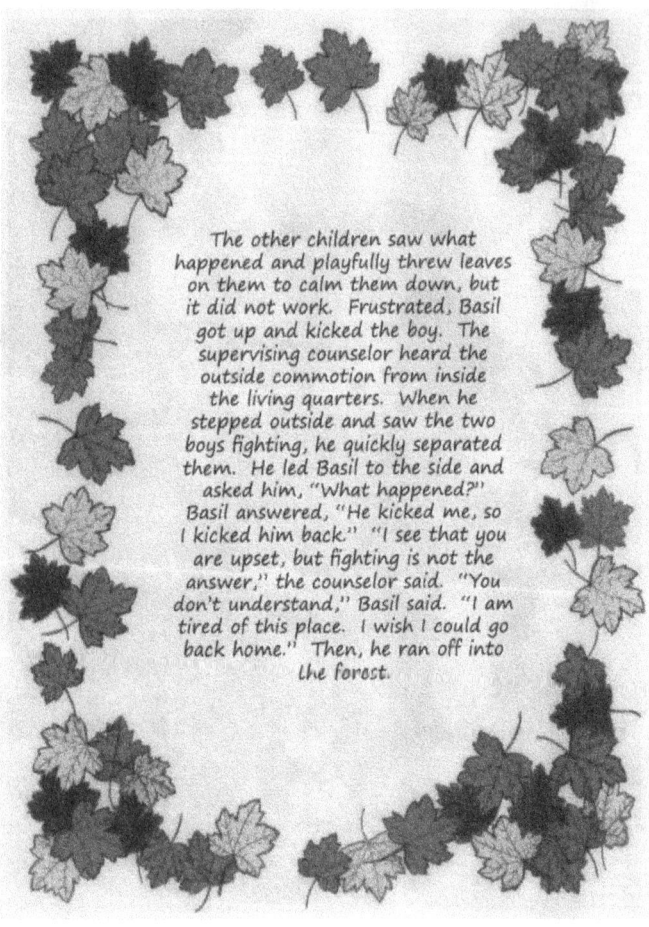

The other children saw what happened and playfully threw leaves on them to calm them down, but it did not work. Frustrated, Basil got up and kicked the boy. The supervising counselor heard the outside commotion from inside the living quarters. When he stepped outside and saw the two boys fighting, he quickly separated them. He led Basil to the side and asked him, "What happened?" Basil answered, "He kicked me, so I kicked him back." "I see that you are upset, but fighting is not the answer," the counselor said. "You don't understand," Basil said. "I am tired of this place. I wish I could go back home." Then, he ran off into the forest.

APPROACHING THE KINGDOM - JTA

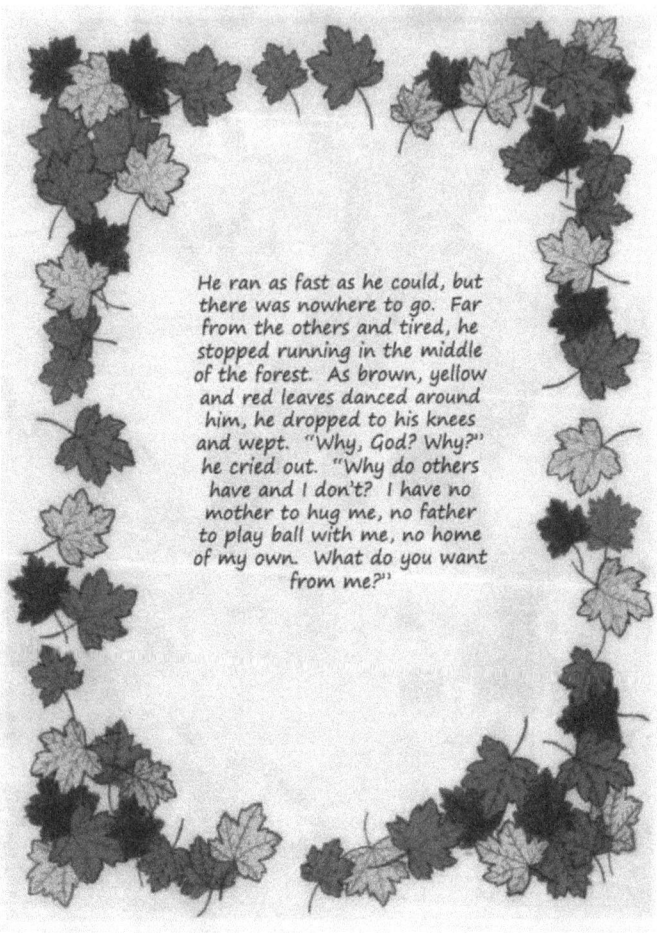

He ran as fast as he could, but there was nowhere to go. Far from the others and tired, he stopped running in the middle of the forest. As brown, yellow and red leaves danced around him, he dropped to his knees and wept. "Why, God? Why?" he cried out. "Why do others have and I don't? I have no mother to hug me, no father to play ball with me, no home of my own. What do you want from me?"

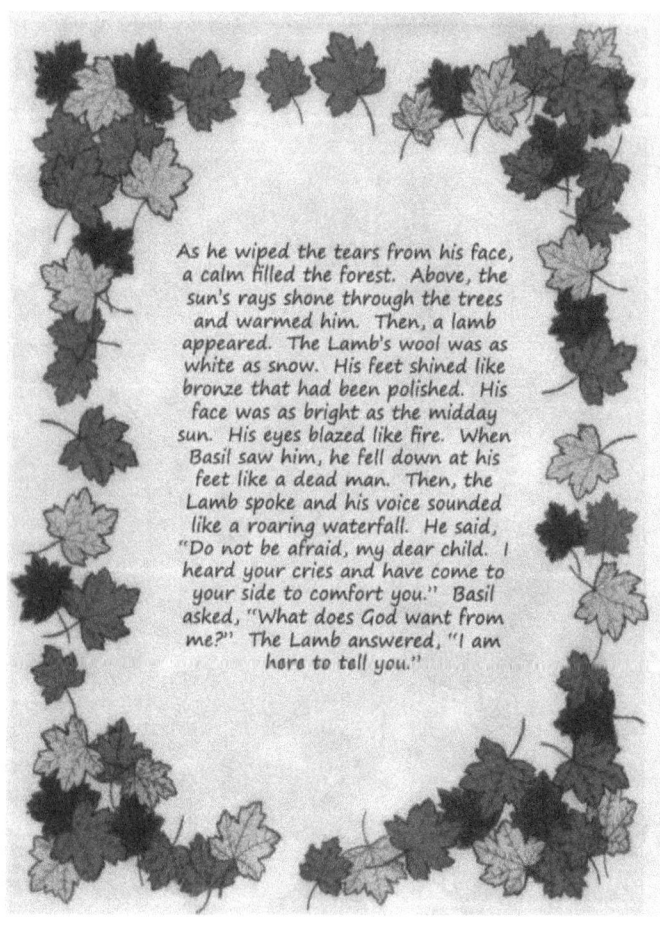

As he wiped the tears from his face, a calm filled the forest. Above, the sun's rays shone through the trees and warmed him. Then, a lamb appeared. The Lamb's wool was as white as snow. His feet shined like bronze that had been polished. His face was as bright as the midday sun. His eyes blazed like fire. When Basil saw him, he fell down at his feet like a dead man. Then, the Lamb spoke and his voice sounded like a roaring waterfall. He said, "Do not be afraid, my dear child. I heard your cries and have come to your side to comfort you." Basil asked, "What does God want from me?" The Lamb answered, "I am here to tell you."

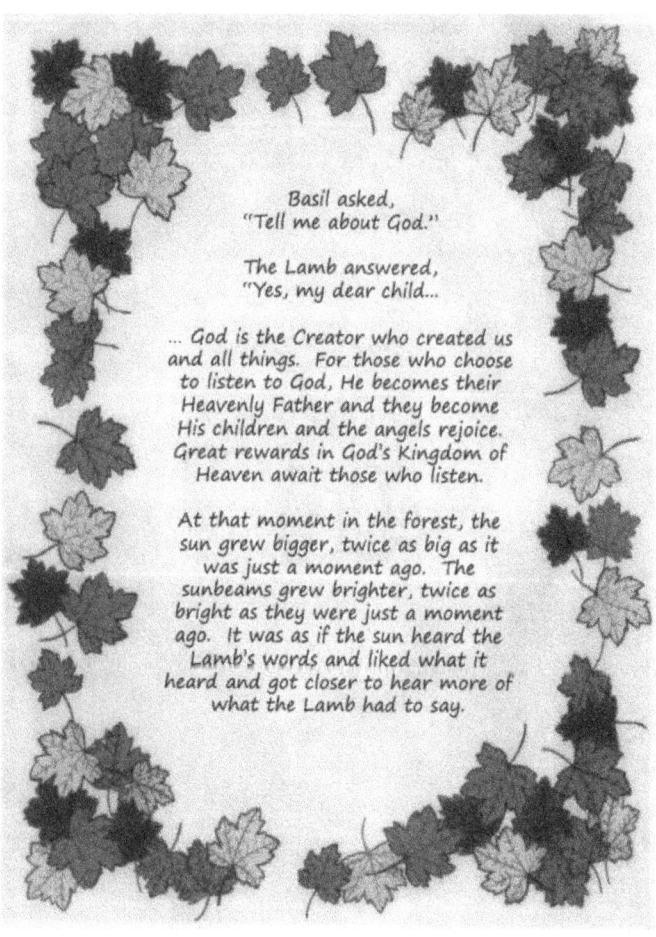

Basil asked,
"Tell me about God."

The Lamb answered,
"Yes, my dear child...

... God is the Creator who created us and all things. For those who choose to listen to God, He becomes their Heavenly Father and they become His children and the angels rejoice. Great rewards in God's Kingdom of Heaven await those who listen.

At that moment in the forest, the sun grew bigger, twice as big as it was just a moment ago. The sunbeams grew brighter, twice as bright as they were just a moment ago. It was as if the sun heard the Lamb's words and liked what it heard and got closer to hear more of what the Lamb had to say.

Basil asked,
"Tell me about love."

The Lamb answered,
"Yes, my dear child...

... God is Love. He wants us to love Him in return. We show that we love God by obeying His commandments. He also wants us to love our neighbor and even to love our enemies.

At that moment in the forest, the big sun grew warmer, twice as warm as it was just a moment ago. The bright sunbeams grew more gentle, twice as gentle as they were just a moment ago. The sun seemed to hug Basil as if it knew that he needed love.

Basil asked,
"Tell me about prayer."

The Lamb answered,
"Yes, my dear child...

... prayer is speaking to God and telling Him what is in your heart. Although He knows everything, He still likes to hear you tell Him. We should pray to God to praise Him, to ask for what we need, including forgiveness when we do wrong, to ask for what others need and to thank Him for what He has done for us.

At that moment in the forest, Basil's fears drifted away with the gentle wind that blew above him. The bright sun and fresh air were in perfect harmony comforting him und he was able to breathe more deeply than he could just a moment ago.

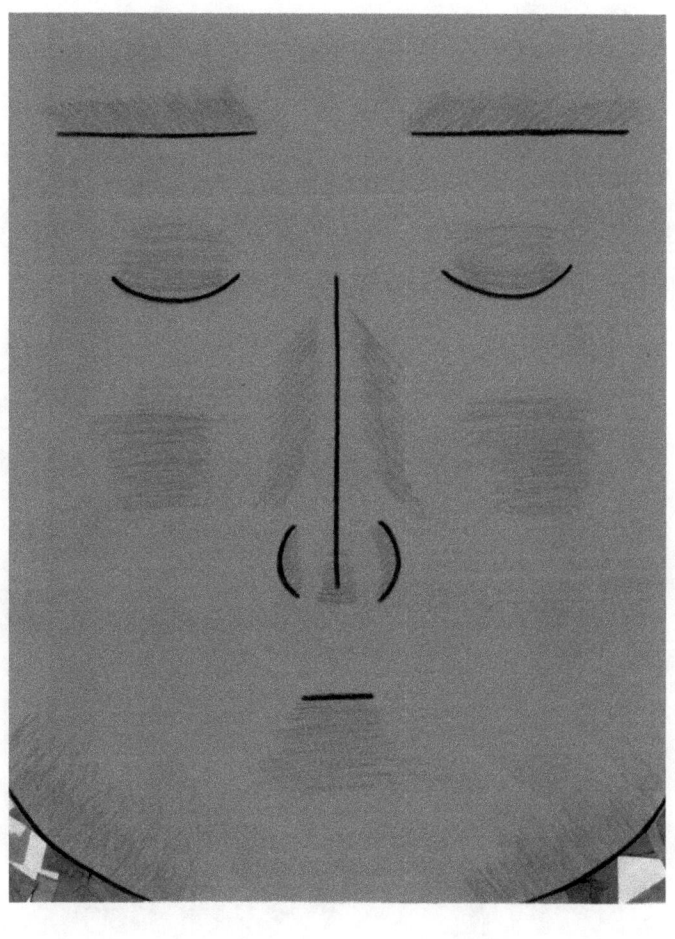

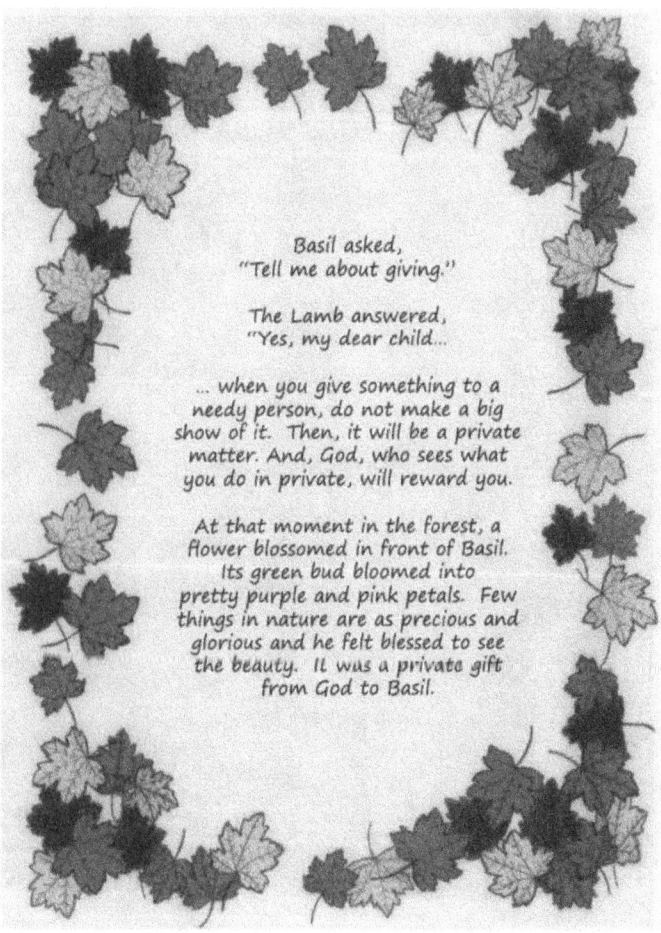

Basil asked,
"Tell me about giving."

The Lamb answered,
"Yes, my dear child...

... when you give something to a needy person, do not make a big show of it. Then, it will be a private matter. And, God, who sees what you do in private, will reward you.

At that moment in the forest, a flower blossomed in front of Basil. Its green bud bloomed into pretty purple and pink petals. Few things in nature are as precious and glorious and he felt blessed to see the beauty. It was a private gift from God to Basil.

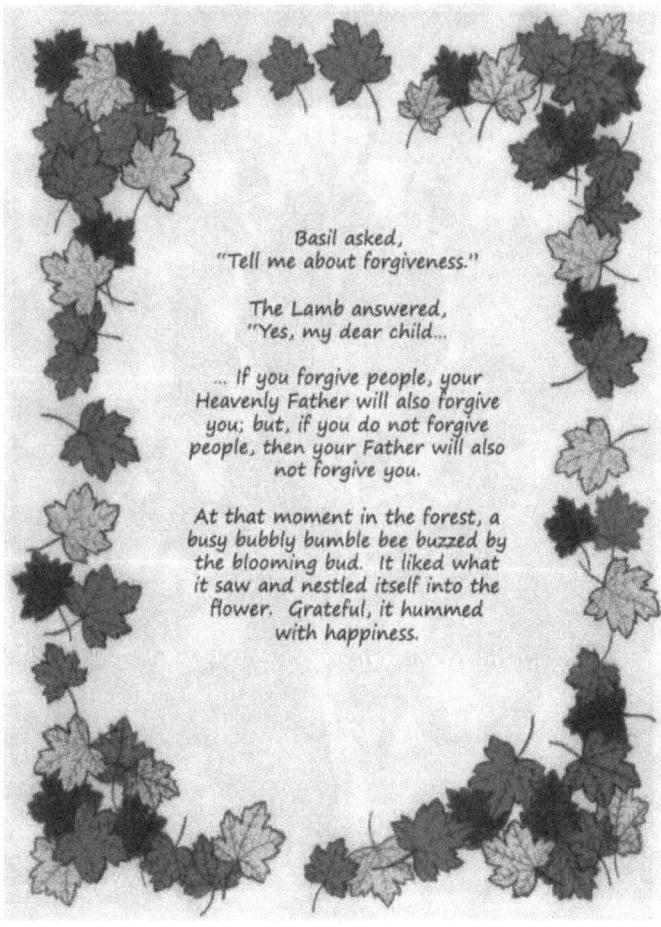

Basil asked,
"Tell me about forgiveness."

The Lamb answered,
"Yes, my dear child...

... If you forgive people, your Heavenly Father will also forgive you; but, if you do not forgive people, then your Father will also not forgive you.

At that moment in the forest, a busy bubbly bumble bee buzzed by the blooming bud. It liked what it saw and nestled itself into the flower. Grateful, it hummed with happiness.

Basil asked,
"Tell me about revenge."

The Lamb answered,
"Yes, my dear child...

... do not take revenge on or do wrong back to someone who has done wrong to you. If anyone slaps you on the cheek, pray for him and be kind to him.

At that moment in the forest, a butterfly floated in front of Basil as if it was saying hello. It was majestic and as it floated away, it kissed him on his one cheek and then on the other.

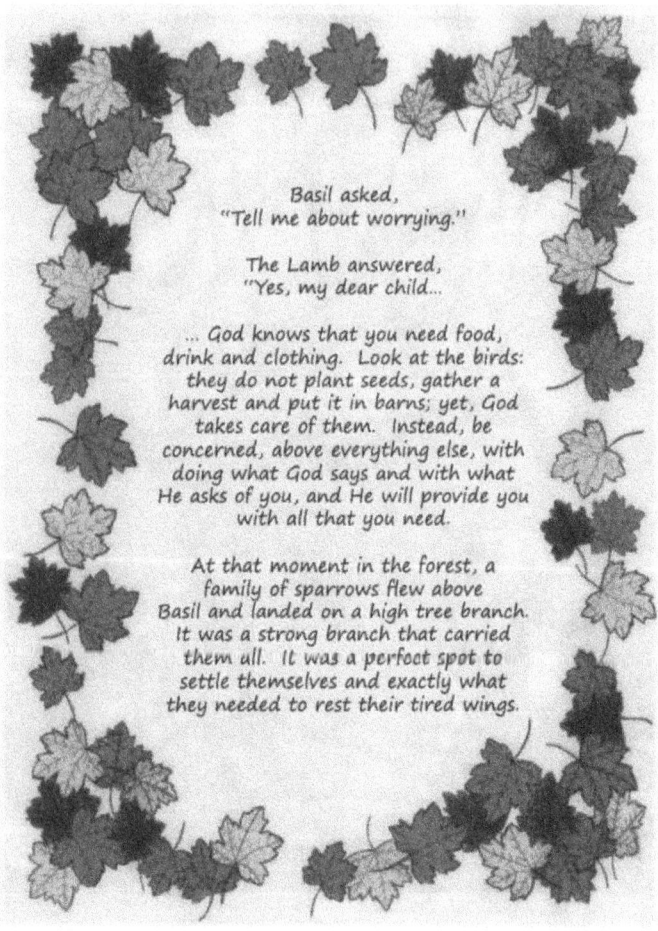

Basil asked,
"Tell me about worrying."

The Lamb answered,
"Yes, my dear child...

... God knows that you need food, drink and clothing. Look at the birds: they do not plant seeds, gather a harvest and put it in barns; yet, God takes care of them. Instead, be concerned, above everything else, with doing what God says and with what He asks of you, and He will provide you with all that you need.

At that moment in the forest, a family of sparrows flew above Basil and landed on a high tree branch. It was a strong branch that carried them all. It was a perfect spot to settle themselves and exactly what they needed to rest their tired wings.

Basil asked,
"Tell me about judging people."

The Lamb answered,
"Yes, my dear child...

... do not judge people or look at other people's wrongdoings or mistakes, so that God will not judge you because God will judge you in the same way you judge people.

At that moment in the forest, a group of dark clouds blocked the shining sun and the air grew thick. Then, it rained with raindrops that were like teardrops.

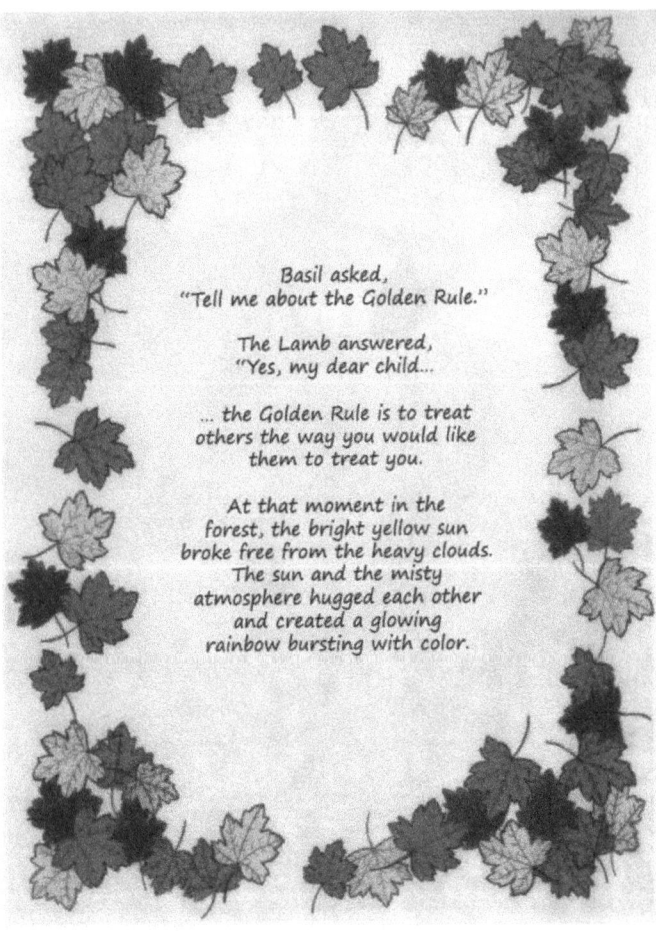

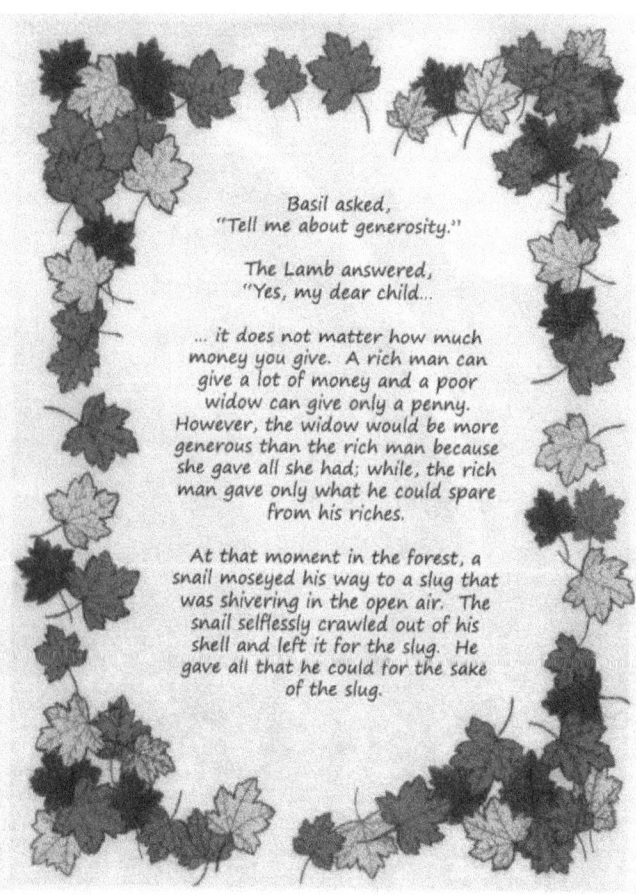

Basil asked,
"Tell me about generosity."

The Lamb answered,
"Yes, my dear child...

... it does not matter how much money you give. A rich man can give a lot of money and a poor widow can give only a penny. However, the widow would be more generous than the rich man because she gave all she had; while, the rich man gave only what he could spare from his riches.

At that moment in the forest, a snail moseyed his way to a slug that was shivering in the open air. The snail selflessly crawled out of his shell and left it for the slug. He gave all that he could for the sake of the slug.

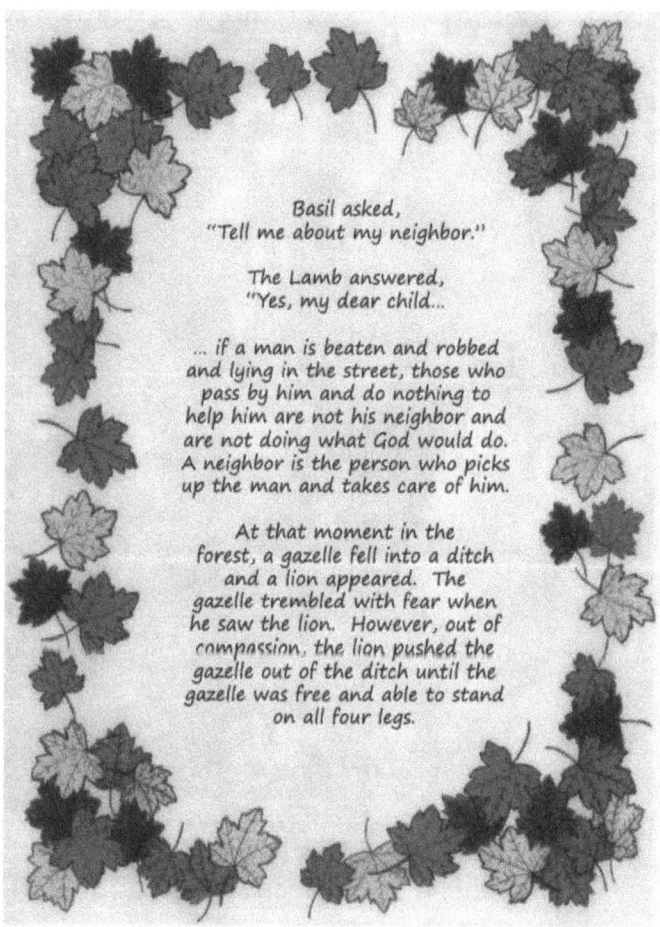

Basil asked,
"Tell me about my neighbor."

The Lamb answered,
"Yes, my dear child...

... if a man is beaten and robbed and lying in the street, those who pass by him and do nothing to help him are not his neighbor and are not doing what God would do. A neighbor is the person who picks up the man and takes care of him.

At that moment in the forest, a gazelle fell into a ditch and a lion appeared. The gazelle trembled with fear when he saw the lion. However, out of compassion, the lion pushed the gazelle out of the ditch until the gazelle was free and able to stand on all four legs.

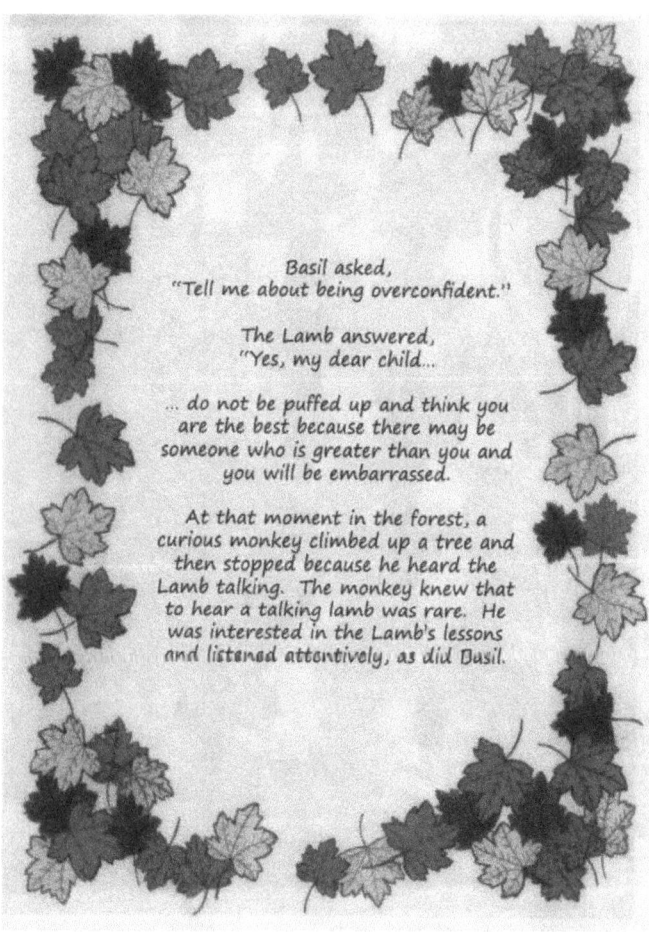

Basil asked,
"Tell me about being overconfident."

The Lamb answered,
"Yes, my dear child...

... do not be puffed up and think you are the best because there may be someone who is greater than you and you will be embarrassed.

At that moment in the forest, a curious monkey climbed up a tree and then stopped because he heard the Lamb talking. The monkey knew that to hear a talking lamb was rare. He was interested in the Lamb's lessons and listened attentively, as did Basil.

Basil asked,
"Tell me about wealth."

The Lamb answered,
"Yes, my dear child...

... true wealth comes from having God in your life and not from having many possessions.

At that moment in the forest, Basil began to pray silently in his thoughts. He prayed to God to give him strength and courage to live life faithfully. He began to realize that life has meaning and that God's ways are higher than our ways.

Basil asked,
"Tell me about how to live
a good life."

The Lamb answered,
"Yes, my dear child...

... a good life is not always easy.
Sometimes, there will be hard
decisions, but if you make the
right choices, God will help you.

At that moment in the forest, a
path of fresh green grass grew
on top of the moist soil and it
led to the children's home.

APPROACHING THE KINGDOM - JTA

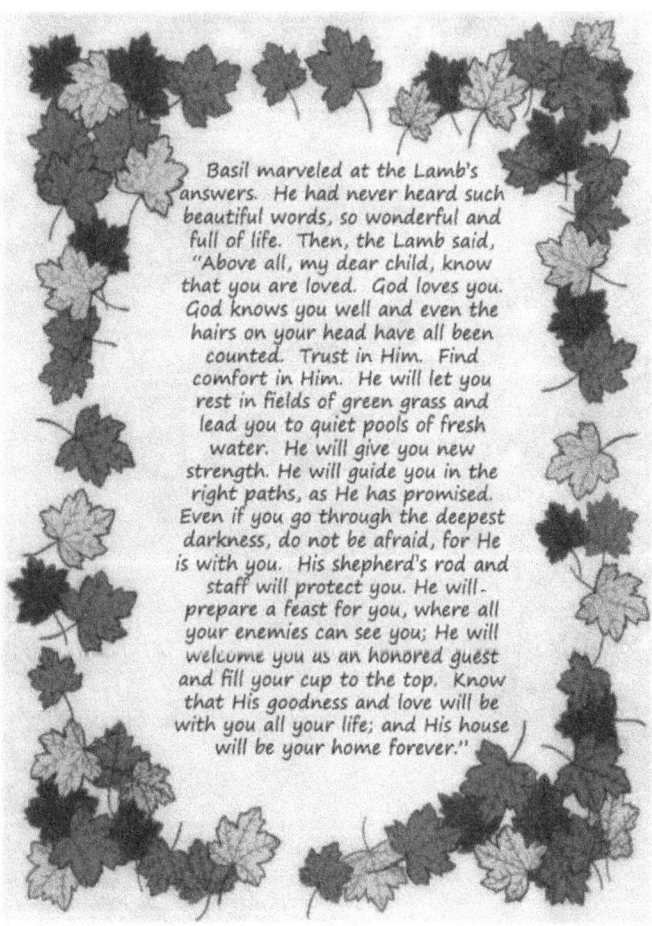

Basil marveled at the Lamb's answers. He had never heard such beautiful words, so wonderful and full of life. Then, the Lamb said, "Above all, my dear child, know that you are loved. God loves you. God knows you well and even the hairs on your head have all been counted. Trust in Him. Find comfort in Him. He will let you rest in fields of green grass and lead you to quiet pools of fresh water. He will give you new strength. He will guide you in the right paths, as He has promised. Even if you go through the deepest darkness, do not be afraid, for He is with you. His shepherd's rod and staff will protect you. He will prepare a feast for you, where all your enemies can see you; He will welcome you as an honored guest and fill your cup to the top. Know that His goodness and love will be with you all your life; and His house will be your home forever."

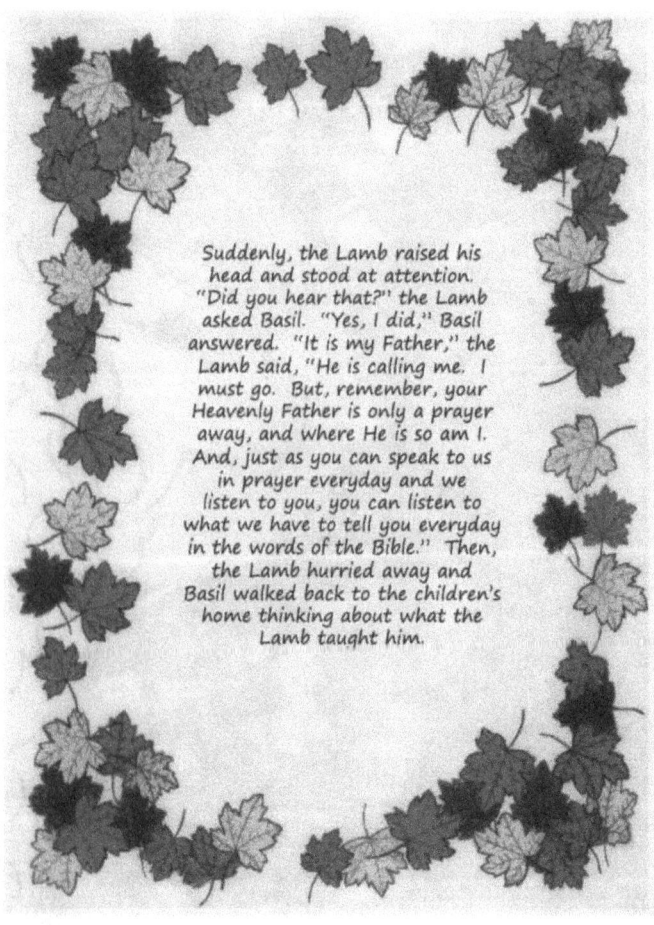

Suddenly, the Lamb raised his head and stood at attention. "Did you hear that?" the Lamb asked Basil. "Yes, I did," Basil answered. "It is my Father," the Lamb said, "He is calling me. I must go. But, remember, your Heavenly Father is only a prayer away, and where He is so am I. And, just as you can speak to us in prayer everyday and we listen to you, you can listen to what we have to tell you everyday in the words of the Bible." Then, the Lamb hurried away and Basil walked back to the children's home thinking about what the Lamb taught him.

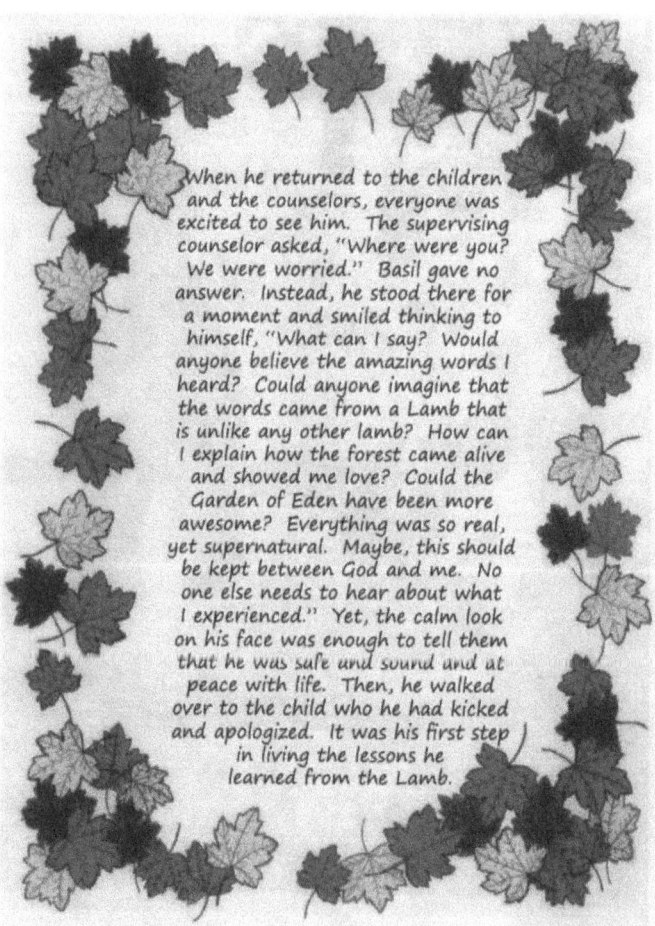

When he returned to the children and the counselors, everyone was excited to see him. The supervising counselor asked, "Where were you? We were worried." Basil gave no answer. Instead, he stood there for a moment and smiled thinking to himself, "What can I say? Would anyone believe the amazing words I heard? Could anyone imagine that the words came from a Lamb that is unlike any other lamb? How can I explain how the forest came alive and showed me love? Could the Garden of Eden have been more awesome? Everything was so real, yet supernatural. Maybe, this should be kept between God and me. No one else needs to hear about what I experienced." Yet, the calm look on his face was enough to tell them that he was safe and sound and at peace with life. Then, he walked over to the child who he had kicked and apologized. It was his first step in living the lessons he learned from the Lamb.

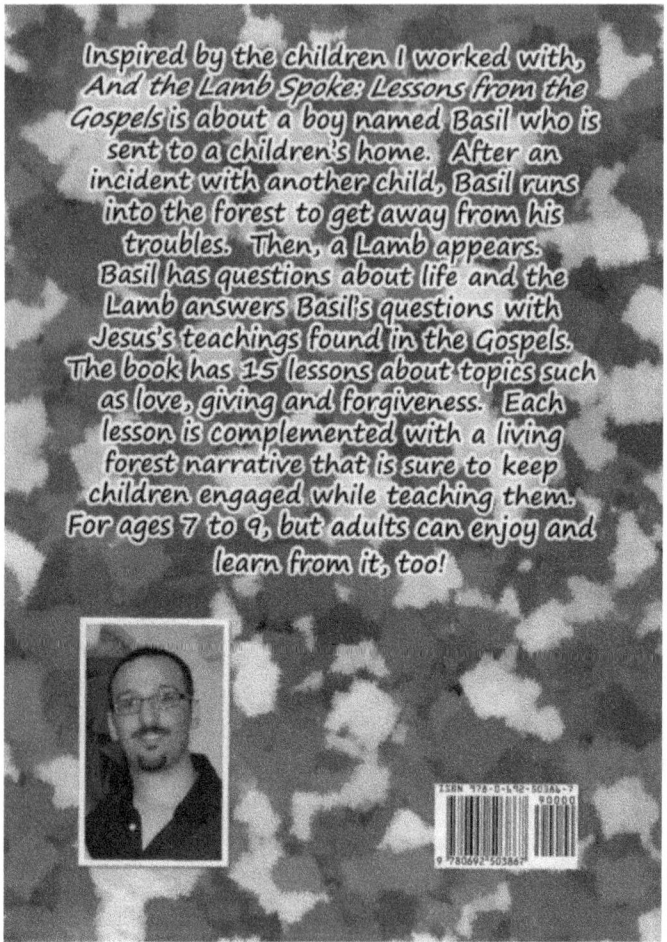

YOUNG EZEKIEL

A LIFE OF LOVES

JAMES THOMAS ANGELIDIS

Young Ezekiel
A Life of Loves

James Thomas Angelidis

Copyright 2016 James Thomas Angelidis.
All rights reserved.
(Edited 2017)

jtangelidis.com

Editorial Assistance from
Craig Cutler &
Sharon Usdan Cutler

Cover Art by
Angela Angelidis (Needlepoint, 1976)

PREFACE

What is love?

Can you describe it?

Do you love your parents, friends, romantic partner and God in the same way?

In the English language, we use the word love in all these relationships, but the ancient Greeks - the first western philosophers - tried to capture, pinpoint and distinguish the different forms of love with four words: storge, philia, eros, agape.

In *Young Ezekiel: A Life of Loves*, Ezekiel will tell you about his life and loves. Though his life is unique, his relationships are like ours and, maybe, through his story, you will learn about yourself and the loves in your life.

YOUNG EZEKIEL
A LIFE OF LOVES

CONTENTS

ONE: STORGE

TWO: PHILIA

THREE: EROS

FOUR: AGAPE

YOUNG EZEKIEL
A LIFE OF LOVES

ONE

STORGE

My name is Ezekiel, which in Hebrew means God strengthens. My parents gave me that name because they believed it would protect me from harm. They believed in the power of a name. They believed it is important to know what a name means or where it comes from and to know who or what it honors. One's name is the beginning of one's identity in the world and represents one for life.

My parents loved me. It was love that was not wasted because it was love that nurtured my soul. Like fertile soil in a flower garden that strengths a lily's roots helping the flower to grow and bloom, their love was vital to my vitality. If I was well behaved or not, they loved me without condition because I was their son. I was not just any boy; I was their boy and that made me special. Their love made me feel that I had value, that they had me just so they could love me. They loved me without reservation, never held it back and would have done more, if it were possible. They praised me when I excelled, supported me when I failed and were patient with me when I struggled. They sacrificed money, time and pleasures to raise me. I'll never be able to repay them, but I loved them in return. Their love has given me confidence that I can do anything, that all things are possible. I was their only child and received their love undivided. I was the center of their lives and they were the center of mine. I was their heart and they were mine. I remember mother squeezing me for no reason other than because she loved me. My parents cherished every moment that was a first and understood how precious life is. They bronzed my first shoes, recorded my first words and videotaped my first steps. Pictures captured our experiences. Some of my favorite images are the candid ones because they are natural and honest. They have no disguise and not one fails to depict our love for each other. I have no bad memories of them. They provided me with food, shelter and love. I lacked nothing.

    Born off the coast of Florida on a small island called Omorfi, I reminisce most about my days on the beach. The walk to the beach was just as much fun as being at the beach. When I was a tot, father would carry me on his shoulders. They made the perfect seat as if shoulders were meant to be sat upon and provided a fantastic view that was superior to what I was accustomed to because of my short height. For those moments, I was a giant and felt indomitable. No one was taller than me, I felt. As tall as the trees,

I would reach high to grab a leaf for no reason other than because I could. It was my natural inclination to a special situation. There was one time when I tested my capacity's limits, stretched for a leaf and almost fell. However, father did not let that happen. He maintained his balance and compensated for my childish behavior. He had it all under control. He could have scolded me because I could have hurt myself, but instead, he said, "Ezekiel, my son, be careful. I need you, just as much as you need me. If you fall, you could get hurt and that would hurt me." I never forgot my father's words because they taught me that our love for each other made us one and that we were an extension of each other. We had to love and take care of ourselves, not just for ourselves, but also for each other. I know now that if I fell and got hurt, it would have hurt father emotionally, just as much as it would have hurt me physically. Perhaps, even more. His love for me was beyond sympathy or empathy. He would have died for me because my life was more important to him than his own life.

    I remember walking in between father and mother and they would swing me with their arms as I held their hands. In the middle of the air, I felt as though I was floating and during that climax, time seemed to stand still. I would hold my breath, my heart would pause and my smile would beam from joy. "Again, again," I would yell and they fulfilled my request without a thought. They would do anything to make me happy. As I grew a bit and got too big to swing from their arms, other games followed. Sometimes, we would kick stones and see how long we could keep one in front of us. I would pass it to mother and she would pass it to father. Our play evolved. Even though the games changed, fun never did. It kept us young. Each of their inner child resurfaced when we played together. They humbled themselves to my level and for those moments, I was their equal.

The beach was a ten minute walk away from home. On the way, we would pass a pasture on the left of the road enclosed by an old weathered wooden fence. A dark red barn with white trim overlooked the pasture, which was made up of gold tinted grass. Cattle roamed the field and they would feed on the grass slowly and carefree. Sometimes, a cow would take a break, look at us and moo and I would wonder what the cow was thinking. Was he trying to say hello or were we interrupting his mealtime? I could also hear the restless chickens heckling in their coop and a couple of dogs replying to their calls. It was the same scene every time we traveled by and because of the expectation of the situation, I was never surprised or let down. The pasture was like a part of my home and I felt I could claim it as my own, but that is what children do. They take possession of the things they are most fond of. It is not their fault because they lack maturity. Unfortunately, some people never grow up and learn to share. It takes a well-adjusted and well-balanced mind to play with others. Some people maintain a selfish and audacious attitude and wars are fought because of such people. Treasures and territory are what they desire and they fail to love their neighbor, which is humankind's second greatest sin after failing to love God.

The beach bustled with activity. Children yelling, water splashing and music playing pulsated through the air. Frisbee throwing, water surfing and volleyball bumping energized the scene. The tourists responded to this the most, but father, mother and I took an unbeaten path known only by the locals. We entered the beach with everyone else, but around a picketed fence, some beach grass and a curiously massive boulder was a coastal strip that was a living dream. The energy was exciting, but a bit much. Father, mother and I preferred serenity over the commotion. Our neighbors frequented it and so did a couple of my schoolmates and their parents. The white unstained sand made the water look blue as it mirrored the color of the blue sky. I could see, beneath the transparent water, the stones and coral that rested on the bottom of the ocean. Every time I saw that sight my natural inclination was to jump in. I would jet to the water and with each step, I would kick up sand behind me. During those hot days, the water refreshed my tanned skin and once I took my first dip, I could stay in there for over an hour. My parents would joke that in a previous life I must have been a fish, even though, I would swim paddling my arms and legs like a puppy dog. While I joined my friends in the water, my parents laid out our beach towels with our belongings by the sand dunes. In mother's bag were suntan lotion, house keys, money and a couple of books. Father carried the cooler stored with baby carrots, cucumbers, cheese and tomato sandwiches with a little mayonnaise and some fresh water. By the time they settled in and got comfortable, I would take a break from playing and mother would see me approach them and ask, "Is my son hungry?" I always nodded my head yes. She knew me better than anyone else; I rarely had to say a word for her to know what I was thinking. Then, we would make a picnic and have our own private party. We would huddle together sitting cross legged on our beach towels with the food in front of us. Sometimes, mother would toss a baby carrot in the air toward father. She would direct it toward his mouth and father would follow, catch, chew and enjoy. Mother would toss them just right and father always caught them. Then, they would look at each other, smile and give each other high-fives for jobs well done. I would laugh and get high-fives, too, because I was their son. As I got older, I would imitate father and soon enough we were all laughing. It was not that we did not want others' company. We just did not need anyone else to have a good time. All we needed was each other.

  As the day passed, father, mother and I would gravitate to the water's edge and sit there while the water washed over our legs. The gentle sweeping waves tingled our skin and calmed our spirits. This tranquil massage will put anyone in a good mood. As we lounged there, father and I often built drip castles out of the wet sand. The powder-like white sand morphed into a mud-like brown when the water touched it. The small grainy consistency was rough, yet smooth - perfect for drip castles. We would grab a fistful of wet sand and guide it off our fingers, so it would drip to the ground where it would accumulate creating the tower of a castle. It was a simple trick that produced an elegant result. The castles resembled 19th century Spanish architect Antoni Gaudi's basilica, "Sagrada Familia." We also filled the plastic cups we brought for our drinking water with wet sand, so we could build miniature forts. The key is to not use dry sand that will crumble or water saturated sand that will get stuck in the cup; but, rather, a consistency in between the two. We would stack one fort or drip castle on top of other forts fashioning many tall structures that were grouped together creating a kingdom. Our kingdom would remain until the water attacked it. Nature's power is mightier than anything humankind can make, even with our overconfident arrogance. Other times, father, mother and I would dig massive pits. We would dig so deep that at the bottom, we would hit water. The first time this happened, I was puzzled. Father told me that if we dig deeper, we would reach the other side of the earth. I paused with my eyes in a daze contemplating the idea. When I got stuck on the thought, father confessed he was teasing me and then smiled, grabbed my neck and kissed my forehead. Sometimes, mother and I could convince father to get into the pit, so we could bury him up to the neck and all we could see is his head above the ground. More often than not, he did not mind looking silly for his family in front of others and that is what made him cool. Silly is not really silly when love is involved.

      Father also showed me how to skip rocks on the surface of the ocean. He was much more coordinated than I. When he threw the rock upon the ocean, it would skip five or six times. When I threw the rock, it would hit kerplunk then fall to the bottom. The trick was to find a flat and smooth rock and direct the throw to the surface of the water. I can do it now the way father did it then, but when I was a child, it was like magic. Another favorite pastime at the beach was looking for sea glass - glass made smooth by years of being tossed around in the sand and sea - on the beach. Mother learned this pastime from her mother and passed it down to me. The beach coast was long. It would take most people twenty-five minutes to walk along it and another twenty-five minutes to walk back, but for mother and I and other sea glass enthusiasts, the full walk could exceed two hours and we enjoyed every minute. The sea glass would settle on the shore beside the pebbles, but the colors of the sea glass would pop and glisten in the sunlight. Browns, greens and whites were common, but rare colors like purple were always prized. During the day, I would carry my favorite pieces in my pocket as good luck charms and at night, I would keep them on my stand by my bed so they would always be near me.

During the weekdays, father worked as a teacher in the town high school. He taught eleventh grade history. He was most fascinated with the American Civil War and legacy of President Abraham Lincoln. He was father's hero. Wisdom, truth and honor are words that father used to describe him to me when I was a child. He used Lincoln to put a face on virtue and integrity that would help mold my character. That was his way of planting a seed in my mind, so I too would strive to be great and make this world a better place.

He explained to me that Lincoln was an avid reader. Lincoln grew up in the American frontier where skills with an axe and hunting were prized, not education. Most children who grew up like him found no value in books because their parents did not find them important, but Lincoln was an exception. Though tall and strong, he had dreams beyond the frontier and he believed that reading would make his dreams a reality. And, when most boys were idling away time, Lincoln was reading diligently. During the summer, he would read outside and at night, he would read under a lamp. He was curious, read with tenacity and reveled in the acquisition of knowledge. At first, Lincoln read because he enjoyed the written word, but as he matured, he realized its greater value.

Books were hard to find in the frontier, but most homes had a Bible. Lincoln read and reread the Bible, memorized large portions of it and could recite them by heart, particularly the Psalms. Though not a church-going Christian, he took Scripture seriously and lived by its principles. During one cold night, he saw a defeated drunk man lying in the road and, without thought, helped the man to his feet, got him into a warm home and cared for him the next day. He was acting like the Good Samaritan who Jesus preached. He believed in God, but was skeptical about miracles and transcendence. The *Dilworth's Speller* was another popular book that Lincoln had access to which taught wisdom lessons that guided him through his youth. It encouraged reading to enhance the self and introduced him to literature outside the Bible, such as Aesop's fables, which became favorites with their sagacity. *Pilgrim's Progress* was another important book that directed his moral compass. He read anything and everything, including biographies, histories, novels and poetry. In fact, he wrote fine poetry himself. He recorded his favorite literature in a journal - a practice that strengthened his later writings and speeches. He absorbed and savored Shakespeare's works, which gave him greater insight into and a more complete perspective of human nature. He was different than most boys and by the time he was nineteen, he had an idea that he would be a great man. Father explained this to me as well as to his students who would soon be off to college where they would discover their potential. He made us believe that, like Lincoln, we could be great if we worked hard and pursued knowledge and wisdom.

Father believed in his profession, in cultivating the young minds of his students who will one day shape the world. He understood he may not make history, but he taught his students that one day they could. He believed inspiration is divine and transformative. It prompts people to act and if it remains, extraordinary things will happen. It is like supernatural motivation. It is a thought that ignites a flame in a person that has the potential to set a group and nation to rise and make change happen.

Father did not make a lot of money and we were not rich, but father was doing what he loved and that love came home with him every night. Some people toil day and day to make money, but are miserable. Money can enhance quality of life, but it is no guarantee of happiness. Father found a healthy balance that few people do. He believed that studying history was noble. He used to recite this one proverb, his favorite, to me by 19th century Spanish American philosopher and writer George Santayana, "Those who cannot remember the past are condemned to repeat it." So, we have a responsibility in this world to be knowledgeable of who we are and what we have done and to be aware of our capabilities - both good and bad - so we can make this world a better place for our children and our grandchildren and so on. Only by knowing history can one change history and prevent the mistakes of the past. 5th century BC Greek philosopher Socrates lived by the ancient Greek aphorism, "Know thyself." This piece of wisdom was the beginning of Western philosophy. Self-knowledge helps one to know one's strengths and weaknesses to make one a better person. One has to examine his own life and history, so he can make better decisions for himself and excel. Santayana's aphorism has roots in the ancient Greek aphorism. They both speak truth about awareness and transformation - one for the individual and the other for humankind.

Another of father's favorite proverbs is from 1st century BC Roman historian Titus Livy who said, "We fear things in proportion to our ignorance of them." The more we know about something, the less there is to fear. Most of us fear the unknown because we are unable to see the next step in the darkness of uncertainty. With knowledge, we become familiar with our surroundings and can confidently take the next step. Familiarity leads to comfort and security. It makes learning possible and prejudice fade. Father always encouraged me to explore and seek out answers to my questions. He taught me the value of books. Mother, too, was well read and, every so often, we would go together as a family to book fairs to buy used books - so much fun.

The school father taught at was a ten minute walk away from our home. Mother would prepare lunch for him and we would walk together to his school to deliver it to him. He would tell us that seeing us was the best part of his day. Mother and I were just as happy to see him.

Before I attended school and mother returned to work, I would spend the weekdays with her. She was a nurse, but chose to leave her occupation to raise me. She and father spoke about expenses and priorities and they decided to sacrifice many of the material pleasures that occupy many. Those days she spent with me are priceless. No money could replace their worth. As a child, I went to sleep early and woke up early and mother was always there. She bathed me, fed me and read to me. We were friends, but she was my mother first. She did not let me get away with misbehavior. If I made a mess of my room, I had to clean it otherwise mother would take away my favorite toys until I learned the lesson about the privilege of possessions. I was disciplined and learned right from wrong from her, but her actions always conveyed love. Few things were as satisfying as her smile and praise. She taught me about how to grow up strong in this world. If I tripped and fell, she gave me the opportunity to pick myself up, but if I hurt myself, she was there to comfort me with her embrace. In the playground, she gave me enough distance to wander around, so I could explore and learn independently. She let me make mistakes, so I could learn from them. If I tried climbing up some apparatus and could not, I learned my capabilities and limitations. In the local playground is where I learned how to interact with strangers, make friends and share. She showed me how to look for the humanity in people. I was sensitive to myself and others and developed the quality of compassion at a young age. I would see children cry or have temper tantrums and look at them with concern wondering why they were upset. Respect is the foundation for a civil society and as I interacted with other children, mother helped mold my character and behavior. I realized sharing was how to make friends. It leads to a peaceful and joyful relationship, but if a child stole my toy, I expressed my distress and often hollered at or chased after them. Mother understood the dangers of strangers, but did not smother or shelter me. I learned quickly from her guidance. For example, when I was around three years old and beginning to verbalize my thoughts, I introduced myself to an older woman and said, "Hello. My name is Ezekiel." And she said, "Nice to meet you Ezekiel. That's a lovely name." I said "I am three. I can count to ten." The woman must have thought this was very cute and she engaged me in conversation. I thought I was a big boy and was proud to express myself, but looking back, this could have been dangerous. For a child, talking to strangers is usually not a good idea. I was not cognizant of it at the time, but in retrospect, I realize mother was there overseeing this interaction and was there to protect me. I was learning about myself and how to communicate under mother's watch.

Behavior modification was important, but fun was the reason we came to the playground. Swings, slides and the jungle gym created a universe of unlimited possibilities. Always excited to visit, I never got bored of the playground. Yelling, laughing and running were common practice. Playing got me tired, so I could sleep soundly, which was good for me, but good for mother, too. It gave her time to gather her thoughts and rest. Being a good mother can be exhausting, but through her hugs and kisses, I know there was little else that she would rather do. She prepared me for preschool and a life beyond our nuclear family. When I began school, she returned to work as a nurse.

Raising a child is the toughest job in the world. To every child, mother is most important. Everyone says his or her mother is the best. Even in his song "Dear Mama," rapper Tupac Shakur praises his mother, a woman many would criticize. It's a deep and sensitive song from a self-proclaimed ghetto thug. Tupac Shakur and I grew up very differently, but I can relate to his song because I have the same love for my mother as he did for his mother. I do not know what it is about mothers. I am not a mother. Where do they get their love? Is it innate? Though often overlooked and taken for granted, no job is more serious and important. Mothers and fathers are responsible for another human being who will one day be a part of society: fact. Will that child be a cancer to the world or bright light? Most of that has to do with the parents. Monsters and saints are rare, but parents have the obligation to raise a child who will contribute to society; otherwise, they will have done an injustice to the child and society. There is no such thing as a perfect parent, just as there is no such thing as a perfect human being. However, if you love your child and raise your child with God and Christ, you will have done your best and what is expected of you by God.

      We lived in a modest one story white painted wood shingled house. Sky blue wood shutters bordered the sides of the windows and we had a matching front sky blue door that accented our home's cozy appearance. There were trimmed bushes in front of the house that had spectacular lemon yellow lilies living below. To the side was a stone birdbath that was frequented by a family of green and yellow colored parakeets with mixed black and white wings. Butterflies befriended them and together they filled the air with compassion. The dainty birds and butterflies were easily flustered and every time I approached them they would flutter away. A palm tree proudly peered over our house enjoying the horizon. A confident, spirited and free American flag swayed in the wind on a pole. Meandering through our green grass was a path made up of smooth beach stones that lead to the front door. On the side of our house was a studio apartment that was once a garage. Our tenant was a fisherman and crew member on one of the island's party boats that catered to the tourists who wanted an adventure at sea and to catch a few fish. He was middle aged with a scruffy beard and had no family of his own. He was a bit of a wanderer and loner, but settled down in Omorfi. We did not spend much time with him, but he was respectful and paid his rent promptly. Father's salary was our primary source of income, but the monthly rent paycheck helped a lot with our expenses and alleviated some pressure for father and mother.

After entering through the front door, one would find a rather large open furnished room with beige short looped durable carpet introducing the inside of the house. There was a mat next to the door where we would place our sandals and shoes, so we would minimize sand and dirt from entering in the house. There was also a coatrack where we would keep our coats and umbrellas that we would use depending on the weather. Spread out, yet carefully positioned clay potted green plants added warmth and life to the atmosphere. Mother and I would water them daily and as I got older, I would do so on my own. For this and other chores, like throwing out the garbage, I would get paid a weekly allowance that showed me responsibility and the reward of work. The walls were adorned with mother's paintings. She painted for pleasure and often imitated her favorite artist, 19th century French Impressionist painter Claude Monet. She would paint in the spacious entrance room sitting in front of an easel. There was usually light music playing in the background. She was very focused, yet at peace. It was like meditation for her. She tried to paint every day and I knew how to keep myself busy by reading, drawing or playing in the backyard, so she could. When she was finished for the day, she would neatly place her work and materials in the corner to the right of the entrance room's front door. This way it was not visible when introduced to the inside of the house. Our house was not very big and the open room was the best place to paint. Two cork colored couches in the far corner of the room leaned against the walls and an oval glass coffee table conveniently sat in front of them. Mother left cashews and almonds in a bowl on the coffee table in case we wanted a little something to nibble on and as a light treat for any guests. Usually open, the windows brought in fresh air and the ceiling fan helped circulate it.

    The most mystical room in the house was the family study room. The floor was wood and three walls were painted white. The fourth wall and the high ceiling were made up of sun windows, so the room was always lit with natural light. It also allowed for a spectacular and tranquil view of the ocean and the sunset. At the square room's center was a square off-white flokati rug with a circular wood coffee table on it. The table was surrounded by three brown leather seats with jade tree plants separating them. There were four small, yet powerful speakers stationed in each corner of the room, so if you sat on one of the seats you would be immersed in musical sounds of mostly classical, jazz, rock or hip-hop. On the walls were framed prints of Gandhi, Mother Teresa and Lincoln, as well as framed prints of Van Gogh, Matisse and Monet paintings. Below the prints stood wood bookshelves that bordered the room and they were filled with father's history books and classics of literature, mother's art and photography books and my children's books. My favorite books were of the Berenstain Bears series. They taught Christian lessons with engaging pictures without being overtly religious. I found the collection of Aesop's fables fascinating and it - with father and mother's commentaries - made me think deeply at an early age. I had a great affinity for picture books, particularly those of dinosaurs. Their bones and muscles and the mystery of their life and extinction spurred my imagination to wander. In the study room on the floor or in my seat, I used draw and color pictures of them and other animals with careful detail. I tried to copy their images as realistically as possible. Mother and father posted my best artwork on the walls with their prints. When they put them up, I stood taller with my shoulders back and chest high. I pledged allegiance to hard work. Few moments were as rewarding as when my parents hung my work on the wall.

    Mother's passion for art extended beyond the modern masters' works to include Orthodox Christian Byzantine icons. Her passion influenced father and they developed a common devotion to the icons.

Mother's love of art and father's belief in inspiration embodied by his heroes seemed to wed well in the icons. Father and mother placed icons of Christ Jesus and the Virgin Mother Mary in their bedroom and mine, too, on top of our bureaus leaning against the wall. The portraits were authentic paintings about the size of a book cover. They carried more than an esthetic appeal - they were there to protect us. My parents were not kooky and their beliefs had nothing to do with superstition, but rather a deep belief in the supernatural and the men and women who embodied it. This same philosophy was applied when they named me. It was given to me to protect me from harm. An icon of the Prophet Ezekiel hung on the wall inside my bedroom next to the door above the light switch to remind me every time I came in and out of the room that my name had a source. It had meaning and was fundamental to my identity. I did not like it as a child because I thought it was weird and felt I had to explain its meaning when I introduced myself to others; however, today, I say it with pride because its uniqueness reminds me of my parents who believed in its value.

When I was very little, mother played a lot of classical music in our home. She learned somewhere that classical music helped the mind grow intellectually. She believed that the way fruits and vegetables were good for the body, classical music was good for the mind. Each provides nutrients that foster good health. She preferred Bach above the other classical musicians because much of his music was Christian oriented and mother wanted to nourish me with as much positive as possible. My parents had eclectic musical tastes. More often than not, jazz played in our study. The type of jazz they listened to varied, but it usually did not have words, which can be distracting if one is reading and trying to concentrate. Jazz seems to help the mind process reading material because it helps the mind flow with the ideas. Like classical, jazz is intellectual, but also spiritual. John Coltrane's music is a perfect example. From its birth, jazz has had soul in it. The artist's honesty and nakedness while performing his piece makes it impossible to not come from the soul. Coltrane, though, elevated jazz's spiritual possibilities and brought that soulful quality to the forefront. His album *A Love Supreme* ends with his track, "Psalm" - praising God's Supreme Love for us. The album is not a peaceful expression, rather an exuberant excitement of devotion to God. It's a piece of art that stands alone, that demands attention, that leaves an impression. We did not listen to Coltrane's *A Love Supreme* while we were reading - it is too intense - but I mention it here to highlight jazz's spiritual nature. Albums like Miles Davis's *Kind of Blue* we played regularly while we were reading in the study because they are soft and subtle. My parents enjoyed the masters of all the popular genres of American music. They were astute and musically knowledgeable. Listening to music was how father and mother spent their alone time together. I remember falling asleep and hearing them listening to music in the entrance room. It was spacious and father and mother would dance together. I know this because more than once I woke up from sleep and walked into the entrance room looking for father and mother and found them dancing. The first time this happened, I was startled because I did not expect it. But, when I saw the activity, it looked like fun and I wanted to join them. Father and mother smiled at me, but swiftly, yet calmly escorted me back to my bedroom. I quickly learned that it was not my playtime. It was their playtime. Music is the strongest medium that speaks to the soul. Books, at their best, teach us about the human condition, but music has the power to amplify or change our condition within an hour depending on what we need. There is always a song that we can connect with no matter what mood we are in. It might be because of the lyrics, the melodies or the rhythms that make us feel alive. It's more than sound because it is an expression of the human spirit. A talented musician is acutely in tune to what is inside of him and creates to share that with his audience. Sometimes, it is so personal that he may not want others hear his music, but if he does and it resonates with others, few things are as unifying. He is a kindred spirit that can hear what is inside of you and speaks for you. Few things can bring people together the way a good song does. Music is the most potent art form. Within seconds, a good song can reach the soul; however, it is the most fleeting art form. It changes with the times. It's like a flashing spark of light that excites, but disappears as quickly as it appeared. On the other hand, books are the most enduring art form. Homer wrote the *Iliad* and the *Odyssey* around 2800 years ago and it still lives, stirs the human spirit and speaks to the soul. As readers today, we can benefit from the wisdom of the people who lived before us. Books make learning about the world, humanity and oneself possible and more complete. And, the best have the potential to pass the test of time, which is the most demanding and authoritative test I know. Both books and music reflect the human condition, but touch us in different ways: music is more emotional, while books are more cerebral.

We lived in the town of Paidi in Omorfi. It was more like the size of a village than a suburb. The roads were narrow, but accommodated for two way traffic. Most of the buildings were one or two stories tall. The houses were not cramped. They had space to breathe, but were close enough and neighbors were comfortable enough that one neighbor could ask another - without strain or reservation - for a cup of sugar. Our house was closer to the beach than the center of town. There were many beaches around Paidi, but we could walk to the beach we frequented. We had to drive a couple of minutes to get to the center of town where there was a large traffic circle that had a gazebo in the middle. It was the landmark everyone referred to when someone needed directions. The traffic circle brought everything in town close together and easy to get to. The locals owned and operated the shops and restaurants. Corporations and franchises had not tainted the setting. The pizza shop was always busy and for good reason because I do not know any person who does not like pizza. Motels as opposed to resort type hotels catered to the tourists. Paidi had a reputation of being a getaway destination. Visitors escaped the busy bedlam of cities to relax. There was no nightlife to attract party people, which is why families gravitated toward it. The miniature golf course called Putt Paradise, which had a tropical theme, and the ice cream house called Cow's Delight, which was painted with a cow like black and white pattern, stood side by side and were very popular. Once or twice a year, father, mother and I would join the tourists for an evening of fun. The miniature golf course was well lit, so you could putt even when the day turned into night. It had nine holes, with a special tenth hole that was elevated above the ground and was inside a large shark's mouth. There was a little ramp and if you hit the ball with a single stroke with the right amount of accuracy and speed, it would coast off the ramp through the air into the hole and you would win a baseball cap with the Putt Paradise logo, which was good business and good advertising. Mother owned that hole. Father and I never won a hat, but mother won two. She would wear them like crowns in our house touting her royalty status and what could father and I say? Very little. She was the queen.

Yard sales were plentiful in Paidi. Mother and I could spend hours hunting for bargains. The old adage, "One man's trash is another man's treasure" carries truth. For a couple of dollars, I bought a snorkeling mask that I used for years. I guess the owner no longer needed it and getting rid of it for a couple of dollars was worth it. That was okay with me. The seller and I both won. My best purchase was a fishing rod and reel I bought for father for Father's Day. Mother saw the set first and then called me over. It was brand new and was being sold for a quarter of the price it was marketed for in stores. Our timing was good because someone else could have easily picked it up before us. We got lucky. Few things are as satisfying as a good deal. It was a perfect gift because father and I would go fishing together on his days off from work, so I knew he would like it. To go fishing, we would walk fifteen minutes from our house along the boat dock boardwalk to our spot near the main docking station. On our way, we would stop at the bait and tackle shop that was next to the fishing party boats. We would pick up a dozen claims, our preferred bait for flounder, our desired catch. Lures in plastic transparent packages hung on the shop's wall. Their shimmers appealed to my eyes. Silver, green and yellow glistened in the light, but the lures were costly. Father stuck with the claims because that was what worked for him. They came in a re-sealable bag and father temporarily stored them in our five gallon white plastic paint bucket that he carried. I carried the small tackle box where we kept fishing line, hooks, weights and other standard equipment. He held his rod and reel and I held mine. We would spend hours fishing and fill our ocean water filled paint bucket with our catch. Tourists would wander through the dock, stumble across us and wow at our bucket of fish. "What kind of fish are those? How many fish is that? What kind of bait are you using? How long have you been here?" were common questions. I answered every question without hesitation because I was proud of our accomplishment. When the day was done, we usually caught dozens of fish, gut and cleaned them on the dock and then brought them home to mother who would fry them up for dinner that night. It was gratifying to work and eat the fruits of our labor. One day, we decided to try something new and board one of the fishing party boats. I had never been on a boat before. I had been waiting for this day all week, got up early that day and had some breakfast. We walked to the dock then got in line to enter the boat. The hair on my arms stood with anticipation and excitement. We stepped in and claimed our spots. The sun was hot that day and in the air was a wind. As the boat got out into the ocean, the waves were beating against its sides. Choppy waters were not a part of our agenda, but we had no choice other than to move on.

About twenty minutes into our trip, as I was leaning against the boat's edge with my pole in hand and line out, I got dizzy, light headed, weak in the knees and my stomach started to turn. I glanced to my side and noticed other guys with the same symptoms. Then, one guy upchucked his breakfast. Then, a second, third and fourth. It was contagious, like an epidemic, from one man to the next. I could not hold it in any longer and succumbed to my illness and upchucked along with them. This continued for the remainder of the trip, which lasted for four and a half grueling hours. I would take breaks from emptying my stomach by lying down groaning on a bench. The merciless waves defeated me that day. That was it. Never again. I learned my lesson. From that day on, I stayed on the dock.

During the day, mother would take me around town as she ran her errands. The post office, laundromat and corner convenience store were regular destinations. The doctor's office was another familiar place where I would get routine checkups. Most of the time, I followed mother dragging my feet. Going to all these places felt like work. I would rather be home playing with my toys. However, I did not mind our weekly trip to the grocery mart.

The only one in town, the grocery mart was owned and operated by our neighbors and we looked forward to seeing them every time we went shopping. Their three children were older than me and helped stock shelves and work the registers. You can make a lot of money owning your own business, but in can be a lot of work because its success depends on you. You reap what you sow. However, even with hard work, success is not guaranteed. As with everything, God's Grace is pivotal. I remember it being built, so it was relatively new to the community and outsold other specialty food stores because it carried most products and produce. Though not the size of a chain establishment, it had its own bakery, deli and fish market inside. Upon walking through the front entrance, I could smell the scent of fresh fish. Since we lived by the ocean, the stock of fish was replenished daily, so the smell was brisk, not spoiled, as it is in some places. We always picked up the staples - like milk and eggs - and took advantage of the in-store bakery and deli.

    My parents were frugal and conservative with money, but not cheap, particularly with food. Any extra money was usually spent to make a good meal. Mother did not hesitate to buy steaks, as long as they were on sale. Good food enhanced the quality of our lives and was something we enjoyed together. Dinner was a formal, yet informal event. We sat together at 6:30 every evening, set the table and said prayer. Food followed and as we spoke about our days, we tended to let loose and indulge in each other's company. New stories as well as old stories about our lives surfaced in dialogue in a way that defines family. Dinnertime was the climax of our day. There was nothing else we would rather do, no place we would rather be and no others on earth who we would rather be with. Mother made a lot of soup, father's choice meal. If father had a long day at work and mother cooked some soup, he would spontaneously brighten up. Chicken noodle, split pea and Cajun shrimp were among the regular dishes. And, if we had a few extra ingredients that seemed to go together, mother would put them together and make some gumbo. She mixed up the menu, so father was always surprised.

In the grocery mart, mother would play question/answer games with me to keep me from causing mischief, which worked, at least, temporarily. She would ask, "What does organic mean?" or "What is poultry?" The questions were not always easy, but I liked the process of learning. When I learned that tomatoes are botanically defined as fruit and not as vegetables, my mind nearly exploded. Chefs may use the savory, unsweet tomato as a vegetable in cooking, but the tomato is the fleshy seed-bearing body of a flowering plant, which makes it a fruit. It is not the root, stem or leaf of a plant, which would make it a vegetable.

For me, our trip to the grocery mart was an adventure that began when we chose our grocery cart. They were large - much bigger than I was - and the key was to find one that had strong wheels - this way it could support my weight as I treated it like my own private chariot. When I was small, I would sit in the cart with the groceries, but when I got bigger and started to crush the groceries, I would stand outside on the front axle and hang onto to the body. Mother was the driver and I was the passenger. It was thrilling and unpredictable because I rode blind with my back in front. It was the only way to grasp the cart. I never knew which direction mother would be pushing. "Faster, faster," I would shout, but mother would tell me to pipe down. I would comply, so she would not got tired of me and kick me off. The ride would freeze when mother stopped the cart to pick up food from the shelves. This gave me the opportunity to run around. With mother busy, I had the freedom to play in the aisle. I would run up the aisle and half way through I would drop to the side of my butt and slide. The faster I ran, the further I would slide. Then, I would run down the aisle and do it again. I did this as long as mother was searching and reaching for the shelved food. This could last minutes and I would slide a half a dozen times. I perfected the skill and considered myself an athlete. I felt like the grocery mart aisle sliding Olympic champion and the other customers were the crowd mesmerized by my athletic excellence. I could hear them chanting my name, "Ezekiel! Ezekiel! Ezekiel!" even if it was only in my imagination. When mother moved on to the next item on her shopping list and restarted the chariot, I would get back on board and the games would continue. Mother would not get angry at me because she was expecting it, but if I was getting too loud and disrupting the other customers, she would give me a look and I would stop because I knew if I did not, I would be in trouble. That look was more powerful than any words she could say and I knew exactly what she meant. If I was relatively well behaved and not disrupting the other customers too much, she would allow me choose a candy. I always picked a chocolate. It could be dark chocolate, milk chocolate, with peanut butter or coconut - it did not matter. I would savor the taste because it was my favorite food.

When I was little, every day was special and every Saturday morning was like a holiday. On Saturdays, I would wake up early without any outside notice - only from my exuberant spirit that could barely wait to begin the day. Slowly, my eyes would open and a smile would break through from within and surface onto my face. I would take a deep breath and inhale the sunlit air that filled my bedroom and yawn a great yawn to fight drowsiness's gravity, which wanted to keep me under the sheets. I would stretch my body straight from the curl it kept itself in during the night, feeling my blood flow through my veins, regenerating my muscles. The light outdoor breeze would strike the palm tree's leaves, which in turn would break the wind. I could hear the confrontation of nature's elements, which seemed to encourage me to get out of bed. I could hear the birds chime into nature's rhythmic commotion and sometimes a bird would peep through the window and chirp hello. My spirit and nature seemed to start the day together and begin the first page of the day's chapter unified. I would savor the surreal quality of my dreams and dance with it until my mind's eye lit out the cloudiness of unreality and dusted off sleep's final phase.

After I broke free from my bed sheets, I would hurry into father and mother's adjacent room and slip into their bed. They would try to sleep into a couple extra dream sequences, but I was too excited to be awake to let that happen. I would cocoon myself in between them as if I was about to go back to sleep, but my restlessness kept my eyes wide open. I can still smell the fresh scent and feel the soft texture of father and mother's newly laundered pillowcases and bed sheets. When mother caressed my cheek with her hand and father brushed my hair with his hand, I knew they, too, were ready to rise and shine. It was the only morning in the week that father and mother would remain in bed later than I. Father did not have work and we usually had no plans, so Saturday mornings were just for us with no distraction from the outside world. We would lovingly give each other butterfly kisses - eyelash kisses on the cheek. It would tickle, but that was how we greeted each other on Saturday mornings. We would also snuggle up together and sing songs. Sometimes they were commercially successful songs and other times we made up our own lyrics to random melodies and beats that popped into our heads, but whatever we sang was always a happy tune about us being together.

Father would get up and walk to the two bedroom windows and slide the window curtains to the side to let the sunlight in. At that moment, I could see the sunrays break into the room through the transparent windows dividing the light and darkness in front of me. Dust particles drifted through the sunlit air and never seemed to land on anything, but rather floated effortlessly continuously harmoniously silently within the sun's rays. One at a time, we would enter the bathroom to scrub our faces and brush our teeth. By then, it would be about half past nine and our taste buds and stomachs would alert us that it was time for breakfast. Mother would cook. She was a genius in the kitchen. Everything she made was good and the meals were as healthy as possible without losing flavor. I can still taste her homemade whole-wheat pancakes. We would dress the pancakes with cottage cheese and maple syrup and have some fresh fruit and a glass of orange juice on the side. As she was cooking, father and I would prepare the table. We were a team in that kitchen and we savored not only the food, but also each other's company. When we finished eating, father and I would clean up the kitchen and put the dishes away while mother put the leftovers in the refrigerator, so we could enjoy them the next day. For the rest of Saturday, we would be at the beach - swimming, building drip castles, skipping rocks on the surface of the water and looking for sea glass.

 Sundays were reserved for spiritual renewal.

My parents did not follow an organized religion, but they believed in the Almighty God of the three great monotheistic world religions - Judaism, Christianity and Islam. They believed He is a Supreme Presence who plays a role in people's lives and that He is Powerful. Most people in the world believe in God and some do not and my parents felt bad for those who do not. Some people deny the existence of God through science. The reasoning mind and the senses are the foundation of science; however, my parents knew that the reasoning mind and the senses are not trustworthy. My parents recognized that science has achieved great things and that it has taught us much from the microscopic to the cosmic. And, they believed in the noble honesty of the scientific method and it's longing for truth to the point of confession of its limitations never knowing if its findings are completely correct. Conclusions are constantly being reassessed by means of new tests and discoveries. Science has not given us all the answers. And, it may never. With science, there is no end in sight. There will always be new realms to explore and more questions to ask. Science desires to see the whole iceberg even though, more often than not, it is only a witness of the iceberg's tip. Plato understood this and allegorized the weakness of perception in his allegory of the cave where people saw truth in shadows and not what was the source of the shadows. I believe that, eventually, science will find that everything began with God. And, I believe science will eventually realize that God will be the end of scientific discovery. Pope Benedict XVI professed that science is "unable to grasp the global nature of reality" (December 22, 2005). My parents believed that God is reality. They believed that God is beyond our comprehension and that He is mysterious, but that He does exist. He who says God does not exist is lost, lifeless and already dead. If God exists, so does the Adversary - Satan. Scripture says so and so does Jesus. Who would dare say that the devil does not exist? As Charles Baudelaire wrote, "the finest trick of the devil is to persuade you that he does not exist." My parents recognized Jesus as the Christ of God and the Savior of humankind, but they did not subscribe to any one Christian denomination. We did not go to church on Sundays, but we did pray and study the Bible. Our Sundays were much like the Jewish Sabbath.

  Like Jews, we left behind the stresses and confines of the world, so we could devote ourselves to God. It was a day of peace when God made us to lie down in green pastures, lead us beside still waters, restored our souls and lead us in paths of righteousness for His name's sake (Psalm 23). It was a day of rest, rejuvenation and prayer that we waited for each week. Our Sunday worship may not have been filled with ceremony and historical tradition, like the Jewish celebration of the Sabbath, but I believe our hearts were in the same place as practicing Jews. My parents were well versed in the

Bible and they felt the same natural piety to observe a holy day that honored God's rest at the end of Creation:

> And on the seventh day God finished his work which he had done, and he rested on the seventh day from all his work which he had done. So God blessed the seventh day and hallowed it, because on it God rested from all his work which he had done in creation (Genesis 2:2).

Music was important in our house and was not neglected on Sundays. Black American Gospel music helped us get closer to God because of the musicians' devotion to God's Son Jesus the Christ and the music's message of the Good News of God's Kingdom of Heaven. Gospel music's depth and power cannot be denied. Those singers and musicians were not merely entertainers, but brothers and sisters who we related to in heavenly ecstasy and worldly pain. Mahalia Jackson, Aretha Franklin and the Five Blind Boys of Mississippi kept us centered in this turbulent world and helped us get by during rough days.

My parents were everything to me, so when they died, my young innocent world crumbled.

I was twelve. It was a Friday night. The weather was beautiful and the stars were as bright as ever - perfect for a romantic evening. My parents decided to go out on a date just the two of them as a couple. Our neighbor was taking care of me. It was the end of the summer, the time of season when kids are preparing to go to college and are saying goodbye to their old friends. The college years is a time when most young adults are living independent of their parents for the first time, when they are on their own making their own decisions. It is a time when many blossom into maturity in front of the community. It is an exhilarating time when everything is new and they are learning about themselves. However, it can also be a reckless time when young adults feel indomitable as though there are no consequences to their actions - youth's greatest lie. Some fail life's lessons and reality confronts them when it is too late. My parents and I paid the price for one such youth's reckless behavior. She was drinking. She was underage. Her friend hosted a party at his parents' house. His parents did not promote the drinking, but neither did they stop it. The girl and a few friends decided to leave the party and get in her car to drive to their respective houses. She was supposed to be the sober designated driver, but she got carried away in pleasures of the party. She told the police that she only had a couple of drinks, but that was enough to dull her senses. My parents, too, were on their way home. Father was a cautious driver. He would tell me, "You have to be careful on the road because you never know who is doing what behind the wheel. When I step into my car, safety is top priority because not only could I injure myself, I could injure someone else and I would have to live with that for the rest of my life." The girl who was driving was not paying attention to the road. Her friends were joking around in the backseat of her car and she turned around to see why they were laughing. She hit my parents' car from the back. It swerved to the right, then to the left into oncoming traffic. A massive truck was driving toward them and hit them head on. Their car was destroyed and they died instantly. They were the only casualties. It was on the local television news. It was horrific. As an adult, I looked for answers and learned details. When I lost them, I was a child. They, too, were young. Both were thirty-four.

    I used to blame the parents who allowed the underage drinking and the reckless college girl for my parents' deaths, but then I stopped because blame will not heal my sickness - my parents are gone and nothing can bring them back. In anger and frustration, I used to ask myself, "Why do good people suffer misfortune? Where is God when there is pain?" In Scripture, there is a parable about how God gave the homeless Lazarus - whose sores were licked by stray dogs - relief and eternal peace after death in Paradise. I believe God is good and just and that righteousness will prevail, even if it must be after death. As I dig deep, I hear Jesus cry out to me and to those suffering in this life in this world, "I know your pain!" because he took the form of a human being in flesh and experienced the peak of human suffering by being nailed to a cross for hours and left to die - a torture reserved for criminals, not something we would imagine for the Sinless One. And, to those who have lost loved ones in their lives, to parents who have lost their children (perhaps, life's greatest ill), God cries out to them, "I know your pain!" because His only Son was tortured and killed. Understanding this about Jesus the Christ and God the Father, I find comfort because I know I am not alone. If God and His Son experienced pain, we are not immune to it either.

      I believe God never leaves us, even when we think He has. This sentiment is illustrated in mother's favorite poem, *Footprints in the Sand*. In it, a man has a dream about his life with God of which is represented by two sets of footprints on a beach. He notices that during his most difficult times, there is only one set and so questions God's presence. The poem ends with God comforting and reassuring the man that when he saw only one set of footprints on the beach, it was not that God was not by his side, but rather that God was carrying him. This poem hung framed on father and mother's bedroom wall. They often referred to it in conversation and they pointed it out to me more than once. As a child, its imagery left an impression on me and now as an adult, I consider it angelic. When I am troubled and in distress, I go to it and it strengthens me and reminds me of mother. It helped her and it has helped me. Even after death, father and mother still teach me about life and love.

They helped shaped my character and helped direct me to God intentionally and unintentionally, in specific ways and in implicit influences. God was the center of their universe and by means of His Grace and Love, He made that possible. God strengthened them and He has strengthened me and He is the center of my universe, as well.

    I miss my parents, but their love for me lives in me and is a part of me coming through with every action I take. I sometimes think about the mystery and power of love. In English, we use the word "love" in many ways. We say we love art, our pets and God with the same word. The ancient Greeks tried to capture, pinpoint and distinguish the many forms of love with four words: storge, philia, eros, agape.

    Many years after my parents' deaths, I had a desire to understand the meaning of love. It helped me cope with my loss. By studying it, my feelings for them were no longer undefinable. I know they loved me and I know they knew I loved them, but I had an ethereal understanding of our relationship. Studying about love was therapeutic and helped me make sense of our love. I was able to extract its meaning through study.

    The ancient Greeks used the term "storge" to describe a fondness, affection and love that holds a family together. My parents' love for me and my love for them is the epitome of storge. My mother squeezing me as a child for no other reason than because she loved me is storge in its purest form. She demonstrated her storge for me when she would labor in the kitchen to make me homemade angel hair pasta with sauce made fresh from the tomatoes in our garden because it was my favorite meal. I have had spaghetti and tomato sauce in restaurants, but it does not compare to my mother's cooking. I felt my parents' storge for me when they would give me butterfly kisses on Saturday mornings and when they would read a story to me at night and then tuck me into bed. I tried to reciprocate their storge for me with hand crafted birthday cards that said things like, "World's Best Father" and "World's Best Mother." Storge is a comfortable, quiet, private feeling that I smelled in mother's perfume and in father's aftershave. It comes to me when I see yellow lilies like the ones that were in front of our home. I found it in father's jokes and in mother's laugh. Father had a dry wit that mother appreciated. He was a master of puns and would play with words. One of father's regular jokes was, "You can tune a guitar, but you can't *tuna* fish. Unless of course, you play *bass*" (Douglas Adams). Mother must have heard that joke a thousand times, but she always laughed, as if to say, "That's my husband, at it again, and I love him."

    Storge extends beyond parent and child to connect all family members, humanity and even animals. As 20th century British author, academic and lay theologian C.S. Lewis explains in *The Four Loves*, storge "ignores the barriers of age, sex, class and education. It can exist between a clever young man from the university and an old nurse, though their minds inhabit different worlds" (Lewis, *The Four Loves*, Harcourt Inc, 32). Storge can be a love shared between a man and his dog. A dog has storge for her newborn puppies and a cat has storge for her newborn kittens. Sometimes, even a dog and a cat can have storge for each other.

YOUNG EZEKIEL
A LIFE OF LOVES

TWO

PHILIA

My parents and I shared a small world inhabited by only the three of us. I never saw any relatives and though my parents had many acquaintances, they had few friends. These things did not matter to them because our small world was filled with storge. We thought that all we needed was each other and our storge. It was a beautiful world that one day was no more.

After my parents' deaths, my future was uncertain and I was vulnerable to the outside world. But, I was lucky. My grandmother's sister - an aunt who I never met - rescued me from the lost life that seemed to be ahead of me. My mother never mentioned her. In fact, my parents never spoke about family because both felt their families were highly dysfunctional. Father never met his father because my grandfather left my grandmother while my grandmother was pregnant with father. My grandfather was a gambler and could not support his wife and son, so he left them. He was a con-man who preyed on women and would take their money and when he had his fill, he would abandon them. My father's mother was irresponsible, as well. She neglected father during his youth. She inherited a family estate with a great sum of money and was very intelligent and made sure father went to school, but she used drugs and failed to care for father. Father pretty much raised himself. My grandmother never fully recovered from her addictions and was in and out of rehabilitation centers for most of her life. I remember father calling my mother his angel because he believed she saved him from his dark life. Mother had great sympathy and compassion for father. He was smart and strong and overcame his hard life and mother fell in love with him because of this.

Mother's family was also troubled and it was money that tore them apart. When my grandfather died prematurely from a heart attack, my grandmother manipulated his will to acquire mother's inheritance. My grandmother said she did so because she was sick with cancer and needed to pay for treatment. The judge sided with my grandmother, but mother was convinced that my grandmother stole her inheritance to sustain her affluent lifestyle. I learned all this from my grandmother's sister, my Aunt Gerontissa, when I was old enough to inquire and understand. My aunt was level headed and gave me her more objective perspective. My aunt told me money tears families apart too often. Money is powerful and can pervert one's character. If one cannot forgive, relationships are doomed. My parents were born and raised near Boston, but moved to Omorfi to start a new life.

My aunt stayed in Massachusetts. When she learned about my parents' deaths, she brought me back. My aunt was not a native of the United States. She was an immigrant born in the homeland and was a child during World War II. She was fifteen when the war ended and grew up in the aftermath when the nations were trying to recover from the devastation. In those formative years, she acquired much of her knowledge about the world and the individual on her own and she matured quickly on the streets. She was street smart. From her life experiences, she gathered information and saw patterns of when people prevailed and lost that helped her to make better decisions. She observed the piety of the priest, the erudition of the scholar, the lasciviousness of the whore and the greed of the miser. No one is perfect and she noticed when the priest was lazy and when the scholar was foolish and she observed redemption in the whore's honesty and the miser's frugality. She applied what she learned to her own life, which made her wise. As I got to know her, Aunt Gerontissa knew what was inside of people because she was keenly aware of herself and to know oneself is to know what is inside others. As Socrates learned from the oracle of Delphi, "Know thyself." To know thyself is to know what dwells inside the individual and to know the human condition. She believed that we are all the same - we are all human beings all living on the same planet. We all experience love and pain and we can all relate to each other's joy and sorrow. She was sensitive to her own feelings and the feelings of others which gave her compassion. To know thyself is easier said than done. It could take a lifetime, but if one perseveres, one will notice treasures multiplying within.

My aunt was a stout and physically strong woman. She reminded me of a bull; not because she had a short temper, but because she had a powerful presence. She demanded respect, but was never rude. She rarely laughed; although, her kindness often shined through her serious disposition. Her hair was short, grey and wavy. Some women dye their hair, but my aunt never got carried away with looks. She had seen so much during her life that looks were of little importance. In the house, she wore robes and slippers that matched. Most of her robes were shades of purple, her favorite color. Outside the house, she wore dark colored blouses and dresses. The weight of the clothing depended on the outside temperature. A seamstress by trade, she worked in a shop, but also in her home for family and friends. She was frugal and wise with money. If a customer had disposable fabric that he or she did not want, my aunt would make a bag, scarf or hat out of it and sell it in the shop she worked in. She was clever and her creations were ingenious. Outside her kitchen door she kept a large clay pot to put banana peels, apple cores and the like as compost. She would use the compost to fertilize her vegetable garden and rose bushes. When my aunt was not working, she was usually tending to her gardens. People around town knew her as the women with the beautiful rose bushes. They grew in her front lawn where people walking and driving by could see and admire them. In the backyard, she grew her vegetable garden, which took up half of the space. It was Edenesque. Cucumbers, eggplants and tomatoes flourished during the warm seasons. She had a pear tree and grape vines, which grew along her wooden fence. She even had a fig tree that in the summer produced the best figs on the east coast. She liked being outside. She did not have a television or computer - things that usually keep people indoors. She rose with the sun and set with the sun. When she was cooking, she had the hands of a magician. But, she never kept secrets. If her neighbor asked her how she put together her chicken cutlet with mushroom sauce, she proudly passed on the recipe. Many people tried to cook her meals, but no one could compare. She was a master chef.

    After my parents' deaths, I was angry with God. But, my aunt was very religious and because of her influence on me during those formative years, my anger did not last long. When I was a child, my parents taught me about God and Jesus the Christ, but they did not follow an organized formal Christianity. We never attended Sunday services, but I never missed a Sunday service with my aunt.

About once a month, my aunt and I visited the nuns at the nunnery. It took about an hour and a half to get there, but it was all highway. It was the furthest my aunt would drive in her car. It was not because the car could not handle it; but because my aunt, at her age, did not have the same stamina to drive as she used to. At the nunnery, we would help the nuns with chores which gave us the opportunity to talk to them and learn from them. Being in their presence was enough to edify. They always wore black, but they were filled with joy because of their relationship with God and Jesus. It was not an easy life. They had to endure the ascetical struggle to purify themselves for the Lord. However, if you asked them, they would tell you there is no other life to live. None of them would leave. Their devotion to God and Jesus was too strong. Annually, my aunt and I would buy from the nuns a homemade vasilopita to celebrate the new year. It was a round sweet bread that had inside it a coin, which would bring the recipient good luck for the year. We also visited to buy icons, books and recorded chanting - not always for us, but also as gifts for loved ones. My aunt's devotion to the Church compelled her to fast. Throughout the year, she would fast from meat and dairy on Wednesdays and Fridays. The Church selected those days to mourn when Jesus was betrayed by Judas and when he suffered on the Cross. Plus, for over forty days during Great Lent, she would fast to prepare for Easter. She would cook, so I adopted her fasting lifestyle.

My relationship with the Church reached a new phase when I was an adolescent; I was skeptical about the Bible and the Church. I thought that because the Bible was written by man, it was not perfect and filled with error. I now reflect on this and it is an understandable objection, but at the time I did not understand the power of the Holy Spirit and how it guides man and moves him to write about God in the Light of God. I believed that the Church, too, was filled with error, but unlearned, I did not understand that the Church Fathers created the Church to preserve the authenticity of the faith. Yes, man created it, but a body was necessary, so the belief and teachings of Christ could continue to guide and teach man here on earth until Christ returns. Though my connection to the Church was weak, during this time in my life, I always knew that God existed. I thought to myself, how could we be so vain to think that we know everything and deny God?

As I was growing up, I had a problem with money and thought money caused people to do wicked things. My family history shaped my perspective and I believe my conclusions were justifiable. However, my aunt explained to me that money does not have to be evil. In fact, it could be valuable and used to do good works. My aunt opened my eyes and showed me a different perspective. She was a member of the Greek Ladies Philoptochos

Society. Philoptochos is a Greek word that means "friend of the poor." It is one of the largest women's philanthropic organization in the United States. The women are known as the mothers of a Greek Orthodox Christian children's home called Saint Basil Academy in Garrison, NY. The children of Saint Basil Academy have troubled backgrounds, like my own, but do not have an aunt, like mine, to adopt them. I thank God every day that my aunt took me in. She did not have to, but her storge for me compelled her. Saint Basil Academy provides a refuge for children whose parents or guardians are unable to care for them due to illness, death, chemical addiction and other problems. Through the guiding light of the Greek Orthodox Christian Church, it provides a nurturing environment where they are strengthened by a support system that allows them to flourish and become meaningful members of society. It provides a beacon of hope and a safe haven for them by ensuring material, spiritual, and emotional support for the development of the whole person: body, mind, and spirit. The staff of Saint Basil Academy provides the structure that they need through hours of selfless giving. Through the behavior modification program, the children are taught accountability and responsibility for themselves. The Director of Saint Basil Academy is Father Costa, a powerful, yet gentle shepherd who leads his flock with love. Saint Basil Academy's mission is to teach, to heal, to bring the light of Christ to young lives. (Saint Basil Academy on-line brochure). My aunt explained to me that money can be a blessing from God and it could be used to fulfill God's will. She told me about Saint John Chrysostom. Born around 350 AD, John was given the name "Chrysostom," which in Greek means "Golden Mouth," because of the sublimity of his preaching. In *On Wealth and Poverty*, John, filled with the Holy Spirit, gives his transcendent view of money. He explains that those who have money are blessed with it by God and to not share one's possessions is theft. God has given the wealthy their money, but it also belongs to the poor:

> He [the rich man] is directed to distribute it to his fellow servants who are in want. So if he spends more on himself than his need requires, he will pay the harshest penalty in the hereafter. For his own goods are not his own, but belong to his fellow servants (John Chrysostom, *On Wealth and Poverty*, SVS Press, 50).

I believe those who give to the children of Saint Basil Academy give from their hearts. They may not need to hear John's theology, but they can find reassurance in his words that what they are doing is divine.

Every Sunday, I went to church services with my aunt. I remember how impressed I was with the icons in the church, particularly the one of Christ Pantocrator - Christ the Almighty. It is the icon of

Christ blessing His people as ruler of all Creation and it is located at the dome of every Greek Orthodox Christian Church. The church is filled with icons and each one is magnificent. The artist's careful attention to detail in creating such an intricate image is awe-inspiring. It is mystifying how the artist can create these massive images with such fine precision, particularly mystifying are those that are mosaics, which are made of tiny stones. As a child, I knew Christ was the Son of God, but I also knew that he was a man and I was always puzzled at why the Orthodox icons did not look realistic. The Orthodox icons are not like photographs. They are in Byzantine style and represent an ideal image, inner spiritual nature and other-worldly quality of the subject. They glorify God, His Son, Mother Mary, the martyrs and the saints. Historically, the icons were meant to help the laity to connect with God and teach them lessons and theology the Church believes are of supreme importance. As a child, they left me captivated and wondering. Closest to my heart were the icons of children martyrs that adorn the walls inside the chapel. These children, who were as young as I was when I was first struck by their images, died because they stood up to persecution and would not deny their love for Christ. They were filled with great strength and I desired to be as strong as them. 2nd century Church theologian Tertullian famously said that "the blood of the martyrs is the seed of the Church." The martyrs' bloody deaths and their strength to not deny their love for Christ propagated the faith. I can envision onlookers puzzled by a Christian martyr's death ask one another, "Who are these people who face death without fear and what do they believe in?" The answer that traveled the land was that they are Christians and they believe in Jesus the Christ. The children whose images adorn the chapel walls were filled with courage and they gave me courage.

Most Sundays, I did not want to go to church, but when the services were over, I felt the Holy Spirit in me. Sometimes, on my way home, I would sing and hum the hymns. I did not realize it, but the Christianity in me was growing. It affected me.

Every season in Massachusetts gave me a different taste of God's Glorious Creation. In the autumn, the colorful leaves brightened the horizon. In the winter, the white snow descending from the sky aroused in me the spirit of Christmas. In the spring, the earth and all that inhabit it came alive in anticipation of Easter. In the summer, the radiant sun warmed me and magnified the sky. Year-round the grounds were bursting with beauty. It was much different than Omorfi and the beaches I knew so well.

My aunt's home was a single story ranch-style house. The surface of the exterior was made of cream-colored stucco. Most of the houses in the neighborhood were ranch-style, as well. They were all built in the 1950s when the architectural design was at its peak of popularity. Other exterior facades included brick, stone and wood. Trees separated the houses. In front of many of the houses, beyond their lawns, were short free dry-stone walls that bordered the roads and peeking out of each entrance stood mailboxes. People jogged along roads and bicyclists pedaled along with them. Cars would wiz by them, but the joggers and bicyclists did not care. Nothing distracted them from their sports. Surrounding my new home was nature. Trees were everywhere and little animals rustled in the leaves and birds chirped in the air. I often saw deer scamper in the forests. Calm and quiet, I would try to get close to them and I always felt special to witness their graceful honesty.

One late summer day, a couple of weeks after I moved into my new home, I was in the public park on the basketball court shooting jump-shots by myself. I was there for about twenty minutes when a group of boys, all about my age, gathered together on the other side of the court. I kept on shooting and after each shot, I glanced over to see what they were doing. One of the boys was tying his shoe. Another one was drinking from his water bottle. The remaining boys were playing on the court. They were all joking around and laughing. I kept to myself even though it looked like they were having fun. Then, from the corner of my eye, I noticed that one of the boys was walking in my direction, but I pretended that I did not see him. As he approached me, he called out, "Hey buddy." I was a bit stunned and said, "How's it going?" Then, he said, "My friends and I want to start a game, but we are short one person. Do you want to play?" I quickly said, "Definitely." Then, he said, "Cool." As I picked up my ball and my stuff that lay on the ground, he took a step closer and introduced himself. "I'm Mike," he said. "I'm Ezekiel," I said. "I never heard that name before," he said. "Yeah, I know. It's a little weird," I said. "No. I think it's cool," he said. Then, we walked over to the other boys and Mike said, "I found a player. His name is Ezekiel." They each gave me a big smile. By the time the game was over, I felt like I was a part of their crew. Mike and the boys were my first friends in my new home.

    Mike's best friend was Gabe and soon, Gabe became my good friend, too. Mike, Gabe and I were inseparable. The three of us were the same age, lived in the same neighborhood and went to the same school. We hung out with other children, but - autumn, winter, spring and summer - we were always together. We did the same things most boys did, but we did them together. We spent a lot of time in the wooded trails that were practically in our backyards. Hundreds of acres of nature were preserved for hiking enthusiasts, wildlife watchers and young explorers and adventurers, like us. We trekked through the trails often and knew the nooks and crannies around every turn. We had our favorite spots and usually gravitated to the waters. There were places where bold brooks fell from high rocks, pounding and pulsating on the stalwart rocks below. In the meandering streams, salamanders slipped and slid through the moss-covered rock faces. Creeks crept around rough rocky corners. And, in the still ponds on the floating lily pads, frogs ribbited and toads croaked. Sometimes, we went fishing and other times, we went swimming. These images remain steadfast in my memory. My love for Mike and Gabe is deep because their friendships helped me recover from my parents' deaths. They were there for me when I needed them most, even if they did not know it. They did not hesitate to love me as their friend. The ancient Greeks called this love between friends "philia." The 4th century BC Greek philosopher Aristotle was one of the first to analyze philia's nuances. In his work *Nicomachean Ethics*, he devotes sections (or books) 8 and 9 to exploring its meaning and its relevance in our lives.

    C.S. Lewis calls philia the least natural love because we can survive without it. Eros (romantic love) begets us, storge (familial love) rears us, agape (Christian love) brings us closer to our Maker, but we can probably live without philia (friendship love). Friends are not obligated to be friends. Mike and Gabe did not have to talk to me at the basketball court. They could have ignored me. I had nothing to offer them, but they welcomed me into their group and I am happy that they did. We chose to be friends. Philia is not bound or confined by natural tendencies the way storge and eros are. Philia is a free love. It is a spiritual love that raises us almost above humanity. "It is the sort of love one can imagine between angels" (Lewis, *The Four Loves*, Harcourt Inc, 77). We do not need friends, yet they enrich our lives. In ancient times, philia was exalted because it is something we all want. As Aristotle points out, "No one would choose to live without friends, even if he had all other goods" (Aristotle, *Nicomachean Ethics*, The Library of Liberal Arts, 214). Even if I was the richest man in the world, I would still want friends. One might say they are "the greatest of external goods" (Aristotle, 263). I felt honored to be Mike and Gabe's friend. Who would not be honored to be chosen to be a friend? They express their philia for me and I reciprocate with my philia for them. This mutual love is praiseworthy and is the sign of a true lasting friendship. Mike and Gabe have integrity and are honest, sincere and true to themselves and because they have these qualities within themselves, they are like that with me, too. We did our best to not lower ourselves below these virtues and we never steered one another toward base activities. In fact, we prevent each other from making base decisions. "What characterizes good men is that they neither go wrong themselves nor let their friends do so" (Aristotle, 230). Furthermore, as 6th century BC Greek lyrical poet Theognis said, "You will learn noble things from noble people" (Aristotle, 265).

There was one time, when Mike, Gabe and I trekked through the woods to the waterfall. It was about a fifteen minute walk from our homes and as one approaches the waterfall, there is a heavy stream running from it. We usually went during the summer and would swim in the shallow pool below the falling water. It is an extraordinary sight. The waterfall is about three stories tall. Each time I went, I was awed. However, the water was cold; nothing like the water at Omorfi, but I would go in anyway. This one time, when we arrived, a group of kids were splashing and fooling around. Mike, Gabe and I stationed ourselves on a giant slab of rock under a tree beside the pool and then we inched our way into the water. We walked over to the falling water and let it beat on our backs. It was the best massage. We mixed into the other group to be friendly, but a couple of guys were standoffish though the girls were nice to us. As I started to talk to one of the girls, one of the guys bumped into me on purpose. He gave me a tough look and said, "Watch your step." I was caught off guard and replied with, "Excuse me." Then, he asked, "What's your name?" I answered, "Ezekiel." "Well, Ezekiel," he said, "I dare you to jump from the waterfall." I was young, fourteen years old, and froze. Mike was big for a fourteen year old and was the star center for the high school junior varsity basketball team. As the guy was pestering me, Mike stepped in and said, "Why are you daring my friend?" The guy said, "I think your friend is afraid" and then he started laughing and looking at his friends. Mike said, "What are you trying to do, impress your friends by making my friend look foolish? It doesn't take much to pick on someone smaller than you." When he confronted the guy, the guy said, "I was just trying to be funny." Mike asked, "Have you ever jumped off this cliff?" "No," the guy answered. "Then how can you dare my friend, if you have never jumped?" Mike asked. At first, when the guy bumped into me, he used his size to intimidate me and was swelling with pride, but when Mike stepped in, his ego deflated and he shrunk in size. After that, they respected Mike and me, too, because I was with Mike. Mike kept it real. He told it like it was and spoke to him with respect. Their cold front warmed and, believe it or not, we all ended up becoming friends.

Aristotle explains that bad people never have true long lasting friendships because they lack integrity and are not constant with themselves and therefore cannot be constant with others. Bad people "do not find joy in one another, unless they see some material advantage coming to them" (Aristotle, 222). Bad people do not have true friendships.

Aristotle explains that there are three forms of philia: love for those who are useful, pleasant and good. There are different motives in each form of philia. For example, philia based on usefulness is concerned with the good gained by the other. The relationships between an employer and employee or a teacher and student are examples of philia based on usefulness. Each party sustains the friendship as long as the usefulness for one another lasts. When one thinks he is getting less than he should, there are bound to be complaints and reproaches. Philia based on pleasure, too, only last as long as each party maintains that sense of pleasure. One who finds pleasure in a funny person feels philia for him up until the pleasure ends. But, here, complaints and reproaches do not usually arise because the two parties will simply no longer spend time together. Philia based on usefulness and pleasure are not based on the type of person one is, but because of what is gained. As a result, friendships such as these easily dissolve. Aristotle suggests that when a friendship ends, one should not treat the friend as a stranger, but rather remember that he was once a friend. We should treat him better than a stranger, unless it was his wickedness that ended the friendship (Aristotle, 252). Mike and Gabe are more than friends of utility and pleasure - though they are useful and pleasant because they are good people. They are my good friends. There are many people who I like and get along with and think are good people, but Mike and Gabe are my truest friends. It is impossible to be perfect friends with many people. Like romantic love, it is "an extreme, and an extreme tends to be unique" (Aristotle, 225). Mike and Gabe always looked out for me. They wanted the best for me and I knew it and they knew I would be there for them. When I was down they picked me up. Those "who wish for their friends' good for their friends' sake are friends of the truest sense" (Aristotle, 219). People who share common interests will be companions, but those who share something more will be friends. Friends share something "more inward, less widely shared and less easily defined" (Lewis, 66). They walk side by side seeking a common truth, sharing a common vision. A person should neither have no friends nor too many. Perhaps, the largest number of true friends is limited to the number one might be able to live with (Aristotle, 268). In true friendships, quality is important, not quantity. In true friendships, just as it is in friendships of pleasure, "a few friends are sufficient, just as it takes little to give food the right amount of sweetness" (Aristotle, 267). Mike, Gabe and I grew up together. From the time I moved to Massachusetts at the age of twelve, I have few memories without them. We were constantly in and out of each other's houses and even our families were close. In our friendship, we were equals. There was no leader in our crew and there were no followers. We each had a voice and we respected each other's opinions. We joked with each other, but we never let our jokes go too far to the point of hurting each other. We knew each other's limits and only joked with each other out of philia.

Like everyone who has a friend, our relationships strengthened as we earned each other's confidence. It starts off small, like how Gabe let me review his class notes for a quiz. Or, how Mike let me borrow some money to buy a drink on our walk home from school. On my fourteenth birthday, they each gave me fourteen birthday punches. My arm was sore with bruises for nearly two weeks, but they did it out of philia because they were also the ones who were ready to back me up when I almost got into a fight with two boys on the basketball court outside of school. This was when I knew they were true friends. I trusted them and they trusted me. They never intentionally wronged me. People who become friends quickly without knowing each other's worth are not really friends even though they want to be. A true friendship takes time to grow.

    We had other friends, for example, in class, on sports teams and in clubs. And, in that extended group, most of our friends were friends with each other. "One's friends should also be the friends of one another, if they are all going to spend their days in each other's company" (Aristotle, 268). There was a group of us that played sports. We were competitive and always tried to outdo each other, but it was always in good spirit. We were constantly racing each other to see who could run the fastest. It made us better athletes and because we were friends, we never let the competition get the best of us. I was athletic and strong with good stamina. I was good at sports, better than most, but not exceptional at any one sport. Autumn, winter, spring, summer - we played whatever sport was in season. We played in the town's recreation leagues, but we mostly played amongst each other. Our town had baseball, football and soccer fields; plus, basketball and tennis courts. After homework, we would call each other and get a ball and play until the sun set. The weekends were more of the same. Weather often dictated the chosen sport. Football during the first snowfall became an annual tradition. Snow often accumulated from inches into feet and all us friends were of the consensus that the more the better. We would bundle up in layers of clothing to protect ourselves from nature's elements, but by the end, the jackets and gloves would come off. We took it serious enough that we would sweat in the snow to the point of being soaked inside and out. However, by the end, rules were relinquished and rabblerousing and fooling around reigned. We would often pounce on each other even without possession of the ball just to fall in the soft forgiving snow. Frozen fingers and drenched threads were normal, but it was always a day well spent. For Mike, Gabe and I, our favorite sport, by far, was basketball. We would play all-year-round: outside on black-tops and inside the town's youth center gymnasium. We each had our own style of play, but we also tried to imitate the moves of our favorite players. Our hero was Michael Jordan - perhaps, the greatest athlete of the 20th century. He was the best at offense and defense, a complete player who lead his team to six championships. He injected creativity and artistry into his play on the court. He played at the highest level in every game because he believed every game was important. He wanted to prove that he was the best and he did while mesmerizing, delighting and awing the crowd (including many of his opponents). He made it look easy, but that is because he sharpened his skills with hard practice. When he failed, he practiced harder and it motivated him to be better. God made him tall and strong and blessed him with a tenacity beyond all other athletes, but he seized those gifts and with a profound work ethic, he made himself the best. In one of his most lauded games, he played sick with the flu and a 103 degree fever and through his indomitable will, he scored 38 points leading his team to victory.

    We loved music, too, and the music of Bob Marley was especially meaningful to us. Marley's music is everywhere: radio, television, parties, movies, friends. It is a part of our culture. By the time I was fifteen, I was already numb to his songs. But, one day, Mike, Gabe and I were in Gabe's house lounging on the couches in his living room, hanging out and passing time. Gabe left for a moment and went to his bedroom. When he returned to us, he said, "Fellas, I've got something you've got to hear." "What's that?" I asked. "Bob Marley," he said with a grin on his face. "What's with the excitement? We know it all," Mike said. "Not this stuff," Gabe said proudly. Gabe hooked up the music to the speakers. We got quite and then the music kicked in. It had a heavy rhythm and then we heard Marley's voice: "I'm a rebel, soul rebel. I'm a capturer, soul adventurer." I liked it. I thought it had value, but after the song ended, I did not think much of it. The following Thursday was the anniversary of my parents' deaths. I was hurting. I was sitting on the stoop of my aunt's house and Gabe passed by and saw me. He asked me if I was alright, which meant a lot because he cared. I told him why I was upset. The next day when the three of us were walking together to school, I was still visibly down. Gabe handed me some music and said, "I've got something that may help out." It was an album of some of Bob Marley's early recordings with songs I never heard before. When I returned home and listened to the album, I noticed that the rhythms were uplifting and the lyrics were spiritual. Much of his music hit home. It was like medicine to my sick soul. I was hooked when I heard the song, "I'm Hurting Inside" because I, too, hurt inside. We were coming from the same place, so when Marley sang, "One Love! One Heart! Let's get together and feel all right," I knew things would get better. He preached love, peace, unity, freedom and Jah (God). In songs such as "Thank You Lord," he proclaimed how he loved to pray. Songs like "Exodus" are powerful and helped me make it through tough times. He was not a saint. He was notorious for smoking marijuana and having affairs with women; even so, most of his music is angelic. The youth are impressionable and Marley's indiscretions may seem cool, but my friends and I did not admire him for the marijuana and women; we thought he was cool because of his music.

We value our friends in bad fortune and in good fortune. They are indispensable in bad fortune because we need their assistance. In sorrow, they can alleviate our pain by sharing our burden or by the pleasantness of their presence. If a friend is tactful, "seeing him and talking to him are a source of comfort, since he knows our character and the things which give us pleasure or pain" (Aristotle, 270). They are a refuge during times of misfortune. I do not know how I would have made it through the trauma of my parents' deaths without the Mike and Gabe. We need them in good fortune, too, because it is the best way to live. They give us the opportunity to share our joy. When I finally passed my test at the Department of Motor Vehicles and got my driver's license, I could barely wait to tell Mike and Gabe. I was excited and feeling their joy for me was just as meaningful as getting the license.

The opinions of my friends, "of this little circle, while I am in it, outweighs that of a thousand outsiders... Theirs is the praise we really covet and the blame we really dread" (Lewis, 79). Lewis illustrates that a group of friends have the power to stir rebellion. With a common vision, they can change the establishment for better or worse. He explains that "the dangers are perfectly real. Friendship (as the ancients [like Aristotle] saw) can be a school of virtue; but also (as they did not see) a school of vice. It is ambivalent. It makes good men better and bad men worse" (Lewis, 80). After Jesus tells his disciples to love one another as he has loved them, he calls them friends and together they changed the world.

I was able to love Mike and Gabe because I loved myself first. A "man is his own best friend and therefore should have the greatest affection for himself" (Aristotle, 260). This may sound selfish, but if a man does not love himself, how can he love another? How would he know what love is? My love for them was an extension of the love I had for myself. A person who acts justly to himself, who acts with self-control, who seeks to be virtuous cannot be called selfish. He desires what is noble, not what is advantageous. A good man's noble deeds benefit himself because he fulfills his desire to be noble and the recipient of those noble deeds benefits, as well, so both parties win. A wicked man's selfish deeds may fulfill his desire, but he fails to feed the greatest that is in him: love, nobility, virtue. If he chooses to not do what is best for himself, he will not do what is best for another. I believe by loving yourself, by doing what is best for yourself, you will make a true friend.

A person does not need to know every detail of another's life to be a friend. As Lewis writes, "the real question [is], *Do you see the same truth?* In a circle of true friends each man is simply what he is: stands for nothing but himself" (Lewis, 70). I did not need to know that Mike had an older sister who was married with kids or that Gabe liked to read books to be my friend. And, they did not ask to know about my past, so I could qualify to be their friend. Of course, we learned these things as we spent more time together during comments, jokes and stories we told one another, but never as questions to pass a test. My friendships with them began neutral with no proof of who we were and no direction, but when our honest selves came out and because we saw the same truth, then we were able to walk side by side as perfect friends. The more I got to know them and the more I experienced with them, the more I appreciated them. Our philia for each other was so great that each of us felt lucky to have the others. Deep inside, I would ask myself, "Who am I to be blessed with such friends?" It was very humbling. We were free to say and do as we pleased without fear of being judged because we knew each other so well - nothing one could say or do would be a surprise to the rest. When the three of us were together, we brought out the best in each other. We talked philosophy before we were aware of philosophy as an enterprise. We talked about our ambitions and girls. We talked with comfort, ease and joy. The richest moments were those when the air was thick with laughter. We would often laugh for no reason other than because we enjoyed each other's company. Lewis calls times like these "the golden sessions" and that "Life - natural life - has no better gift to give" (Lewis, 72). We knew friendships like ours were rare and I remember saying to myself and to them that these are the best moments of our lives.

There is a movie that Mike, Gabe and I enjoyed called *Stand by Me*. It is a story about four young boys, friends who journey together through prairies and forests to find a dead body, one they learned about in their hometown. The substance of the story is the boys' relationships and their loss of innocence. At the end of the story, one of the boys who was now a man, a writer, reflects on this experience and says, "I never had any friends later on like the ones I had when I was twelve. Jesus, does anyone?" This sentiment was shared between me and my friends and is an insight that has remained with me throughout life.

One of my favorite childhood memories took place outside Gabe's house. There were four of us: myself, Mike, Gabe and our friend Alex. It was a beautiful summer day and the breeze in the air alleviated much of the sun's heat. It was after lunch, but before dinner. At that age, playtime revolved around breakfast, lunch and dinner because my aunt and their mothers wanted to make sure we did not miss a meal. It was a little past mid-summer when the excitement of summer started to subside. We were bored and spent a good half of an hour tossing a football around. Mike interrupted the rhythm and threw the football at the backboard of the basketball rim that was set up in Gabe's driveway. A new game began. We all took turns trying to throw the football at the backboard and after each successful throw, we increased the distance between us and the backboard.

However, this, too, got boring. Our attention spans were sizzling. Gabe's parents were not home, which was an added ingredient to spice up our mischievous dispositions. Mayhem was inevitable. Gabe had a bunch of plum trees on his property, so instead of throwing the football, we decided to throw the fallen plums at each other. I don't know who fired the first shot, but we all picked up ammunition and aimed it at one another. The weapon was chosen. I got hit once and the plum juice stained my shirt and I was upset, but then I hit Mike, which was gratifying. Soon, we realized we had to set parameters and rules to our game; otherwise, it would be chaos and a disorganized game never lasts long because someone always gets hurt. We incorporated bases and timeouts; however, there was no objective to our game and no points or penalties. It was just an excellent idea. I asked myself, "Why did we not think of this before?" We split up into two teams. It was Mike and Gabe versus Alex and me. On his property, Gabe had a car garage that was separate from his house. The garage was one story tall, as was part of his house. Between these two buildings - these fortifications - were the driveway and a vegetable garden. It was brave to run though the driveway because we would be exposed, but we could quickly escape. The vegetable garden was a good place to hide, but it was difficult to run through. And, on the roofs, our only protection was prayer. The space was small enough where we could reach each other from one edifice to the other, yet large enough to make the game challenging. It was an ideal combat zone. We decided to climb onto the roofs and commence battle. Courage and confidence were clutch to conquering and claiming conquest. I think a lot of people would have freaked out being up so high, but not us. We were comfortable running on the roofs, jumping up and down one story buildings and dodging small inanimate objects aimed at each other because we were athletes with good balance. There were many trees and countless plums. Our arsenal was limited to plums, but we exploited our resources by the tactics we used. We hurled some of the plums into the air as grenades, released others with rapid fire and spread handfuls of others with a single throw. My principal strategy was to attack then immediately defend. I often employed a blitzkrieg, but then required a short reprieve to muster my military might and gather arms. Mike was always on the move and employed a moving target theory, which made him difficult to track and attack. Alex stationed himself under one of the trees which supplied unlimited ammo and he used a shovel he found in the open garage as a shield to protect himself. Gabe was less strategic and consequently slipped a few times on the mushed fruit. Fortunately, he was on the ground and not on one of the roofs. We probably would have been there until someone broke a bone, but a police officer heard us and saw us from a distance and commanded us to come down from the roofs -

disrupting our fun. At the end, we sat on the war torn landscape and the plum remains and juices that saturated the sun scolded cement and roofs, which emitted a unique mist and fruity smell. There was no victory claimed and no spoils won - other than a good time. As an adult looking back at my youthful years, I have scenes in my mind that emerge from my memory, but there are only a few events that are always with me which I will never forget. The plum battle is one of them.

I know I said philia is a freely chosen love, that we pick our friends, that we select those whom we might connect with. But, sometimes, I think something more transcendent, mystical and divine takes place. Life seems to be very delicate and complex. The slightest change can change the outcome of the following events. Everything has consequences. It is the principle of cause and effect. There are an infinite number of ways of how my parents could still be alive. And, there are an infinite number of ways of how I would not have met Mike and Gabe. If you asked me before my parents' deaths what my life would be like in the future, I never would have guessed the reality. Mike and Gabe are like family and I believe this is not by chance. C.S. Lewis said it best: "for a Christian, there are, strictly speaking, no chances. A secret Master of the Ceremonies has been at work. Christ, who said to the disciples 'Ye have not chosen me, but I have chosen you,' can truly say to every group of Christian friends

'You have not chosen one another but I have chosen you for one another'" (Lewis, 89).

    For me, living with my aunt was a blessing on many levels. Geographically, it made a difference. As a child, the last thing I wanted to do was to leave Omorfi. It was my home and all I knew. But, looking back at my situation, I was better off moving away from Omorfi . Living in Massachusetts separated me from my parents' car accident. It alleviated the situation. It was the case of out of sight, out of mind. The physical distance between Omorfi and Massachusetts provided for me an emotional distance. And, the stark contrast between one another's landscape gave me a new start.

    I revisited Omorfi when I was an adult, when I felt I was prepared to deal with the trauma, strong enough deal with the pain. As an adult whose wounds had managed to heal with a scar, I visited the roads and paths I traveled along as a child. They caused scenes of my life to flash before my eyes reminding me of my parents. The smell of the salt water, the feel of the rough sand sifting through my toes, the sound of children laughing and splashing water, the taste of the fresh fruit and the sight of my old house ignited a love in me that I missed. It was like a lucid dream that receded to the back of my mind that was reawakened. I cried when I revisited for the first time, but it was a good cry. During that first visit as a mature man, I felt as though my parents were with me, once again. I could feel their presence.

I am not one for sentimentality. I do not believe it does any good. It only makes one woozy with longing. The love in me that I felt when I returned to Omorfi was empowering. It reminded me of who I was that lead me to become who I am. No other place in Omorfi affected me as much as the beach I played on as a boy. As I got closer to it, I could smell and taste the salt water air, which tantalized my anticipation of my desired destination. I remember stepping on the sun beaten sand and it being hot. The vibrant sun was mightier than any cloud in the sky. The drifting clouds seemed to disappear in despair because they could not compete with the sun. I hurried through the grainy pebbled earth to the ocean's edge to relieve my feet's bottoms. The stark contrast of the hot sand to the cold water would tingle my feet, shoot up my legs, pass through my spine and flutter into my heart making me feel alive. The excitement of being at the beach was equally emotional and physical. I remember being fixated on the rhythmic waves and moment by moment, they would rush on to the shore gently covering and refreshing my feet. The waves would console me - "Shhh… Shhh… Shhh" is what they would say - reassuring me that all is good. I stood there for a bit and watched the water approach me and then recede. Slowly, it would breathe in and just as it caught its breath, it would exhale with relentless consistency. Sometimes, the tide is high and sometimes, it is low, but I would never say that the ocean gets tired because it never stops. It never gives up. The ocean knows better than anyone that life is not a sprint. It is a marathon. It knows that tomorrow is another day. The ocean has been around longer than life itself and it marches on with confidence. I do not know what will happen tomorrow, but the ocean might. It is older, stronger and wiser than I am. I stood in front of the water and looked out to the ocean looking for answers and they came to me. My cares seemed to drift away with the wind. The ocean whispered to me reassuring me that all is not lost. It told me that there are things that I do not know, but that I should not lose faith. My heart murmured inside me, "meditation, meditation, meditation." I trust the ocean because it has never lied to me. Before I reached the ocean, my mind was in a fuss, but as I stood there gazing at and pondering into the triumphant ocean, it knew what to say to me to return my mind to peace. Day and night I see it in my mind's eye. As I approached it, it reminded me that it has answers. Nothing on earth is wiser than the ocean, but in all of Creation, nothing is wiser than the stars. They dwell in the heaven of heavens and shine bright reminding me of God's Eternity. I look up to them and like the ocean, they speak to me. The stars are kind, gentle and have never let me down. They do not run. They shine unapologetically. Even the ocean listens to the stars because the stars oversee it, too. I look up and the stars bring me to the edge of my thoughts encouraging me to find my own answers. The stars, tranquil and sublime, speak softly and humbly to me. Sometimes, I think I found the answers on my own, but when my troubles return, I know I must go to the stars who know me better than I know myself.

My aunt was not formally educated, but she understood the value of an academic education and encouraged me to pursue a university degree. She believed it is something that I would always have, something that no one could take away, something with undisputed value. She nourished an orphaned boy's body, mind and soul to good health and helped bring me closer to God. In many ways, I am who I am today because of my aunt. She gave me the opportunity to live a full life. Mike and Gabe, too, helped to define my life. They were fundamental to my recovery from my parents' deaths and still further, they enriched my life. They are an invaluable gift to me from God. My philia for them is limitless. I would lay down my life for them. After my parents' deaths, God blessed me with a new life and I thank Him every night in my prayers.

YOUNG EZEKIEL
A LIFE OF LOVES

THREE

EROS

After I graduated from high school, I attended a small private university near the valleys of Pennsylvania. I earned high grades in high school and was offered a full-tuition scholarship with room and board. I had never been as excited as I was the moment I read the words, "Congratulations! You have been accepted…" I began to experience the fruits of my labor and it felt good. A high school teacher told me in life, if you persevere, you will "make" things go your way. I was beginning to realize the truth in his words. Life is both art and sport and the more we put in to it, the greater the masterpiece. We just have to care about life to make our lives worth living.

When I moved to Pennsylvania, Mike and Gabe stayed in the Boston area. Mike became a carpenter's apprentice. He was good with his hands and was skilled with tools more so than with books. Gabe entered the culinary trade and started out by assisting a chef in a French bistro with the goal of becoming a chef himself. We each had different strengths and contributed to the world in different ways.

During my first semester at the university, I noticed a change in myself. I was growing up. My clothes were more adult and I was standing taller. I developed a stride. It was the brash swagger of a college kid who was discovering his potential, but who had not yet been tested by the world. It was a wonderful time and everything was new. It was unknown territory for me and I was ready to explore. Never shy as a youth, but, perhaps, a bit reserved, I made a conscious effort to make friends. I developed an outgoing spirit and became more gregarious. I was meeting new people and reading the works of some of the greatest thinkers of all time. When I was accepted to the university, I was undecided on what subject I wanted to study, so I entered the liberal arts program. I figured, by doing so, I would learn a little bit of everything. This passive decision turned out to be a blessing. In the program, we studied the most influential ideas and the greatest works of all time from the East and the West and from the humanities and natural sciences. I relished in my books and was most enchanted with philosophy. It was exhilarating to read 5th century BC Greek philosopher Plato's *The Republic* and I saw myself as a philosopher king. My mind was like a sponge in that I was absorbing all kinds of information from many directions sometimes with little discretion. The ideas of those influential

Western philosophers seemed most enlightening. More than once, I remember saying to myself, "Ah, yes. There it is. Now, I see. Here is truth," but I was naïve and impressionable. Philosophy at its best opens discussion. It rarely provides answers; rather, it provokes one to think more deeply and ask further questions. A professor of mine once told me that confusion is a good thing because it means you are still thinking. If you are no longer confused, it means you have stopped thinking and you should not be satisfied, but alarmed. For a while, I believed that. But, then, through life's trials and tribulations and some self-examination, I discovered truth in Jesus's words and I am no longer confused and I am at peace with that; moreover, I am happy.

The program was a stepping stone for me. It was the catalyst for a dazzling period in my life of thoughtful inquiry and desire for knowledge. It paved the way for greater intellectual expeditions later in life. The program accomplished what it intended to do, which was to open my mind to possibilities and shift my thinking from a parochial view to a world view, and I greatly appreciate it for that. It was essential to my learning development. But, when one discovers Jesus as the Christ, all other knowledge is unfulfilling. When one accepts Jesus as the Christ, the goal is no longer the acquisition of knowledge or anything else; rather, it is to be his loyal servant.

There are two philosophies about success in life: work for money or do what you love. Some people are blessed and they make money by doing what they love, but for most, it is a fork in the road. The world tells us, "Make money" and I want to tell the world, "I have dreams." In our world, money is a necessity - it is how we share resources - but money should not be the goal. There will never be enough money. If a person can find a passion, he must not let it go to make money - the risk of losing his passion is too great. So, at the university, I studied the liberal arts because that was the only material that I was excited about. I may not have developed a practical skill, but the knowledge that I acquired was an investment in myself.

      I spent a lot of time in the school library. It gave me access to thousands of books for free. I could reference dozens of books without leaving the building. It made it easy to build, expand and focus my knowledge and compare histories, ideas and philosophies. I could jump from the Chinese dynasties to communist Russia, from classical Greece to modern Germany. I could explore at my own pace; sometimes in an excited frenzy and sometimes in deep hard contemplation. I was hungry for knowledge and at times, I wanted to physically consume the books as if, with every swallow, the answers would come to me more quickly. Some of the books were worn because of their popularity; while, others were covered in dust. On the shelves, every book was a coffin with words inside, but once one was opened, it found air and was given new life.

In each book, death and immortality fought every time a patron entered the library.

When I was not in the library, I was with my friends meeting girls and trying to figure them out. God knows my heart wanted to love, but my mind was poisoned with lust. Love and lust are not the same. Love comes from the soul, while lust is all physical. Love is about both people in the relationship, while lust is just about oneself. If one is only concerned with what one can get, the relationship between the couple is doomed. Lust has no positive attributes - it only corrupts male and female. It is fantasy and deception that is contrary to love. Fleeting and ultimately unfulfilling, lust is one of the greatest lies. Because of my sexual liaisons with the girls, my confidence grew and I thought of myself as a real man, but I was far from being a real man, I was far from God.

After graduation, I had a degree, but no job. I was filled with knowledge from my liberal arts classes and now I had to figure out how I was going to apply this knowledge. I knew finding my place in the world was going to take time, but I was following my heart and gut. I wanted more than money. I moved to a town next to Philadelphia and had some random jobs here and there, but my first substantial job was when I was twenty-three in a hospital. My mother was a nurse and I saw how important the profession was to her. I followed her lead because I, too, want to help those in need. Working there, I learned about life's dignity and value and I think there are few places where one can witness greater heights of life's dynamism. Life and death fill every corner of the quarters. I've seen babies enter the world and people leave the world. Every day there is celebration and mourning. Life is respected and God is reverenced in hospitals. The evil of disease is visible, but so, too, is the kindness of nurses. People are healed to good health. Modern medicine and technology thrive in hospitals and the ancient wisdom of doctors to "first do no harm" is practiced.

My job mainly consisted of filing documents, changing bed sheets and tending to patients. It was not a prestigious job, but I felt it was noble. I felt like I was making a difference, even if it was one patient at a time. My co-workers and I were a team with the goal of making our weak patients strong. There was a doctor in my unit who often carried *The Little Flowers of St Francis*. He wore his white coat and the book stuck out of his pocket, just enough, so I could make out the title. That image has stayed with me. He figured it out. He made the connection between healing the body and the soul. During the most troubling times, he was able to comfort his patients. I bought the same book the doctor had and during my down time, I did a little reading.

I was having a good time at work. Barry, my supervisor, was a good guy and in many ways, I considered him a friend. We were not true friends, but that's okay. The circumstances of our relationship prevented that. We were friends of utility. We had an agreement with certain expectations that had to be met for the relationship to last. As long as I worked hard for him and performed well at my job, he would allow me to continue to work for him. But, it was not only about business. We were also friends of pleasure. We talked sports and current affairs and our senses of humor were the same. The day would pass quickly when we worked together.

One of my favorite people at work was Olivia - the lady at the greeting desk in the lobby. We had the same work schedule. She was a heavy lady, very sociable and well liked. She was also a big basketball fan, like me. One morning, I walked into the hospital's lobby and she saw me and asked,

"Ezekiel, honey, did you see Michael Jordan last night?"

"I certainly did. He scored 49 points," I answered.

"He's a pleasure to watch. I look forward to Chicago Bulls games," she said.

"Who would you rather see win, the Philadelphia 76ers or the Chicago Bulls with Michael Jordan?" I asked.

"Ezekiel, honey, you know I am a Philly native, but I have to admit: I sometimes catch myself cheering for Michael Jordan. I just hope he takes it easy on my Sixers," she replied.

"I understand," I said with a chuckle.

Olivia was usually inundated with visitors, phones and messages, but that day we had a few minutes to catch up. It was her daughter's fourth birthday a few days before and she showed me some photos of the party. She purchased a piñata and she had a couple of great photos of her daughter and friends scrambling to collect the falling candy from the broken piñata. Catching up with Olivia was a good way to start the day, which would turn out to be a great day. I was busy and time seemed to be flying by. I did not even realize that I missed lunch. The unit was running like a well-oiled machine with everybody working together. There are few highs that are greater than when everyone is working together with each other for each other. However, time stopped when I noticed a beautiful girl sitting in the waiting room in my unit of the hospital. She looked great: hair flowing, good posture, legs crossed. She was a natural beauty with inviting features. Sitting there, she opened her bag, reached in and pulled out a book. She held it in front of her, flipped a few pages and began to read. "Perfect... I love books... there's my opening," I said to myself. "I'll just ask her what she is reading." So, I made like I was working and walked into the waiting room to tidy up the magazines, seats and pillows. Then, I walked over to the girl and as her eyes ran across the page, I asked,

"What are you reading?"
"Oh," she said, "*The Alchemist*."

It was as if all the stars in the sky directed me to her at this moment in our lives at this point in history because *The Alchemist* was one of my favorite books.

"That's a great book," I said. "Where in the story are you?" I asked.

"Just the first few pages," she said.

"If you're a dreamer, you will like it. I'm a dreamer and I like it. It will inspire you to be what you always knew you should be. It's deep, but accessible. I've recommended it to friends. It will place you somewhere, but not here and will draw you in with mystical phrases like 'Personal Legend' and 'Soul of the World.' And, it's not too long, which is always a plus."

I looked into her eyes. She had beautiful eyes - pools of caramel. I could swim in her eyes. And, she welcomed me with her eyes - growing bigger and brighter.

"Sounds amazing," she said. "I look forward to reading it."

We both took a deep breath.

Then, I asked, "What's your name?"

"Julie," she answered. "And you are?"

"I'm Ezekiel."

"That's a unique name," she said.

"It's Hebrew. It means 'God strengthens,'" I said.

"I like names that mean something or represent something. The name Julie is not very interesting."

"I like it. It reminds me of Juliet and star-crossed love," I said.

"I guess so," she replied demurely.

We spoke for a bit and then her cousin entered the waiting room. The two came to the hospital because her cousin got into a bicycle accident. She was on the road training for a race when a car got a little too close. She got startled and fell to the ground. The doctor gave her some antibiotics for lacerations on her elbows and knees. She was pleasant, but was in some pain and wanted to head home.

Then, Julie said, "Well, it was nice to meet you."

"Same here," I replied.

"I'll see you around," she said.

As she was walking away, but before I lost my chance, I asked, "Hey, Julie. Would you like to get some coffee some time?"

"Sounds nice," she said with a smile.

Then, we exchanged phone numbers. I was cloud high. Few things are as exciting as making that first connection with a girl. In these moments, the unknown is thrilling. Anticipation becomes intoxicating and the imagination takes over. I gave her a call and we made plans to meet Friday after my shift at work ended. We were going to meet in the hospital's lobby and walk to the local coffee shop.

Friday finally arrived. I could barely wait to see her. All day at work I thought about her. I got a little nervous, but it was a good nervous because I felt alive. All my senses were rushing and when I saw her in the lobby, I felt like a gush of cool water washed over me. I saw her, she saw me and she smiled. That was all I needed - her smile lit me up.

We walked together down the road to the coffee shop. It was spring and there was a gentle breeze in the air. The sun was setting turning the sky into pale purple and pink. Feathery clouds caressed the sky, which was melting into the horizon. Beside the sidewalks, shrubs bloomed flowers and above, trees housed singing sparrows. It was a quiet neighborhood where bakers baked bread and window shopping was a pastime. People nodded hello and couples held hands. I was walking taller than usual with Julie by my side.

We entered the coffee shop, stepped to the counter and ordered drinks. I paid and then we took our drinks, found a table with a couple of seats, sat down and got to know each other. I learned that she liked art and I like art, so we talked art much of the night. The previous summer, she journeyed to Florence, Italy to visit family.

I said, "I hear Florence is amazing with its Renaissance history."

"It is," she replied. "In Florence, I saw Michelangelo's *David*. He's much taller than I expected, much taller than any man. He stands unaffected, self-assured and with poise. He's young, the age when he killed Goliath. I was awestruck knowing that he was once a block of cold marble stone, but Michelangelo brought him to life. Michelangelo saw his subjects in the marble and carved them to set them free. In the museum, along with the *David*, are Michelangelo's "unfinished slaves," which show the chisel to stone marks that illustrate his vision to release life within the living stone.

She was excited to share her experiences with me and I enjoyed listening.

She said, "We also stopped in Rome in Vatican City in Saint Peter's Basilica where there is one of Michelangelo's Pietas, which is powerful. It depicts a youthful Mother Mary - majestic and regal - as she cradles her lifeless son. She is sorrowful and in disbelief and with her hand's gesture, she says, "Look at my son. They have killed him." Her gesture also says, "Here he is. He has done it - that which he was meant to do." And, with her demeanor, she glorifies him. I never studied art formally, so I may sound naive, but Michelangelo's work spoke to me."

I said, "One day, I would like to see what you saw. Michelangelo was a genius and his masterpieces are divine. He may not be a saint, but I am sure his art has inspired saints."

She said, "I'm lucky, I know, to have seen these wonderful things. One day, I would like to go to Amsterdam in the Netherlands where there is the Vincent Van Gogh museum. You should come with me. Vincent Van Gogh is my favorite artist."

I added, "He's one of my favorites, too. Like Michelangelo, he was a genius, but his story is deeply dramatic and tragic. I read that even though he painted something like 900 paintings in 10 years, he sold only one in his lifetime. I also learned that he may have suffered from seizures and mental illness, which may be why he cut off his ear and shot himself in the chest killing himself. Some of my friends and I visited the Museum of Modern Art in New York City and got up close to *Starry Night*, which is unlike anything from any other painter."

We sipped our coffees and long after we were done, we stayed in the coffee shop talking. Our conversations were unhurried, effortless and free. Never was it an "interview" as if we were applying for jobs. Our conversations did not go back and forth as if we were playing tennis, which as conversation, can be repetitive and exhausting. I mentioned I liked her purple knit scarf and she told me that her student's mother made it for her because of her dedication to the young girl. Julie was a fourth grade teacher who was passionate about her job and was devoted to her students. It is meaningful work and I let her know. I told her my favorite teacher, when I was young, made me believe I could be great one day. As an adult, her voice stayed with me and she made me believe in myself. When I doubted myself or failed, I thought of her. The greatest adults help children see their potential. It is like planting seeds and strengthening roots. It worked for me and is something I pass on to those younger than me. Not once did Julie and I force our conversations or did they end up at dead ends. Sign posts appeared which turned into new topics. We were enjoying each other's company and the slight pauses added a playful tension that only heightened our attraction for each other. I learned she liked to sing. When she was little, she would sing to entertain her family during gatherings and holidays. She and her cousins would put on a show for the older generations and it became a tiny tradition for them and something they all looked forward to when they got together. I told her I sang, too, but only in the shower because the acoustics made my voice sound just right. She liked poetry and told me one night she performed at an open mic in a bar in Philadelphia. She said she was nervous, but excited. I told her I would love to hear her poetry, but she shied away suggesting that she wanted us to get to know each other better. I asked why she was shy if she could stand in front of a crowd of strangers. I would be just as welcoming as they were and she told me it was a possibility allowing the thought to marinate in my mind. We spoke about pop-culture and the inanity of certain celebrities and learned that we shared common opinions. I told her I liked her car. It was a Mini-Cooper. She told me it was her first new car purchase. Her previous car she inherited from her grandparents. Then, I told her about my first car, which was a 1988 Dodge 600 that had fuzzy dice hanging on the rearview mirror. At some point, the passenger door stopped opening and to sit in the passenger seat, my friends would have to jump through the open window. The car had character, to say the least. When Julie and I communicated, we listened to each other and did not just wait to talk. And, not once did either of us look at our watches or phones looking for the time waiting for the date to end. The only clue that revealed the passing of time was when the sun was setting and night was filling the air. The glistening stars were beginning to break through the dark sky. It was as if God scattered diamonds over the heavens and left them there so we could venerate His Glorious Creation. The lucid evening was transformed into a brilliant night while we were together in the humble coffee shop.

We walked back to the hospital and as we walked, we talked some more. Our steps gradually aligned in sequence as we walked side by side together as a pair. We reached our cars and said goodnight. Our first date could not have turned out better for a first date. The future looked good for me and Julie, but it was still too early to tell if my dreams would materialize.

After our first date, we were eager to reunite. We spoke on the phone every day when we were not together. I learned we lived not far from each other. A few days later on our second date, I picked her up at her apartment at around 8:30PM. I parked my car on the side of the street, walked to her doorstep, rang her doorbell and she answered. Seeing her again, I felt alive. I almost forgot what that felt like when I was not with her, but it came back in full force when I saw her. "Did my heart love till now?" (Shakespeare, *Romeo and Juliet*, 1.5.50). When she saw me, she smiled with her rose tinted cheeks and I smiled back. The night had begun and we were ready to celebrate because we were together, again.

    Her apartment was about twenty minutes away from our destination, a suburb near Philadelphia. It was a quaint town that by day, was mild tempered, but by night, its Main Street was hopping with energy. There were about a dozen bars and restaurants on that street that catered to young adults, like us. Each establishment pulsated with rhythms and melodies that snuck out of each entrance, that teased the people outside to step inside, that invited patrons to join the party. The atmosphere was fun and it was an environment that was hard to dislike. The spring air was crisp, far from humid. People wore jeans. The young men casually wore collar shirts and the young women wore scarves around their necks, draped over their shoulders. I parked my car, we crossed the road and walked together down Main Street to the bar I chose for the night. I opened the door and we were greeted by a doorman. He was a friend of mine and let us in without charging us an entrance fee. We walked in and the lights were dim and the place was filled with people - talking, laughing and dancing. I noticed a couple of unoccupied bar stools, so I held her by the hand and we navigated through the sea of people to claim our seats. A band was playing that night which is why I chose the venue. Live music always enhances the vibe in a bar and the band that night was talented which made the night even more special. We settled in and were enjoying the atmosphere. I bought myself a bottled beer and her a vodka gimlet. She told me she liked the place and I told her it was one of my favorite spots. Her incandescent smile was complemented with her subtle laugh and she styled herself with class that was elevated by her quiet confidence. As the evening passed by, our conversations got more playful. We sat shoulder to shoulder. During a moment of silence between us, I slid my hand down her arm, extended my fingers and grasped her hand and she grasped mine.

> If I profane with my unworthiest hand
> This holy shrine, the gentle sin is this:
> My lips, two blushing pilgrims, ready stand
> To smooth that rough touch with a tender kiss
> (Shakespeare, 1.5.91).

She turned her head toward me and I leaned in. Then, we kissed. Paused. And, then, we kissed, again. From that moment, I was hers and she was mine.

When we left the bar, the avenue was bustling with young adults, but we were one. We did not want to leave each other. Love is relentless and euphoric.

It is those moments of eros that we wish would last forever. There is no earthly high that is higher and it is not something that happens often. It takes the right person at the right time. I drove her to her home and we kissed goodnight. With that kiss, I felt complete. She stepped out of the car, walked to her door, unlocked it and entered safely. Then, I drove home in bliss.

The next time we got together, a few days later, I picked her up at her apartment and we went out for dinner. We decided to get sushi, so I took her to a Japanese restaurant that had a more traditional atmosphere than most. When we walked in, near the entrance, there was a rock fountain and a few bonsai trees. We were greeted by the hostess and took off our shoes. The hostess guided us to our dining area, which was enclosed by white screens. This allowed for privacy from the other patrons in the large open room. Some of the screens were decorated with calligraphy and along the walls were prints of nature scenes like mountains, trees and waterfalls. At the center of our dining area was a table that was near to the ground because there were no chairs. Instead, there were mats and we sat with bent knees on our legs. Our server handed us moist towels to wash our hands. We began with a bowl of edamame. Then, we each ordered two sushi rolls with a miso soup and green tea. The restaurant was quiet, not because it was empty, but because everyone spoke softly and so, we did, as well. It was different than most Western restaurants, which made the experience fun. After dinner, I took her to a small family-owned cafe that was known for its homemade cheese-cake. We had dessert and some coffee, but the night was young and we did not want it to end, so we went to my apartment.

    We walked up a few steps and entered through the front door. In my living room, there was a black couch and a couple of black seats that sat around a rectangular dark brown wooden coffee table. There was a window with a large plant beside it and hanging on the walls were some prints. Pictures rested on top of end tables. I gave her a tour of my apartment and then we walked back into the living room. I asked her if she wanted something to drink and she asked for a glass of water. I served her water with some ice and a lemon wedge. In the living room was my vinyl record collection. I like jazz music, so I put on John Coltrane's *Stellar Regions*. I clued her in to the artists and the various genres. We sat on the floor listening to music and telling stories. She hummed as she thought and such endearing intimacies made me feel like we had known each other forever. They are intimacies that not everyone gets a glimpse of or could appreciate, little things, like a gesture or look, that make eros special. During a moment of silence, she got up and walked over to the music shelves to check out my records. Then, she walked around the room to get a closer look at the pictures.

    "Is that you?" she asked.

I walked over to her and looked at the picture that she was pointing to and said, "Yes, it was."

"You were cute," she said with a smile.

"And, that must be your mom. She was beautiful. And, your dad - he looks like a proud papa," she said.

"They were great people," I said.

"What do you mean 'were?'" she asked.

"When I was twelve, my parents died in a car accident. A reckless college girl was drinking that night and hit my parents from behind. My parents' car swerved into oncoming traffic and hit a truck and they died instantly. I loved them very much. They were all I knew and their love remains with me every day."

"Oh my, I did not mean to pry," she said.

"I do not mind," I said. "I like talking about them. I do not get to talk about them much. It feels good when I do because it helps me to remember. It makes me feel like they are still alive."

I told her about Omorfi and how we lived by the beach, how father was a high school history teacher and how father, mother and I would sing songs on Saturday mornings. I told her about all the storge we had for each other.

Then, I said, "When my parents' lives ended, so did mine, but my aunt stepped in and adopted me and provided me with a new life. She nurtured my body, mind and soul into good health. I've been through a lot, but I'm still here. I'm a survivor."

She looked me in the eye and I could feel her love.

She said, "I'm sorry, Ezekiel, that you had to go through all that. The world is a difficult place. Some days, I believe I have found Heaven here on earth and other times, I question if Hell could be worse. Life can be unfair. I know. When I was eleven, my father was diagnosed with brain cancer. He was a sincere man who lived for his family and always had a loving disposition. Slowly, he lost mobility, then speech, then his ability to respond to our presence. The cancer was killing him and stealing his life from us. He fought for three years and then God freed him from his battle and he left this world when he was only forty-one and I was only fourteen. But, I have faith and I believe that when my journey here on earth ends, I will be with my father, again, in Paradise with God where there is no more pain and life is everlasting. Some days are tougher than others, but I believe the love of those close to us has the power to heal and I realize, more than ever, how delicate, tender and special life is. I'm so happy I found you. My days with you are pure joy and I thank God that you are in my life. I have never been as happy as I have been with you. I have never felt this way before."

Then, I said, "I am no merchant of the sea, yet wert thou as far as that vast shore washed with the farthest sea, I should adventure for such merchandise as you" (Shakespeare, 2.2.81).

Then, she said, "My kindness is as boundless as the sea, my love as deep; the more I give to thee, the more I have, for both are infinite" (Shakespeare, 2.2.132).

For the rest of the night, we said no more. We gazed into each other's eyes and stayed up kissing and caressing. Then, we fell asleep in each other's arms. The next morning, Julie woke me up with a kiss and she told me that she loved me and I told her that I loved her. It was a perfect moment.

My relationship with Julie was my first real romantic relationship. It was the first time I experienced the love form eros, which is the Greek term for romantic love.

I was in love with Julie, in eros with her, but my feelings for her were more than sexual. We are more than animals. She was not just a body. She was a soul. Certainly, I desired sex, but more than that, I desired her, her presence, her love. I fell for her and she fell for me. I could see it in her eyes, feel it in her touch, hear it in her voice, taste it in her kiss and smell it in her perfume. We communicated on multiple levels and we had our own world. When I was with her, I did not want be with any other girl. She was all I wanted. All I wanted was her and I wanted her to feel the same way about me. I would have done anything for her, not just so she would reciprocate my love, but so she, too, could genuinely experience eros and feel what I felt because it felt so good.

It was as if I knew Julie before we met and when I met her, it was as if we were reuniting. But, at the same time, everything was new and fresh. With her, a new chapter in my life began, an exciting, ecstatic and exhilarating chapter. I did things with Julie that before her, I never would. I love the melodies and rhythms of music, but I was uncomfortable with dancing. Julie got me to dance with her when we were alone and sometimes when we were in public. She brought out a different side of me. She helped me grow. She was beautiful on the outside and in the inside. She caught my attention because of her looks, but I fell in love with her because of her soul. I considered her a friend because we saw things in the same way, walked the same path and shared a common vision. We were friends, not in the way that I considered Mike and Gabe friends - sexual attraction and tension prevented that - but I considered her my equal. Julie and I were a pair, a couple, partners in a way that only a man and woman can be. We complemented each other and were a match.

The first time Mike and Gabe met Julie was when Julie and I visited Massachusetts. Julie and I had been dating for about a year, so I must have been twenty-five. While I was studying and then working in Pennsylvania, I would return to Massachusetts during summers and holidays because it was my home and to see my aunt, Mike and Gabe. This time, I returned when it was Memorial Day weekend and

Julie and I stayed at my aunt's house. Mike and Gabe had apartments not far from where we grew up. On that Saturday night, we decided to go to a bar that Mike, Gabe and I frequented when I would return home. It had over twenty beers on tap, which were backed up by over sixty different bottled beers. We sat at the corner table and ordered a bunch of appetizers - no meals, just a sampling of the house specialties. Julie was a natural fit into our crew. She quickly picked up our sense of humor. They each told stories about me pushing my comfort zone and keeping me on the edge of my seat. However, because they loved me, they also told stories that elevated me to royalty status, even hero status. We spent hours together and talked about the past, present and future, about politics, principles and popular culture. We had fun and laughed a lot. It was like the best party with the best company. I remember looking at Julie and thinking to myself how lucky I was to have her as my woman. I was deeply in eros with her and when I looked into her eyes, I saw the world and myself and everything made sense.

    In Greek mythology, Eros is the god of love. He appears in different forms in history. He is first identified as one of the primordial cosmic gods who was there at the beginning of time as an agent of procreation. The 700 BC Greek poet Hesiod refers to him in his *Theogony*, meaning "Birth of the Gods:"

    Verily at the first Chaos came to be, but next

> wide-bosomed Earth, the ever-sure foundations of all the deathless ones who hold the peaks of snowy Olympus, and dim Tartarus in the depth of the wide-pathed Earth, and Eros (Love), fairest among the deathless gods, who unnerves the limbs and overcomes the mind and wise counsels of all gods and all men within them (2.116).
> (Translation H.G. Evelyn-White [http://www.greekmythology.com])

When I was with Julie, I was unnerved and overcome with eros and she was the center of my universe; nothing else mattered when I was with her. Time and responsibilities disappeared and all that remained was our eros. Later on in *Theogony*, Eros and Desire are with goddess Aphrodite at her birth. Aphrodite is also known as Venus and the scene of her birth is famously depicted in Sandro Botticelli's Renaissance painting.

In later mythology, Eros was depicted as goddess Aphrodite's mischievous young winged son who, with his bow and arrows and flaming torch, sets the hearts of gods and men on fire with passion. Today, we know this Eros as Cupid and see him commercially on Valentine's Day gift cards.

There is also a story of Eros who, as a young deity, falls in love with Psyche who falls in love with him. Love falls in love and is loved. The tale was first penned by Latin philosophical writer Apuleius during the 2nd century AD, but as far back as 4th century BC, it appeared in Greek folklore and popular art. It is one of the most famous love stories in classical antiquity and it remains influential. It is echoed in fairy tales, such as *Cinderella* and *Beauty and the Beast*. In Greek, "eros" means love and "psyche" means soul. When I learned this, the story of Eros and Psyche became more interesting and I wanted to see if I could learn anything about the relationship between love and the soul.

I asked myself, "What can I learn from Psyche, if psyche means soul?" The story tells us that Psyche was the most beautiful women on earth. Words could not describe her radiance. Many people believed that she was not of this world and prayed to her, worshiped her and compared her to goddess Aphrodite. Can we say that all souls are as beautiful? Can we say that all souls can be mistaken for the divine? I believe so.

When the tale begins, Psyche longed and waited for love. Because of her radiant beauty, men did not approach her and she feared that her dreams of love would never be anything more than dreams. She woefully sat at home all alone weeping in despair because she wanted to love, be in love and be loved. Can we say the same is true for every soul? Do all souls long for love? Do all souls search for love? I think so. I think all souls desire love.

When Eros left Psyche and the two were separated, Psyche vowed to herself that she would do anything to get him back. She endured the trial of the mixed seeds, the trial of the golden wool, the trial of the black waterfall and the trial of the box in Hades. Can we say that all souls will do anything for love? Can we say that all souls will confront all challenges for love? I am not sure, but I know that at the peak of my relationship with Julie, I did not want to let her go and if we were separated, I would have done anything to get her back. I would have done anything for her love.

At the end, when Eros and Psyche were reunited, Eros took Psyche to heaven. All the gods were with them and there was a great banquet with savory foods, flowing wine, fragrant flowers and angelic music. Can we say that love takes all souls to heaven? Can love bring all souls closer to the gods? I do not know, but I will tell you that at the peak of my relationship with Julie, we felt as though we were experiencing heaven on earth and with her, I felt as though I was bursting with great light. We felt as though we were living in a timeless realm.

For a while, Julie and I thought we would be together forever - even after death because not even death could separate us and our love for each other. We thought mighty Eros would keep his promise to be with us forever. At his highest, in many ways, he was our god. Eros took over and everything we did, all the time we spent and every thought we had revolved around Eros. It was like a religion that we followed. We followed his rules, so he would bring us joy and we followed his rules out of fear, so as to not disrupt him. We were helpless to the powers of Eros. Who are we to deny the god of love? Eros invites us and teases us to join him and for some, it can do more harm than good, it can go wrong. But, for Julie and I, Eros was heavenly. The god of love was good to us. However, the magnitude of his initial impact did not last. Ironically, "he is notoriously the most mortal of our loves" (Lewis, 113). When Eros's power faded, we became disenchanted with him and each other. Julie and I were not able to stay together without Eros. We tried, but we were young and not able to handle our eros's descent. Little issues grew to become big issues. Then, we spoke about marriage and children. I did not want children. I gave it tremendous thought. Because of the pain I experienced and ugliness I saw in the world, I loved my children so much to not have them. I understood how hard life can be and the great responsibility and duty to be a good parent, which is the hardest and most important job in the world. I did not want to take that risk and fail my children and the world with that most serious task. Then, I asked myself, "If I did decide to have children, would it be for myself or for them?" Something that has to be considered. After that, we realized that we did not see our futures in the same way, so we broke up.

  The eros I felt for Julie surpasses the eros I felt for any other female in my life. After Julie, I questioned if I would ever find a better woman. I had more love for Julie than lust. Eros is tricky and complicated in that way. Lust plays a role. It is seductive, like an intoxicating drug or potion. If another woman entered my life, I knew it would have to be because of love and not based on lust. Real men do not lust after women. They have agape love for them as handmaids of God.

YOUNG EZEKIEL
A LIFE OF LOVES

FOUR

AGAPE

> By this we know love [agape], that he [Jesus] laid down his life for us.
> (1 John 3:16)

One Friday - specifically, Christian Great Friday - I was working in the hospital's emergency room. It was an unusually quiet day in my unit, so I volunteered to work in the ER in case the staff there needed help. It was understaffed because a few people took off from work to go to church. I planned to go to church, too, but not until late at night.

After the sun had set, the paramedics rushed in with an old man on a stretcher. The old man was wearing a brown suit and his white dress shirt was saturated in blood. The nurses hurried to get to him and evaluate his condition. Skin the color of bronze and body tall and thin, he had full head of white hair that was in disarray. He had a grimace on his face and after each inhale of air, he held his breath trying to block the pain he felt from his wound. The nurses called the doctor and pointed out what they noticed. The doctor examined the old man. As he made his assessments, he was calm, but intensely focused. Then, they entered the operating room. At the time, I was stocking up and organizing medical supplies, so they would be easy to get to and ready for when needed. I was working in the background supporting the nurses and doctors, so they could save lives. A bit later, the old man was brought out from the operating room. No longer in his suit, he was clothed in a blue gown with his right side bound up. He was incapacitated in an anesthetic slumber. He laid silently in recovery for a couple of hours and then started to groan in his sleep, but was unresponsive to outside stimuli. Three hours after surgery, he woke up. Drowsy, but awake, he rolled around a bit in his stretcher wanting to sit up, but unable. One of the nurses approached him, held his hand, supported his shoulder and said, "Take it easy, friend." He calmed down, then sighed. I asked the nurse if there was anything I could do for him and she said I can stay with him and tend to him. Not sure how to help, but eager, I let him know I was there,

"Hello, sir," I said softly.

With murky eyes, he mumbled, "Oh my, where am I?"

"You are in a hospital, sir," I said.

Stroking his gaunt face with his heavy hand, he was slowly putting the pieces together and making sense of his current situation.

"How are you feeling, sir?" I asked.

"Not well," he answered.

"Is there anything I can do for you?" I asked.

"I thirst," he said.

I walked away and then returned with some water in a paper cup and a straw. I held the water in front of him and he grasped my hand and sipped the water. After each swallow, he cleared his congested throat. When he let go of my hand, I took away the half-empty cup. Then, he dropped his head back onto the pillow and fell back asleep. He was exhausted. He fell in and out of consciousness for a while and finally awoke alert. He rubbed his eyes with his hand, took a deep breath and adjusted his position in the bed. I helped him. After he was settled, I gave him water, again, and as he drank, I could see it satisfied him. After each mouthful, he sat there and looked at the cup. After his final gulp, he said, "Nothing replenishes like water."

"Yes, sir," I said.

Then, he said, "Did you know, my young friend, that the human body is predominantly made of water? Depending on build, a person's body is between 50 to 70% water."

"Sounds familiar, sir," I said.

"I always found that fascinating," he said slowly. "Life is filled with fascinating facts. I have learned many things in my many years on this earth. I have been blessed. God has been good to me.

What we old people say about good health is true. It is more valuable than money, fame or any pleasure. And, the older you become, the more clearly you will see the truth of this insight. I have had many healthy years - more than most - however, I am afraid that my remaining moments here on earth are few."

His side hurt. He tried to lift his arm to test his body's limits and could not and then he shouted in pain. A nurse heard him and walked over. She checked his vital signs, but there was little more she could do for him. She adjusted his blanket, clasped his shoulder and then walked away. He started to cough and after each cough, he cleared his throat. We sat together for a moment in silence. I could see that the old man was thinking and reflecting.

After some time, he shook his head and said, "It all happened so quickly."

"What's that, sir?" I asked.

"The way I was shot on my way to church to celebrate Great Friday," he answered.

Great Friday is the most solemn and poignant day of the year for Christians. It is the day we commemorate Jesus's crucifixion and death. He was killed like a guilty criminal, but the Cross is a symbol of victory. Our reasoning minds tell us the way Jesus died is a curse and a disgrace; however, over two billion people wear the Cross around their necks with pride because Jesus was killed on the Cross for us because of his agape for us. Easter may be the most sublime and reverent day of the year because it is a day of hope and promise that there is eternal life with God in Heaven and that one day our bodies will resurrect. However, we love Jesus not for what he can give us, but because of his incomprehensible agape for us. His self-sacrificial death defines agape and he is worthy of adoration and adulation. The Cross is a sign of victory because on it, Jesus completed his mission for our salvation. Not even death could stop Jesus from fulfilling his mission. In fact, death made it possible. Dying for us is why he came into the world.

"How did it happen, sir?" I asked.

He explained, "The day started off well. I was in good spirits all day and all week because this year all Christians are celebrating Holy Week together and are going to celebrate Easter on the same day. This happens only every few years and it brings me great joy when the Christian community is united in brotherhood. My house is an eight minute walk from the church. I know because I walk to it for every Sunday service. All day it had been very foggy, so I could not see very well. I was focusing on each one of my steps trying to break through the misty air. My glasses began to fog up and I was having a difficult time seeing through them. I removed them from my face and from my breast pocket, I took out a handkerchief to wipe them. Then, I heard a ruckus behind me, so I turned around quickly, got distracted and dropped my glasses. I was in front of the neighborhood liquor store, which has been robbed in the past. I'm rarely out at night because the area is not safe, but today, service was at night. Usually, I walk that route on Sunday mornings when it is quite and danger is asleep. I bent down to pick up my glasses and was pushed from the back. I heard yelling in the background and then a gunshot. My side was pierced by the bullet. The young man that shot me did not mean to. I know because he looked stunned after the gun fired. He looked me in the eye and froze. There was a moment between us and I told him, "I forgive you." He ran and then the owner of the liquor store ran to me and pressed my side. I felt pain and saw blood on his hand. He hollered to his son, who was working with him in the liquor store, and a little while later the ambulance found us."

Blood from his pierced side was coming through the bandage. I called a nurse and she quickly entered the old man's room to remedy the issue. I left them, so they could have some privacy as she rebound his torso with gauze. I could hear the old man grunting in pain. When she was finished, she told me I could go back inside his room. The old man saw the Cross around my neck, so he knew I was a Christian and asked,

"My young friend, have you been to church to celebrate Holy Week?"

"Yes, sir. I was able to attend most of the services," I said.

"How beautiful was Palm Sunday?" he asked.

"Very beautiful, sir, very beautiful," I

answered.

    Palm Sunday is one of the most beautiful and moving days in the year for Christians. It commemorates Jesus's triumphal entry into Jerusalem trumpeting his arrival as our King, Savior and God. He enters the city sitting on a donkey announcing that he is the King that Jerusalem had been waiting for. Prophet Zechariah prophesied:

> Rejoice greatly, O daughter of Zion!
> Shout aloud, O daughter of Jerusalem!
> Lo, your king comes to you;
> triumphant and victorious is he,
> humble and riding on an ass,
> on a colt the foal of an ass (Zechariah 9:9).

    The crowd that greeted Jesus glorified him shouting, "Hosanna! Blessed is he who comes in the name of the Lord! Blessed is the kingdom of our father David that is coming! Hosanna in the highest!" (Mark 11:9b). They spread palm tree branches on the ground and hailed him as their king.

    When I was young and attended church with my aunt, we would make palm leaf Crosses the day before Palm Sunday. That was Saturday of Lazarus. After church services and a light brunch in the recreation hall, our church community would gather to split palm leaves into strips - thin enough so we could fold them into Crosses. I only did this once a year - every Saturday of Lazarus - and the first few took a little time to shape. I had to refresh my memory and once it came back to me, I would make dozens of palm leaf Crosses, which would be handed to the church parishioners the next day on Palm Sunday. I would keep the Cross I received all year - sometimes, more than a year - because I felt its holy power would bless me.

For Christians, Palm Sunday is a day to celebrate, but the days following Palm Sunday are sad because we know that our King will soon be killed. Jesus is better than a political king who can gain territory or peace for his subjects in this world. He is our King and Priest who can save us from death and give us eternal life. Most did not understand this at first. Not even Jesus's disciples were fully aware of his eternal power. Not until Jesus rose from the dead and appeared to his disciples, did they fully understand his power. Truly, his kingship is not of this world. Jesus's reign is in the Kingdom of God and not in a kingdom of man.

Only through Jesus's suffering can we understand his kingship. As Prophet Isaiah prophesied,

> [God] will divide him a portion with the great,
> and he shall divide the spoil with the strong;
> because he poured out his soul to death,
> and was numbered with the transgressors
> (Isaiah 53:12).

> Behold, my servant [God's servant] shall prosper,
> he shall be exalted and lifted up,
> and shall be very high.
> As many were astonished at him -
> his appearance was so marred, beyond human semblance,
> and his form beyond that of the sons of men -
> so shall he startle many nations;
> kings shall shut their mouths because of him;
> for that which has not been told them they shall see,
> and that which they have not heard they shall understand (Isaiah 52:13).

This world's kings may be baffled by Jesus - Isaiah's prophesied Suffering Servant of God - and his resurrection and the miracles worked in his name by the Holy Spirit, but for Christians, they are as real as God's Kingdom of Heaven.

Jesus was and is the only perfect man. He is the only true king. The rest of us are small. None of us can compare. Many men think they are big, but truth is the best we can be are servants of the Great King Jesus. He was selfless and is the ultimate king because he paid the ultimate price with his life for his servants. All we have is our life in this world and Jesus laid his down for us, so we could have a meaningful life with God. He loved us so much, which is why he is the greatest king and for those who choose to serve the Great King, the reward is God's Kingdom of Heaven. There are many leaders - both good and bad - in the world, but Jesus is the only Christ and Son of God. He is the strongest man ever for no one else can be crucified as he was and retain his love for God the way he did with patience and grace. He is our Savior, who saves our souls from hell, death and eternal suffering. It is a sublime mystery that God chose to humble himself to become man - for Jesus truly was God. And, a still deeper tragic glory that he died, so we could have life. He entered this world to teach and show us the meaning of agape and since his advent, the world has never been the same. Glory to thee, our God, glory to thee.

After we settled in, the doctor came over to tell the old man about his condition. The bullet missed his organs, but his wound, nonetheless, would not stop bleeding. His future did not look good and the doctor asked the old man if there was any family he would like to call. The old man said he was a widower and he and his late wife never had children. His friends had all died. He was one of the last of his generation and his social sphere was limited to the church. He had no one, so I had great sympathy for him and decided to stay by his bedside so he would not be alone.

"Do you know why we call it Passion of the Christ, my young friend?" he asked.

"I believe so, sir. I think it refers to Jesus's zeal, love and devotion for God," I answered.

"I understand why you say that, my young friend. It is true: Jesus loved God, but that is not why we refer to it as his Passion. The word 'passion' comes from a Greek word meaning 'to suffer.' Do you understand suffering?" he asked.

"Yes, sir. It means to go through pain, to hurt, to feel close to death," I answered.

"You are right, my young friend, but do you understand the glory of suffering?" he asked.

"What do you mean, sir?" I asked.

The old man took a deep breath and exhaled slowly. His pain was barely manageable. His pierced side would not stop bleeding. Then, he said, "Suffering brings us closer to Jesus who suffered. With suffering, we have the honor of emulating Jesus. If he could endure his Cross, we can endure ours. Perhaps, this is my Cross. Though I am anxious about death, Jesus is near to me and I know God will never leave me. Because of Jesus, I understand suffering and I know that after death, I will find peace with God and Jesus in Paradise."

I realized that if the Son of God experienced suffering, we are not immune to it either. It is a part of life. When my parents died, God gave me strength. God and Jesus understand my pain because of the pain they experienced when Jesus died. The Son of God lowered himself to reach us, so when we die we can be elevated to be with him. One who suffers to death and believes in Jesus is not far from Paradise and everlasting life.

Pain and struggle add depth to the soul. Recovery is strength. Jesus makes recovery possible. He is Salvation. Few people know pain, struggle, recovery and Jesus better than Black Americans. Like the Jews, they were once slaves, but God and Jesus saved them and have saved us all. Black American Gospel music is one of the greatest gifts any people has given to the world. The best songs are as powerful as the Psalms and they overflow with agape. To the shock of some, Jesus was not a white European. In truth, he was a Jewish man of color born in Palestine. And, revered by most, Mary was a Jewish teen virgin of color who gave birth to God.

Jesus knew what he was getting into and the suffering that was ahead of him. This makes his agape more compelling than if he did not know because most people, if they knew, would have run. As Prophet Isaiah prophesied,

> He was oppressed, and he was afflicted,
> yet he opened not his mouth;
> like a lamb that is led to the slaughter,
> and like a sheep that before its shearers is dumb,
> so he opened not his mouth (Isaiah 53:7).

There are a few times when the Gospels say that Jesus prophesied his own death and how it would happen. For example, Jesus told his disciples,

> "Behold, we are going up to Jerusalem, and everything that is written of the Son of man by the prophets will be accomplished. For he will be delivered to the Gentiles, and will be mocked and shamefully treated and spit upon; they will scourge him and kill him, and on the third day he will rise" (Luke 18:31b).

Even in agony, Jesus's faith in God his Father remained steadfast. In Gethsemane in anticipation of his "cup" of suffering and death, he "prayed more earnestly; and his sweat became like great drops of blood falling down upon the ground" (Luke 22:44). To God, he prayed, "Abba, Father, all things are possible to thee; remove this cup from me; yet not what I will, but what thou wilt" (Mark 14:36). He was obedient to God's will and submitted to God's power. He was God's perfect servant and a son who adored his Father.

When Jesus was questioned about who he was, even if it meant suffering, he fearlessly told the truth:

> The high priest then questioned Jesus about his disciples and his teaching. Jesus answered him, "I have spoken openly to the world; I have always taught in synagogues and in the temple, where all Jews come together; I have said nothing secretly. Why do you ask me? Ask those who have heard me, what I said to

them; they know what I said." When he had said this, one of the officers standing by struck Jesus with his hand, saying, "Is that how you answer the high priest?" Jesus answered him, "If I have spoken wrongly, bear witness to the wrong; but if I have spoken rightly, why do you strike me?" (John 18:19).

Still further:

> Now the chief priests and the whole council sought false testimony against Jesus that they might put him to death, but they found none, though many false witnesses came forward. At last two came forward and said, "This fellow said, 'I am able to destroy the temple of God, and to build it in three days.'" And the high priest stood up and said, "Have you no answer to make? What is it that these men testify against you?" But Jesus was silent. And the high priest said to him, "I adjure you by the living God, tell us if you are the Christ, the Son of God." Jesus said to him, "You have said so. But I tell you, hereafter you will see the Son of man seated at the right hand of Power, and coming on the clouds of heaven." Then the high priest tore his robes, and said, "He has uttered blasphemy. Why do we still need witnesses? You have now heard his blasphemy. What is your judgment?" They

answered, "He deserves death." Then they spat in his face, and struck him; and some slapped him, saying, "Prophesy to us, you Christ! Who is it that struck you?" (Matthew 26:59).

Jesus, my King, not only experienced physical pain for us, but was also belittled, mocked and disgraced for us:

> Then the soldiers of the governor took Jesus into the praetorium, and they gathered the whole battalion before him. And they stripped him and put a scarlet robe upon him, and plaiting a crown of thorns they put it on his head, and put a reed in his right hand. And kneeling before him they mocked him, saying, "Hail, King of the Jews!" And they spat upon him, and took the reed and struck him on the head. And when they had mocked him, they stripped him of the robe, and put his own clothes on him, and led him away to crucify him (Matthew 27:27).

My King is the Son of the Most High, yet he was stepped on like dirt. He suffered many things for me. The soldiers spat on him. How could they spit on my King? He lowered himself for me. Who am I? I am little and he is great. A devoted servant would lay down his life for his king, but my King laid down his life for his servants. What have we done to deserve such grace? How can we repay him? The only way I know how to repay him is to emulate him. We must be willing to sacrifice ourselves for him and the brethren. They treated him less than a human being when in reality he was God. It makes no sense, but if you listen to his words, you will see he did it out of agape. He was disgraced, but that is why I glorify him.

The climax of Jesus's Passion was his crucifixion - an incomprehensible suffering where the sentenced one dies slowly. With his limbs nailed to and his body hanging from a wood, Jesus cried with a loud voice, "My God, my God, why hast thou forsaken me?" (Mark 15:34 and Matthew 27:46). It would be hard to find greater suffering - suffering so great that the Son of God is praying for mercy. However, Jesus never curses God or His authority. Knowing he was innocent and was sentenced unjustly to death, Jesus never separated himself from God. On the Cross, with a loud voice, Jesus cried out, "'Father, into thy hands I commit my spirit!' And having said this he breathed his last" (Luke 23:46). It was finished. Triumph. Jesus accomplished what he was meant to do. To his very end, he was a messenger of the truth and fulfilled his mission for the forgiveness of our sins, so we can have eternal life.

Patients came and were treated as the old man and I sat and spoke. In the ER, things were always in motion and each patient's problem was unique.

Doctors qualified conditions into categories, but no two cases were the same. Most of the night, the regular staff had things under control and they let me stay with the old man. They understood that it was important for me to be there for him. They could see that the old man needed to talk to keep himself alert and lift his spirit. All my other responsibilities could wait. The old man was my top priority.

"Do you know who is the Good Shepherd, my young friend?" he asked.

"Of course, sir. It's Jesus," I answered.

"Do you know why he is called the Good Shepherd?" he asked.

"Not exactly, sir," I answered.

"It's because he laid down his life for us, his flock," he explained.

The old man was referring to John's Gospel 10:11, where Jesus says, "I am the good shepherd. The good shepherd lays down his life for the sheep. He who is a hireling and not a shepherd, whose own the sheep are not, sees the wolf coming and leaves the sheep and flees; and the wolf snatches them and scatters them. He flees because he is a hireling and cares nothing for the sheep. I am the good shepherd; I know my own and my own know me, as the Father knows me and I know the Father; and I lay down my life for the sheep. And I have other sheep, that are not of this fold; I must bring them also, and they will heed my voice. So there shall be one flock, one shepherd. For this reason the Father loves me, because I lay down my life, that I may take it again. No one takes it from me, but I lay it down of my own accord. I have power to lay it down, and I have power to take it again; this charge I have received from my Father."

    The old man told me, "My young friend, meditate on Prophet Isaiah's prophecy of the Christ known as the Suffering Servant prophecy. See how this passage, older than 500 BC, describes Jesus's life and death, his mission and glory. If you open your heart, you will see Jesus. He fulfills the call, role and prophecy. At the end of the prophecy, Isaiah explains that "he bore the sin of many, and made intercession for the transgressors" (53:12c). We are the transgressors - the sinners in this world - and are far from God, but Jesus interceded for us, so we can have a way to unite with God. Sinful man has no way of entering Heaven and uniting with God on his own. We are unworthy of God because we have rejected Him, as did our parents Adam and Eve, and have no way of making amends with Him. God and His Son Jesus knew this and made a plan to save us from our wicked ways that lead to hell, so we can be with God forever in Heaven. The plan was for perfect Jesus to die for us. He was the only worthy sacrifice to God to redeem sinful man. It hurts God and Jesus for Jesus to be tortured and killed, but they did so willingly to retain justice in a God centered universe. God's Justice required punishment for sin and Jesus took our place.

> Surely he has borne our griefs
> and carried our sorrows;
> yet we esteemed him stricken,
> smitten by God, and afflicted.
> But he was wounded for our transgressions,
> he was bruised for our iniquities;
> upon him was the chastisement that made us whole,
> and with his stripes we are healed
> (Isaiah 53:4).

Only perfect Jesus was a satisfactory substitution for humankind. "The LORD has laid on him the iniquity of us all" (Isaiah 53:6). He satisfied the debt due to God for human sin. "He makes himself an offering for sin" (Isaiah 53:10). His blood was "poured out for many for the forgiveness of sins" (Matthew 26:28). Jesus paid the price for our sins. As Paul explained, "You are not your own; you were bought at a price" (1 Corinthians 6:19b). We dishonor God, as did our parents Adam and Eve, with our sin of disobedience. Jesus makes reconciliation possible between God and us. He was perfectly obedient to God's will to the very end of his life. His obedience mends the rift of our disobedience. This is known as atonement, which refers to our redemption and salvation. "By his knowledge shall the righteous one, my servant, make many to be accounted righteous" (Isaiah 53:11). This was made possible because of God and Jesus's agape for us. God loved us because He sent us His Son and Jesus loved us because he sacrificed himself for us. The only way for us to show our love for God is to honor and believe in His Son. We must accept Jesus as our Savior to be put right with God. Jesus makes atonement possible. We just have to believe in him, live his message and emulate his love. If we do, we will live forever in Paradise with God and Jesus. As taught in John 3:16, "For God so loved the world that he gave his only Son, that whoever believes in him should not perish but have eternal life."

     Everything the old man said was profound and it meant more to me than it would have at any other time because it was Great Friday when we commemorate Jesus's self-sacrificial death. I sat with him for hours and as the night passed by, I was getting anxious because I wanted to go to church. However, when the end of my shift arrived, I was compelled to stay with him and miss the church service. I could not leave him. The thought that entered my mind was that, perhaps, it was more important to be with the old man. God seemed to have brought us together. He had no family, but I was there. I felt like I had a duty to be there for him. As I let that thought linger, another thought entered my mind: maybe, the old man was here to help me. He opened my eyes to many mysteries about Jesus. I had never had conversations as deep with another person as I had with the old man. I can think of nowhere else where I would have learned as much about Jesus, his Passion and the meaning of agape.

A nurse joined us. He overheard the old man and I talking about Jesus throughout the night. The nurse was raised Muslim and confessed to us that Muslims do not believe it was Jesus who died on the Cross. They believe it was someone else that was just like Jesus, someone else God transformed to be exactly like Jesus put in Jesus's place. As I have grown older, this confession has left me uneasy because of the virulent forcefulness of radical Muslims who pledge allegiance to Muhammad and his revelations. I have asked myself, "How can it be that Muslims do not believe Jesus died on the Cross? For who professed his Sonship to God? Who was accused at the trials and then carried the Cross? Who did Mother Mary weep to? Who spoke to John on the Cross to care for his Virgin Mother?

The nurse knew what he knew because of Muhammad's Qur'an, which says,

> And their saying: Surely we have killed the Messiah, Isa [Jesus] son of Marium [Mary], the apostle of Allah; and they did not kill him nor did they crucify him, but it appeared to them so (like Isa) and most surely those who differ therein are only in a doubt about it; they have no knowledge respecting it, but only follow a conjecture, and they killed him not for sure.

> Nay! Allah took him up to Himself; and Allah is Mighty, Wise.
>
> (Qur'an, Surah 4, 157-158. Translation M.H. Shakir)

But, the details of Jesus's final hours and death are well documented. It is the most well documented period described in all four Gospels and one of the most well preserved events in human history. The death of the Christ can be difficult to fathom, but it is authentic. It does not agree with conventional human wisdom and can be difficult to make sense of, but it was instituted because of God's Providence and Wisdom. It is not an event that we may like or want to accept or be proud of unless we are seekers of truth. His role was prophesied in the Old Testament and he fulfilled it. Those who have examined the Jewish Scriptures know it and so do those who have seen his workings in the world. The Cross is fundamental. If Muhammad, the author of the Qur'an, was wrong about the fact of Jesus's death, how could he have claimed that God gave him the revelations of the Qur'an? God is Truth, so did Muhammad make up what he wrote? What else could he have feigned divine revelation of? This Muslims must confront for themselves. It is their only path to Salvation. I pray they see the truth for the saving of their souls and the souls of their children.

      The most valuable thing we possess is our souls. If we ask ourselves, "What is the soul?" we can conclude that it is the divine part of us - still further, it is the agape in us. The soul is the only part of us that can make us immortal. And, if we ask ourselves, "How do we reach immortality?" the answer is Jesus Christ. Jesus is the only way to become immortal and attain eternal life because he fills us with agape and only those who are filled with agape can become one with God who is Agape. Immortality is union with God and that is only possible through agape. To be filled with agape, we have to be reborn in spirit with God's Son Jesus. We do not know agape or how to give agape until Jesus enters us. It begins with respect and recognition of his suffering. Consider his suffering and it will lead to empathy. Agape compelled him and his agape will fill you with agape. Then, you will understand that he was no ordinary man. He will transform your mind and heart. And, when you pay attention to his teachings, you will hear truth in his words. No man spoke like this man. No man died like this man. No man loved like this man. Reflect and embrace him and you will understand why we Christians call him God's Suffering Servant, the Christ and God's Son.

      As the hours of Great Friday were coming to a close, I read out loud to the old man the Gospel accounts of Jesus's crucifixion. Then, the old man asked me to read Psalm 22. He told me, "My young friend, meditate on this psalm, which is often referred to as the Passion Psalm. When you read it, try to hear Jesus's suffering and agony when he prays in Gethsemane and when he is hanging on the Cross. As the perfect Jew, the Lord quotes it as he is dying. He was always teaching, even to his very end." The old man inhaled, exhaled, took another deep breath and then continued. "You will see Jesus's humanity as he suffers as a man, but you will also see his confidence in God as God's Son. He never separated himself from God and was always one with God. He has nowhere to go. God is all he has. He trusts in God who gives him strength before he falls apart. Jesus endured to show us that we have the power to endure and that we must endure. God was with Jesus and God will always and forever be with those who love Him."

> Psalm 22 (RSV)
> Plea for Deliverance from Suffering and Hostility
> To the choirmaster: according to The Hind of the Dawn. A Psalm of David.
>
> My God, my God, why hast thou forsaken me?
> Why art thou so far from helping me, from the words of my groaning?
> 2 O my God, I cry by day, but thou dost not answer;

and by night, but find no rest.
3 Yet thou art holy,
 enthroned on the praises of Israel.
4 In thee our fathers trusted;
 they trusted, and thou didst deliver them.
5 To thee they cried, and were saved;
 in thee they trusted, and were not disappointed.
6 But I am a worm, and no man;
 scorned by men, and despised by the people.
7 All who see me mock at me,
 they make mouths at me, they wag their heads;
8 "He committed his cause to the Lord; let him deliver him,
 let him rescue him, for he delights in him!"
9 Yet thou art he who took me from the womb;
 thou didst keep me safe upon my mother's breasts.
10 Upon thee was I cast from my birth,
 and since my mother bore me thou hast been my God.
11 Be not far from me,
 for trouble is near
 and there is none to help.
12 Many bulls encompass me,
 strong bulls of Bashan surround me;
13 they open wide their mouths at me,

like a ravening and roaring lion.
14 I am poured out like water,
   and all my bones are out of joint;
my heart is like wax,
   it is melted within my breast;
15 my strength is dried up like a potsherd,
   and my tongue cleaves to my jaws;
   thou dost lay me in the dust of death.
16 Yea, dogs are round about me;
   a company of evildoers encircle me;
   they have pierced[a] my hands and feet—
17 I can count all my bones—
   they stare and gloat over me;
18 they divide my garments among them,
   and for my raiment they cast lots.
19 But thou, O Lord, be not far off!
   O thou my help, hasten to my aid!
20 Deliver my soul from the sword,
   my life[b] from the power of the dog!
21 Save me from the mouth of the lion,
   my afflicted soul[c] from the horns of the
wild oxen!
22 I will tell of thy name to my brethren;
   in the midst of the congregation I will
praise thee:
23 You who fear the Lord, praise him!
   all you sons of Jacob, glorify him,
   and stand in awe of him, all you sons of
Israel!
24 For he has not despised or abhorred

> the affliction of the afflicted;
>
> and he has not hid his face from him,
>> but has heard, when he cried to him.
>
> 25 From thee comes my praise in the great congregation;
>> my vows I will pay before those who fear him.
>
> 26 The afflicted[d] shall eat and be satisfied;
>> those who seek him shall praise the Lord!
>> May your hearts live forever!
>
> 27 All the ends of the earth shall remember
>> and turn to the Lord;
>
> and all the families of the nations
>> shall worship before him.[e]
>
> 28 For dominion belongs to the Lord,
>> and he rules over the nations.
>
> 29 Yea, to him[f] shall all the proud of the earth bow down;
>> before him shall bow all who go down to the dust,
>> and he who cannot keep himself alive.
>
> 30 Posterity shall serve him;
>> men shall tell of the Lord to the coming generation,
>
> 31 and proclaim his deliverance to a people yet unborn,
>> that he has wrought it.

The old man's teaching about this psalm was the final lesson he spoke to me. The psalm reveals the author's inner struggle, turmoil and suffering. It begins with pain, is filled with deep faith and ends with reverence. I saw it in the old man and Jesus went through it. Jesus's Passion (or Suffering) cannot be separated from his love because it is proof of his love for God and us. We meant the world to Jesus which is why he left the world for us.

By the time it was 11:20 PM, the old man was drifting in and out of consciousness. Our conversations had deteriorated into occasional looks at each other. I could see that he was getting weak as his eyes rolled around behind his heavy eyelids. Sweat beaded above his brow, so I put a damp cloth on his forehead hoping that it would bring him some relief. Then, he started to shiver, so I got an extra blanket and tucked it around him. When his skin started to turn pale, I did not know what to do to ease his pain. I sat with him trying to comfort him as best as I could even if he did not know I was with him. I knew his end was approaching. Then, for a brief moment, his eyes opened and he took a deep breath. In a voice not much louder than a whisper, I heard him pray: "Into thy hands, O Lord, I commend my soul and my body. Do thou thyself bless me, have mercy upon me, and grant me life eternal. Amen." Then, just before midnight, the last minute of Great Friday, he stopped breathing, his heart monitor flat lined and he departed from this world. I had never seen anyone die before and I had mixed feelings about the old man's death. I can best describe my feelings as a joyful sadness - sad because he died, but joyful because I knew he was with God and Jesus in Paradise.

For me, Great Friday is normally emotionally heavy because I mourn Jesus's death. However, witnessing the old man die on Great Friday, I developed a deeper understanding about death that was transformed from a scene that I saw in pictures and film into a raw and permanent reality. This man lived and died as did Jesus. Being with the old man during his final hours helped me to better know Jesus during his final hours. The next day, my spirit still felt heavy, but when I was in church that night for the Easter vigil, God strengthened me. Like fresh air into empty lungs, my spirit was rejuvenated because with my fellow Christians, I was celebrating Jesus's resurrection. In the dark church at the moment of midnight when it became Easter Sunday, the priest came out of the altar with the Sacred Light lit on candles and passed it to the congregation. From one candle to the next, the once dark church was filled with light and light overcame darkness, just as Jesus has overcome death. For we Christians, Jesus's death is the saddest day of the year, but his resurrection is the most joyous. From the moment of the Sacred Light for the next forty days, we Orthodox Christians greet each other with "Christ is Risen!" and respond with "Truly, He is Risen!" I wait all year to proclaim this truth with my fellow Christians. By rising from the dead, Jesus has destroyed Death.

YOUNG EZEKIEL

What is love?

Can you describe it?

Do you love your parents, friends, romantic partner and God in the same way?

In the English language, we use the word love in all these relationships, but the ancient Greeks - the first western philosophers - tried to capture, pinpoint and distinguish the different forms of love with four words: storge, philia, eros, agape.

In Young Ezekiel: A Life of Loves, Ezekiel will tell you about his life and loves. Though his life is unique, his relationships are like ours and, maybe, through his story, you will learn about yourself and the loves in your life.

ISBN 9780997372700

WRITINGS

JAMES THOMAS ANGELIDIS

WRITINGS

A THEOLOGICAL MEMOIR

DANTE'S *DIVINE COMEDY*

HIERARCHY OF TRUTHS

JAMES THOMAS ANGELIDIS

jtangelidis.com

Copyright 2016 James Thomas Angelidis.
All rights reserved.
(Edited 2017)

A THEOLOGICAL MEMOIR

JAMES THOMAS ANGELIDIS

Copyright 2016 James Thomas Angelidis.
All rights reserved.
(Edited 2017)

The following is an article about my journey through the six great world religions' sacred scriptures.

After I graduated from the university, I moved back to my hometown and spent the next few summer months with friends. Up until this phase in my life, there was structure in my life that was as predictable as the seasons in a year. Since I was five years old, I had gone to school every year. Summer would arrive, then pass and school would begin, again. However, this year, after summer passed, my routine changed because school was over. At first, it was liberating. Few things are as sweet as graduating from a university. All that hard work is certified: you have accomplished something. The future is wide open and all things seem possible. However, as the months passed and I could not find a job, I realized things would not be as easy as I thought they would be.

After school, the next step is to get a job, but that next step is easier said than done. The economy was poor which made my task difficult and when I did have interviews, I was telling my potential employers what I thought they wanted to hear, but I had a tough time convincing them I was passionate about the work because I was not. I just wanted a job. For a while, I felt lost. The direction I was heading towards was not leading to anything. I had few "connections" that could have led to a "job." Though I was not "working," I began to make connections in my mind of how I saw the world. I used the information I learned in school and early on in the "real world" little by little, I made connections regarding money and success and aspirations. Relationships appeared and I began to formulate in my mind an idea of the life I wanted to lead.

The next two years of my life are difficult to clearly describe. There was little structure. I was working, but I had little direction. I eventually found work at a marketing department of a law firm in New York City, but this was a temporary job that only lasted for a few months. I had various jobs around town. I painted for a while and even considered making a career out of it, but I was not very sure of how to start a business. I even worked as an electrician's helper for a week. My most substantial job lasted for about one year. I was a laborer at an airline cargo warehouse. It was all manual labor, but I did not mind. It was a simple job. I put in my hours and got paid. I would finish my day then go home and eat dinner. It was honest work. I knew I had potential, but things were moving slowly. This period of my life lasted for about two years, but most of the real work was done in my bedroom with my books in my parent's house as I was coming to know God. It would be a very intense two years with great highs and great lows as I tried to figure out what was real and not fake, true and not false.

    I read extensively and intensely after university. Many of the ideas and philosophies that I was introduced to in my liberal arts classes, I used to help me navigate through the "real world." And, that was the true value of my university education. What I learned in those liberal arts classes, I applied to my life. As students, we were not expected to be experts on anything, but be aware of the people, events and literature that changed the world, so we, too, could contribute to the world.

    My interest in philosophy matured into a passion for religion in my search for truth. I forced myself to read - I learned how to read - not as a means to get a grade in a class, but for knowledge and wisdom that would help to create a foundation from which I could build my life. It started off little, like reading before bed. Then, it became a habit and I read every night before bed and each night I read more than the previous night. Sometimes, I would read at my desk, but I usually read facing down in my bed. Beside my bed, books piled and piled and were stacked one on top of another. I made sure they were always near me in case I changed direction in thought or needed to confirm some knowledge. I was an active reader taking notes and saving pages, so I could go back to the information that I found valuable and relearn it. This way, it would remain with me.

The more I was reading, the more I was learning and the more I wanted to learn. I was hungry for knowledge and sometimes, I wanted to physically consume the books as if, with every swallow, the answers would come to me more quickly.

Every day for two years, I took a literary journey into the greatest literature that has ever been written. I journeyed through the great world religions' sacred scriptures. Below, I have displayed the concepts and beliefs that I find most provocative. I studied all the major religions. I learned that the great world religions can be classified into two types: those that come from human inquiry and those that are God attributed. Hinduism, Taoism and Buddhism are mainly the result of human inquiry and Judaism, Christianity and Islam are God attributed. I spent day and night learning about God and His ways and I felt closer to Him than ever before. Reading those amazing books was like finding treasure. There were nights that I could barely sit still because I was so elated by the jewels of wisdom and theology revealed in those sacred texts.

At the time, I was not a proactive participant in my faith. I was raised a Christian and never considered conversion to any other faith, but I was open to each faith. I never judged the religions and I was eager to examine each of them. My focus was in their sacred scriptures. I never stepped into a church or temple or mosque looking for answers and I never considered traditions or holidays. None of that ever occurred to me. Maybe, I was naive. But, I was hungry for knowledge and I knew I would find that knowledge in the scriptures. I dove into the scriptures themselves and not secondary literature. I wanted to know what made the religions they preached so powerful and why people lived and died for those religions.

I began my search with the religions that come from human inquiry. I was drawn to them because they were philosophical and because their sacred scriptures were short - their size was appealing. I learned that though their pages were minimal, they were potent.

Hinduism

For Hinduism, I studied the *Bhagavad-Gita* and the *Upanishads*. Of all the literature I examined during my journey, the Hindu *Bhagavad-Gita* was my favorite. I studied two different translations and read each translation completely at least twice and I referred back to the texts many times. I was first introduced to the *Bhagavad-Gita* during my studies at the university. Though I did not fully understand it when I was in school, I realized its importance once I began my investigation into eternal truths. It is life changing and life enhancing revelation. It is a spiritual warrior's guide and instruction manual to reach union with God. It teaches asceticism and mysticism. Chapters include: spiritual discipline, discipline of action, knowledge, infinite spirit, sublime mystery. It is also referred to as *Krishna's Council in Time of War.* In it, Lord Krishna councils Warrior-Prince Arjuna on how to transcend earthly desires and fight the spiritual battle within him, the same spiritual battle that takes place in each of us. Most inspiring is when Krishna tells Arjuna to:

> Look to your own duty;
> do not tremble before it;
> nothing is better for a warrior
> than a battle of sacred duty.
>
> The doors of heaven open
> for warriors who rejoice
> to have a battle like this
> thrust on them by chance.
>
> If you fail to wage this war
> of sacred duty,
> you will abandon your own duty

and fame only to gain evil.

People will tell
of your undying shame,
and for a man of honor
shame is worse than death.

The great chariot warriors will think
you deserted in fear of battle;
you will be despised
by those who held you in esteem.

Your enemies will slander you,
scorning your skill
in so many unspeakable ways -
could any suffering be worse?

If you are killed, you win heaven;
if you triumph, you enjoy the earth;
therefore, Arjuna, stand up
and resolve to fight the battle!

- *The Bhagavad-Gita*, 2.31-37
(Translation B.S. Miller)

I feel compelled and believe I have the responsibility to emphasize and make clear that these words of encouragement are for a spiritual battle that takes place in one's soul and not a physical war with weapons. I know that those inclined to read my story are, most likely, not war minded, but I stress that this speech does not encourage physical war because of the time in history we live in. With the unrighteous madness of terrorism inflicted upon the innocent in our time, the inspiring words of Krishna may be taken out of context; however, I refuse to shy away from this speech because it is intended for good and can help one get closer to God. In our age, Muslim radicals have decided to terrorize the world by declaring a holy war in the name of God. They have used the term "jihad" to justify their actions. The Islamic term jihad means "struggle" and is a religious duty for Muslims. There are two forms of jihad in the Muslim faith. One refers to an internal struggle to live a moral and virtuous life and is called the greater jihad. The other refers to an external struggle to fight a holy war against the enemies of Islam and is called the lesser jihad. I pray that we all chose to fight the greater jihad within to live a moral and virtuous life and apply Krishna's advice to Arjuna to our personal lives and forget the lesser jihad of Muslim radicals who have dishonored God.

    What I found most compelling in Hindu theology is the relationship between Atman and Brahman. Atman is the soul within a person, the innermost reality of a person and Brahman is the soul of the universe, the supreme infinite reality of the universe. Most compelling is the belief that Atman and Brahman are of the same essence, the same substance. Man's goal is to unite his soul with the soul of the universe. This can only be done if man can free himself from the bondage of worldly attachments and actions. Once freed, Atman becomes one with Brahman. The *Bhagavad-Gita* and the *Upanishads* teach the principles that will help one to free Atman into Brahman. The *Upanishads* - known for being the eternal wisdom of the Hindu mystics - is the most comprehensive text of theology behind this goal. It is the oldest scripture that I studied, but it remains fresh.

Taoism

Taoism is an ancient Chinese philosophy that became one of the great world religions. Its principal text is the *Tao Te Ching*. Probably a compilation of wisdom and insight from many sages, the *Tao Te Ching* began to take shape as far back as the seventh century BC, but most likely did not reach its final form until the mid-third century BC. However, tradition ascribes the authorship of the text to Lao Tzu, a seemingly legendary figure who is said to have been a contemporary of Confucius during the early sixth century BC.

With 81 short poem-like chapters, the text is primarily concerned with the Tao and Te. Taoism adopted its name from the Tao, which translates into English as "Way," as in the way the universe operates. It is the natural rhythm of the universe, the absolute reality of the universe. From before the beginning of time, it is the mysterious source of

Heaven and earth and the fountain of life for all life in the universe. The Tao is ethereal, yet substantial. It is invisible and vague, yet it has form and essence. It is unknowable, yet pervasive and trying to understand it can be difficult, but not hopeless.

In English, Te translates into "Virtue," as in the virtue characteristic of one who abides by the Tao. Te is the manifestation or power of the Tao in one who acts in accordance with the Tao. The underlying characteristic of Te is "wu-wei," which literally means "non-action," in essence, not to strive, like water, which does not contend. A person who is cautious, hesitant, polite, yielding, blank, open, and mixes freely (Addiss 15) is one who practices "wu-wei" and is called a sage. Like the Tao, Te is unfamiliar to many, if not most, and is difficult to comprehend and just as difficult to practice. The sage practices wu-wei and all things in the universe settle themselves and return to their natural state; harmony returns to the natural rhythm of the universe and all is restored, as it was meant to be. Wu-wei is not a form of apathy or recklessness. It means to take no unnatural action and to be one with the universe, with the Tao, which is "solitary and silent" (Addiss, 25). Understanding this, the world "moves without danger in safety and peace." (Addiss, 35). Everyone who reads the *Tao Te Ching* is encouraged to follow the example of the sage who is praiseworthy as benefactor to universe.

Ching means "classic work," so the *Tao Te Ching* neatly, yet roughly translates into "The Classic work of the Way and its Virtue."

Because of the great difficulty in translating Chinese into English, there are more than 100 translations of the *Tao Te Ching* in English. I first scrutinized the translation that I was introduced to at the university. Then, after extensive research, I scrutinized two additional translations that were popular and critically well received. Initially, I read each one like a novel from one chapter to the next, but when compelled, I returned to chapters that stuck with me. For years, I returned to the texts and I estimate I read the *Tao Te Ching* with earnest resolve at least twenty times. The *Tao Te Ching* was the most elusive, yet enlightening text I was reading at the time and it left a deep impression in my mind. I felt like I was unlocking the secrets of the eternal and I think that is the intention of the text. It is esoteric in nature and I believe few have delved into or have even been introduced to the profound depths of its wisdom. In addition to the *Tao Te Ching*, I read the *Chuang Tzu*, which is made up of brief stories and anecdotes, a delightful read and an important text in Taoism. However, no text, Taoist or otherwise, was as captivating as the *Tao Te Ching*. Its sublime beauty is exemplified in chapter 67, a favorite of mine. Though God the Father does not exist in Taoism, chapter 67 reminds me of a Christian sermon:

Everyone under heaven calls my Tao great,
And unlike anything else.

It is great only because
It is unlike anything else.
If it were like anything else
It would stretch and become thin.

I have three treasures
To maintain and conserve:
The first is compassion.
The second is frugality.
The third is not presuming
To be first under heaven.

Compassion leads to courage.
Frugality allows generosity.
Not presuming to be first
Creates a lasting instrument.

Nowadays
People reject compassion
But want to be brave,
Reject frugality
But want to be generous,
Reject humility
And want to come first.

This is death.

Compassion:
Attack with it and win.
Defend with it and stand firm.

Heaven aids and protects
Through compassion.

- *Tao Te Ching*, 67
(Translation S. Addiss and S. Lombardo)

Buddhism

Over four hundred years before Christ in South Asia by the Himalayas, a child was born named Siddhartha from the Sakya tribe, a prince of the Gautama clan, who would grow up to be known as the Buddha, meaning the "enlightened one" or "awakened one." When I first started studying the great world religions, I was quickly drawn to the story and teachings of the Buddha. I think what I found so appealing was his venerable goal to rid suffering from life. When the Buddha discovered the Four Noble Truths, he attained Enlightenment/Buddhahood/Nirvana. He taught these to his followers and if they were able to fully grasp them and experience them, they too would attain Enlightenment/Buddhahood/Nirvana and as a result, freedom from suffering. The Four Noble Truths are:

One, suffering is a part of existence: "Birth is suffering, aging is suffering, sickness is suffering, death is suffering: likewise, sorrow and grief, woe, lamentation and despair. To be conjoined with things which we dislike, to be separated from things which we like - that also is suffering. Not to get what one wants - that also is suffering. In a word, this body, this five-fold mass which is based on grasping - that is suffering."

Two, craving causes suffering: "It is that craving that leads back to birth, along with the lure and the lust that lingers longingly now here, now there: namely, the craving for sensual pleasure, the craving to be born again, the craving for existence to end."

Three, freedom from suffering is attained by letting go of craving: "It is the utter passionless cessation of, the giving up, the forsaking, the release from, the absence of longing for this craving."

Four, the way that leads to freedom from suffering is the Noble Eightfold Path's Middle Way: "Right views, right aim, right speech, right action, right living, right effort, right mindfulness, right concentration… This is that Middle Way which giveth vision, which

giveth knowledge, which causeth calm,
special knowledge, enlightenment, Nirvana."
The Middle Way is midway between
indulgent desire and extreme asceticism.

I appreciate Buddhism because it makes sense. The Four Noble Truths constitute a sound argument. As I studied them, I understood them, intellectually. And, when I applied them to my life, my experience affirmed their value. It takes a lifetime, some Buddhists believe more than one lifetime, to reach the Enlightenment/Buddhahood/Nirvana of the Buddha. Monks devote their lives to the teachings of the Buddha and some never reach complete freedom from suffering, the state of Enlightenment/Buddhahood/Nirvana. I was no monk and I know I was no further along the path to Enlightenment/Buddhahood/Nirvana than they, but during my earnest, humble quest, I believe I got a taste of that sublime state and it was beautiful.

I was first exposed to the Four Noble Truths at the university. Although, the class did not assign any Buddhist scripture for study, we learned from lectures and secondary readings. During my quest for wisdom and truth and to better understand Buddhism, I found a good book that included portions of authentic Buddhist scripture. Of prime importance is "The First Sermon." This was when the Buddha expounded the Four Noble Truths for the first time to five monks. This moment marked the Setting in Motion the Wheel of Dharma, which refers to the unceasing advancement of the Buddha's message taught by the faithful until the end of time. Through the book and further investigation, I discovered three important and influential sacred Buddhist texts: the *Dhammapada*, the *Lotus Sutra* and *The Way of the Bodhisattva*. The *Dhammapada* is an essential text in Theravada Buddhism. It reflects the essence of the Buddha's teachings. It is poetry and meditation. Reading it was rejuvenating like a cool breeze or a breath of fresh air or a tall glass of fresh water. Most uplifting is the teaching:

> Better than the sole rulership over the world,
> Better than going to heaven,
> Better than lordship over all the worlds,
> Is the fruition of the streamwinner's path.

- *The Dhammapada*, 13.12
(Translation A. Maitreya)

During my journey, with the *Bhagavad-Gita* or the *Dhammapada* in my pocket and reading daily during my travels, I felt like the streamwinner who is coming into his own.

While the *Dhammapada* is intimate as if the Buddha were speaking directly to you and guiding you, the *Lotus Sutra* relates the Buddha's teachings on a cosmic scale. It is a fundamental text in

Mahayana Buddhism. With poetic parables and speeches, it depicts multiple immortal spiritual Buddhas who are a part of an eternal massive spiritual universe. It illustrates the Buddhas' relationships with the universe and the role the individual plays in the universe with the Buddhas as his Light. Of great importance in the *Lotus Sutra* is the Bodhisattva who is "a being destined for Enlightenment/Buddhahood/Nirvana."

The clearest description of the Bodhisattva is in eighth century Indian Buddhist scholar Shantideva's *The Way of the Bodhisattva*. The Bodhisattva heroically postpones Enlightenment/Buddhahood/Nirvana out of great compassion for others in order to help others toward Enlightenment/Buddhahood/Nirvana. He vows to reach Enlightenment/Buddhahood/Nirvana for the benefit of all conscience living beings. In Mahayana Buddhism, everyone is encouraged to become a Bodhisattva. As I read *The Way of the Bodhisattva*, I did not want to put it down and when I was not reading it, I could barely wait to read it, again. It excited me to believe that I, too, could be a Bodhisattva and help save the world.

The *Dhammapada*, the *Lotus Sutra* and *The Way of the Bodhisattva* are very different, but all adhere to the teaching of the Four Noble Truths.

Human Inquiry
in Comparison to

God Attributed

Religions that come from human inquiry and religions that are God attributed have striking similarities and differences. When I decided to examine the great world religions, I had an innate belief that they have similarities because we are all human beings all living on the same planet. Compassion, wellbeing and eternal wisdom are cornerstones of each of the great world religions. As Plato recognized, we all inherently seek the Good. However, the great difference between the religions that come from human inquiry and the religions that are God attributed is belief in the One Almighty God. The religions of human inquiry (Hinduism, Taoism and Buddhism) do not teach that there is One Almighty God; while, the religions that are God attributed (Judaism, Christianity and Islam) do teach that there is One Almighty God.

Judaism

In my search for wisdom, truth and God, I was eager to examine the Jewish religion. Its value was obvious to me: it was the religion of my Lord - Jesus the Christ. As a Christian, I was familiar with Judaism and the monumental and grand stories in the Pentateuch (the first five books of the Old Testament), known in Judaism as the Torah. But, it was not until I inquired about Truth and the meaning of life that I decided I had to read the Jewish Scriptures for myself. I understood that the Old Testament in the Christian Bible was the Jewish Testament, but I was also aware that Jews do not study the Old Testament in the Christian Bible. I was vaguely aware that Jews study and worship from their own text. After some research, I discovered the Hebrew-English Tanakh from the Jewish Publication Society. To the average Christian, the only noticeable difference between the Old Testament in the Christian Bible and the Jewish Tanakh is that the Christian Bible's pages are ordered from left to right while the Tanakh is ordered from right to left. But, after scrutinizing the texts, I learned that there are subtle differences. So, I studied from the Tanakh because I wanted to study what Jews study. I focused on the book of Genesis and the book of Proverbs.

    I studied the book of Genesis because I wanted to learn about the great stories and figures that are fundamental to all three monotheistic religions - the lessons to be learned from God's glory as Creator, from Adam and Eve's fall from grace, from the tragedy of Cain and Abel, from the righteous Noah and the great flood, from the megalomania of the Tower of Babel, from the lives and devotion of Patriarchs Abraham, Isaac and Jacob, and from the rise of Joseph. Each of these narratives is so important to the three monotheistic religions that I knew I had to learn them if I earnestly wanted to understand God and the wisdom and truth that I believed are inherent in each of the great world religions. The book of Proverbs, was of supreme value for my mission to find wisdom, truth and God. As I studied the great world religions' sacred scriptures, I found Proverbs to be the most accessible. It was clear and direct and I believed what it taught. It was practical. It was exactly what my mind was looking for. It taught me,

> 13 Happy is the man who finds wisdom,
> The man who attains understanding.
> 14 Her [Wisdom's] value in trade is better than silver,
> Her yield, greater than gold.
> 15 She is more precious than rubies;
> All of your goods cannot equal her.
>
> - Proverbs 3:13-15
> (JPS Tanakh - Hebrew Bible/Old Testament)

Proverbs is a part of the wisdom literature found in the Jewish Scriptures. It was intended as instruction for, primarily, young men on their way to adulthood. At the time, I was a young man on my way to adulthood and I felt that Proverbs was made for me. I read Proverbs with joy and I applied its lessons to my life right away, but it would take me years to fully understand its teachings and utilize its value.

Islam

Islam's sacred scripture is the Qur'an. Like the Jewish Tanakh, the Qur'an's pages are ordered from right to left instead of left to right. When I first examined the Qur'an, I was surprised how important and integrated the Jewish and Christian Scriptures are to it; however, the style of writing is very different. There is constant repetition in the themed chapters. Its structure is poetic and Allah (God) is constantly addressed within the writing style. We are taught that Allah is Beneficent, Merciful, the Lord of Worlds, Master of the Day of Judgment, Creator, Protector, Lord of Mighty Grace, Forgiving, Ample Giving, Knowing, Hearing, Mighty, Wise, Affectionate, Grateful and is described in many other ways. Ultimately, we are taught that Allah is Powerful and that we must submit to Him and be obedient to Him.

Muslims believe that the Qur'an is Allah's final revelation to humankind and that Muhammad was chosen by Allah to deliver that revelation. In the Qur'an, believers and unbelievers of the revelation are strictly divided from another, but as a young Christian who was looking for answers, I focused not on the divide, but on the truths I saw in the Qur'an.

Islam is unmistakably linked to the previous monotheistic religions: Judaism and Christianity. I was most surprised to see Jesus and Mother Mary in the Qur'an. Jesus is referred to as Messiah and

Mother Mary as Virgin. For example, in chapter 3 of the Qur'an, we are told,

> 45. When the angles said: O Marium [Mary], surely Allah [God] gives you good news with a Word from Him (of one) whose name is Messiah, Isa [Jesus] son of Marium, worthy of regard in this world and the hereafter and of those who are made near (to Allah).
>
> 46. And he shall speak to the people when in the cradle and when of old age, and (he shall be) one of the good ones.
>
> 47. She said: My Lord! when shall there be a son (born) to me, and man has not touched me? He said: Even so, Allah creates what He pleases; when He has decreed a matter, He only says to it, Be, and it is.
>
> 48. And He will teach him the Book and the wisdom and the Taurat [Torah] and the Injeel [Gospel].
>
> 49. And (make him) an apostle to the children of Israel: That I have come to you with a sign from your Lord, that I determine for you out of dust like the form of a bird, then I breathe into it and it becomes a bird with

Allah's permission and I heal the blind and the leprous, and bring the dead to life with Allah's permission and I inform you of what you should eat and what you should store in your houses; most surely there is a sign in this for you, if you are believers.

50. And a verifier of that which is before me of the Taurat, and that I may allow you part of that which has been forbidden you, and I have come to you with a sign from your Lord, therefore be careful of (your duty to) Allah and obey me.

51. Surely Allah is my Lord and your Lord, therefore serve Him; this is the right path.

- Qur'an, Surah III, 45-51
(Translation M. H. Shakir)

I never finished reading the Qur'an - there is so much - but I read approximately 65 percent of it.

Christianity

I was born a Christian. My roots are firmly secured in the Christian religion, which is why I decided to study it last in order to give proper attention to the other great world religions and learn what they had to teach. I never lost sight of Jesus.

He was always with me, but he was not in the forefront of my thoughts as I investigated the other religions. When I finally decided to examine my Christian religion, I concentrated on the four Gospels. Eventually, my enthusiasm grew and I searched for any and all types of literature to satisfy my hunger for knowledge of Jesus the Christ.

I believe in God Almighty. And, I believe that Christianity is the means to God Almighty. When I have a question, I first refer to the Bible, particularly the New Testament. Jesus's words are never far from my heart and mind. There is no doubt that Jesus walked the earth, that he existed historically, but some people doubt that he is the Christ.

I knew that Jesus was the Christ - God's Anointed One - when I discovered the Old Testament prophecy of God's Suffering Servant. It depicts Jesus's suffering and death and his mission and scope - even though it was written over 500 years before he arrived. It reads:

> [Isaiah 52]
> 13 Behold, my servant shall prosper,
>   he shall be exalted and lifted up,
>   and shall be very high.
> 14 As many were astonished at him[b]—
>   his appearance was so marred, beyond human semblance,

and his form beyond that of the sons of men—
15 so shall he startle[c] many nations;
 kings shall shut their mouths because of him;
for that which has not been told them they shall see,
 and that which they have not heard they shall understand.

[Isaiah 53]
Who has believed what we have heard?
 And to whom has the arm of the Lord been revealed?
2 For he grew up before him like a young plant,
 and like a root out of dry ground;
he had no form or comeliness that we should look at him,
 and no beauty that we should desire him.
3 He was despised and rejected[a] by men;
 a man of sorrows,[b] and acquainted with grief;[c]
and as one from whom men hide their faces
 he was despised, and we esteemed him not.
4 Surely he has borne our griefs[d]
 and carried our sorrows;[e]
yet we esteemed him stricken,
 smitten by God, and afflicted.
5 But he was wounded for our transgressions,

he was bruised for our iniquities;
upon him was the chastisement that made us whole,
    and with his stripes we are healed.
6 All we like sheep have gone astray;
    we have turned every one to his own way;
and the Lord has laid on him
    the iniquity of us all.
7 He was oppressed, and he was afflicted,
    yet he opened not his mouth;
like a lamb that is led to the slaughter,
    and like a sheep that before its shearers is dumb,
    so he opened not his mouth.
8 By oppression and judgment he was taken away;
    and as for his generation, who considered
that he was cut off out of the land of the living,
    stricken for the transgression of my people?
9 And they made his grave with the wicked
    and with a rich man in his death,
although he had done no violence,
    and there was no deceit in his mouth.
10 Yet it was the will of the Lord to bruise him;
    he has put him to grief;[f]
when he makes himself[g] an offering for sin,
    he shall see his offspring, he shall prolong his days;

the will of the Lord shall prosper in his hand;
11   he shall see the fruit of the travail of his soul and be satisfied;

by his knowledge shall the righteous one, my servant,
    make many to be accounted righteous;
    and he shall bear their iniquities.
12 Therefore I will divide him a portion with the great,
    and he shall divide the spoil with the strong;
because he poured out his soul to death,
    and was numbered with the transgressors;
yet he bore the sin of many,
    and made intercession for the transgressors.

- Isaiah 52:13-53:12
(RSV Bible)

When I first read this, my heart broke open and a flood of tears poured out. I could barely read it once, but when I did, I needed to read it again and again. Truly, Jesus is the Christ. He fulfills the Old Testament promise. He replaces Israel as the means of Salvation. He is God's Suffering Servant.

Jews and Muslims overlook the truth that Jesus is the Christ and the Son of God because of the hardness of their hearts denying His Love and Passion. Jesus explains to us that,

40 "He who receives you receives me, and he who receives me receives him who sent me. 41 He who receives a prophet because he is a prophet shall receive a prophet's reward, and he who receives a righteous man because he is a righteous man shall receive a righteous man's reward. 42 And whoever gives to one of these little ones even a cup of cold water because he is a disciple, truly, I say to you, he shall not lose his reward."

- Matthew 10:40-42
(RSV Bible)

But, I say to you that Jesus is not just a righteous man and he is more than a prophet; he is the Son of God and he who receives the Son of God because he is the Son of God shall receive the Son's reward. All who believe in Jesus and live according to his teachings will be given the right to enter Paradise because they acknowledge him as the Way, the Truth and the Life. He is the Door of the Sheepfold and all who enter through him will enter Paradise.

As I accrued all this information about the great world religions, connections between them became apparent and the world became a smaller place. I was growing spiritually and confidently. I believed that the religions that I was learning were making me wiser. As I was growing up, I desired physical strength, but now, I sought mental and spiritual strength. My priorities had changed and I devoted myself to the teachings of God seeking the fruits of my spiritual labor.

I was inspired by my heroes and I would cry when I heard about their greatness. There was kinship between me and my heroes in the world - revolutionaries, athletes, artists, musicians - because I, too, wanted to be great and at times, I saw their greatness in me. I wanted to be like these men - men like Mohandas Gandhi, the Mahatma, the Great Soul. He carried the Indian nation to freedom from the British Empire - one of the most powerful empires in recent history - without a sword. His wisdom paralleled that of King Solomon. It was said that during the peak of Hindu and Muslim strife in India, a Hindu anarchist confessed to Gandhi that he killed a Muslim child by smashing the child's head against a wall because the Muslims killed his son. Gandhi told the man that he knew a way out of Hell. He told the man, a Hindu, to find a Muslim boy, his enemy's son, whose parents had been killed in the strife and to raise and nurture the boy as his own, only to be sure that he, a Hindu, raise the boy to be a Muslim, the faith of this enemy. The brilliant Albert Einstein was quoted saying, "Generations to come will scarce believe that such a one as this ever in flesh and blood walked upon this Earth." All my heroes had a passion for life and each one touched my soul. But, no one meant more to me than my Lord Jesus the Christ who taught me about God and the true love between God and man and love between neighbors.

My soul was filled with joy because I knew I was on the right path. I was absorbing the teachings that I learned from the great world religions and the seed of inspiration was budding. I needed to express my internal religious growth and maturity externally. The first stage was keeping a journal, but before formulating my own ideas and interpretations, I cataloged what I learned. And, in my bedroom with my books as I was coming to know God, I posted on my walls many of the wonderful teachings I learned and retained. I surrounded myself with those beautiful and powerful sayings that meant the most to me. They were becoming a part of me and I loved it. However, I was torn between the realities of Heaven and earth and all the euphoric beauty of heavenly wisdom that I learned would conflict with a world that was concerned with its own self interests.

There is a triumph of truth's consistency among the great world religions that there is something with us that is greater than the universe, yet intimately connected to oneself. As a Christian, I believe this is God and that He is our Father, but the other great world religions are not wrong when they describe His Power. All the great world religions aim to unite us with God. Union with God is the reason for living and the final goal. However, it is only possible through Jesus the Christ who is the Way to God the Father.

Every day, I try to serve God. There are many ways to serve Him. We are each gifted with different strengths. The Christian saints are proof of this. No two saints are the same. Each is a person with his or her own identity, but each one serves God. I read and write and try to help those in need. Your path may be different. I tell you to take life seriously and get to know yourself. Find your passion and become all you can be. Take that passion and direct it toward God. Make God your first priority and everything else will work itself out. As long as God's love is in you and it remains in you, you will not go wrong.

DANTE'S *DIVINE COMEDY*

JAMES THOMAS ANGELIDIS

Copyright 2016 James Thomas Angelidis.
All rights reserved.
(Edited 2017)

The following is my graduate school paper about the allegorical nature of Dante's Divine Comedy - a trilogy about Hell, Purgatory and Heaven.

Most people are familiar with Dante's *Inferno* - a fascinating book with vivid imagery about one man's journey through Hell. The mood is dark because Hell is dark, but it is only the beginning of the protagonist's journey. Dante wrote two other books called *Purgatorio* and *Paradiso* and they are about the protagonist's journey through Purgatory and Heaven. Together, the three books complete a set that is known as the *Divine Comedy*. The meaning of the word "comedy" in the title is not the same as the word comedy used in common daily dialogue that refers to amusement and humor. Comedy from the

Divine Comedy refers to a literary genre where the story has a happy ending - unlike a tragedy that ends badly. This is true of Dante's work because at the end, the protagonist encounters God. Dante titled the work, simply, *Comedy*. The word divine was added by a fellow Italian poet, but was not incorporated into the title until over 200 years after Dante wrote the work.

I studied the *Divine Comedy* as a theology student in graduate school. For one semester, along with my other classes, I worked independently with my professor and wrote a 30 page paper on the set. Below is the product of a fascinating and enlightening four months. The *Divine Comedy* can be read on a literal level and on an allegorical level. Dante wrote the work to turn people away from sin and seek God. He wants to wake people up before it is too late and their eternal fates are finalized. The work is a piece of art - an epic poem that stirs the imagination. The protagonist is Dante - a shadow of the author himself - who journeys through Hell, Purgatory and Heaven. However, below the surface are hidden truths and lessons to be learned. The protagonist Dante represents the whole of humankind in the world and his journey is an allegory for humankind's journey toward God. In my paper, I focused on Dante's three guides. They represent the three lights in the world that help people see - with the brightest light at highest height that we can reach. The protagonist Dante sees what he sees because of the guides. They show him. Through them, he sees. These guides allegorically represent the light of Reason, the light of Faith and the light of Glory. They are the means to union with God. Dante is an artist at the highest level because through his art he is able to teach.

Introduction

Dante Alighieri was born in 1265 and died in 1321. He is one of Italy's greatest poets and his *Divine Comedy* is considered a "masterpiece of world literature"[1] and the "greatest Christian poem."[2] The narrative of the *Divine Comedy* describes Dante's journey through the deepest depths of Hell, up Mount Purgatory and then to Heaven where God dwells. This narrative is an allegory for every individual in this world, for his journey and often times, his struggle to find peace in this world with the hope of Salvation. Allegory abounds in the *Divine Comedy* and recognizing it is essential to understanding the many meanings in the text. Like all allegories, it tells a story in which "characters and events stand for abstract ideas, principles, or forces, so that the literal sense has or suggests a parallel, deeper symbolic sense."[3] Ultimately, the protagonist Dante in the

---

[1] Christopher Ryan, "Dante Alighieri," in *The Oxford Companion to Christian Thought,* ed. Adrian Hastings, (Oxford: Oxford University Press, 2000), 149.
[2] *Encyclopedia Britannica*, "Dante," 1970.
[3] *American Heritage Dictionary*, "Allegory," 1996.

Divine Comedy is "the image of every Christian sinner and his pilgrimage is that which every soul must take."[4] In *Journey to Beatrice*, Singleton explains that the story has,

> a meaning for all to see who may happen to find themselves in a dark and bitter wood of sin, who by God's grace may be privileged to turn, in a dawning light, toward a summit where justice and grace and reunion with God may be attained, and who from that first summit may be further privileged to rise to the higher peak of perfected grace and of final beatitude, *while still in this life.*[5]

Yes - "*while still in this life.*" Dante's story is for the living not the dead. With the help of Singleton and other scholars, I will investigate the allegorical nature of Dante's *Divine Comedy*. Dante's journey is not merely a mesmerizing story of a character's journey through the afterlife among the souls of the departed. More importantly, the journey is what medieval theologians called *Itinerarium Mentis Ad Deum* - the journey of the mind and heart, the will and intellect to God. In this work, I will investigate

---

[4] Dorothy Sayers, Introduction, *The Divine Comedy I: Hell,* by Dante Alighieri. ed. and trans. with notes, by Dorothy L. Sayers. (London: Penguin Books, 1949), 67.

[5] Charles S. Singleton, *Journey to Beatrice* (Baltimore: The John's Hopkins University Press, 1977), 7.

the three lights that lead Dante to the unmediated vision of God granted through the gift of what is called the Beatific Vision. Those three lights are personified by his three guides: Virgil as an allegory for the light of Reason, Beatrice as an allegory for the light of Faith and Saint Bernard as an allegory for the light of Glory.

Virgil as an Allegory for the Light of Reason

Virgil represents the light of Reason - the most natural light in man in his journey to God. In comparison to the light of Glory, which is exemplified by Saint Bernard, and the light of Faith, which is exemplified by Beatrice, the light of Reason is the least bright light in man's journey to God.

Historically, Virgil is considered Rome's greatest poet. He was born near Mantua and lived from 70 BC to 19 BC. He is the celebrated author of the *Aeneid*, a national epic and considered one of the greatest pieces of literature in world history. It tells of the origin and destiny of the Roman Empire and its role as leader in the civilized world. The main character is Aeneas who is a "paragon of Roman virtues - familial devotion, loyalty to the state, and piety."[6]

In the *Divine Comedy*, Dante uses Virgil to show that man has the ability to improve himself and

---

[6] *Concise Columbia Encyclopedia*, "Virgil," 1994.

ascend to God through Reason. However, it is important to understand that Reason does not make man perfect. Reason has limits. Virgil's strengths and weaknesses symbolize the strengths and weakness of Reason. As Glazov explains, "Virgil emerges in the poem as the kind of light which 'philosophers' had, who did not have the second and higher light of faith and of sanctifying grace - a fact already apparent in Virgil's confessed limits as guide."[7] Singleton explains,

> Such a light would remain with man even after Adam's sin and after the privation of sanctifying grace which resulted from that sin. Thus it is the light by which the "philosophers" saw whatever truths they did see, since they were deprived of the light of faith or of revelation or of sanctifying grace, and could move in the way of intellect only by the natural light of reason. That light was their only guide *in via*. Plato, therefore, and Aristotle, and all the other virtuous pagans "who did not sin" had this light, natural to man, and no other light of intellect than this. Because this is so, these "philosophers" shall never enjoy that higher light which is Beatrice

---

[7] Gregory Glazov, "The Spiritual Journey in the Divine Comedy Part II: The Three Lights." A Microsoft Office PowerPoint presentation. South Orange, New Jersey. 18 January 2011. Slide 10.

> and which is the light given to the "saints" *in via*; nor of course shall they ever see by that yet higher light of glory which is man's last beatitude. What was denied them in this life is denied them in eternity. Every reader knows the pathos that attaches to the figure of Virgil because of this hard truth.[8]

Singleton is a celebrated scholar. Hatzfeld's calls *Journey to Beatrice* a "most splendid Dante interpretation" and Singleton "one of the great explicators of the medieval mind and art in our time."[9] Singleton points out that Dante did not invent the analogy of three lights; rather, it was a notion he adopted from the theology of his day. Any reader of the *Divine Comedy* who is introduced to Saint Thomas Aquinas's *In Isaiam Prophetam* will clearly see the parallels between the theologies in the two works, both of which seem to have adopted it from a common theological tradition. Though perhaps not obvious today, Dante seems to have taken the familiar theology of his day to create the allegorical *Divine Comedy*.

The author Dante chose Virgil to be the protagonist Dante's guide through two-thirds of his journey in the afterlife - through Hell and up to the

---

[8] Singleton, *Journey to Beatrice*, 33.
[9] Helmut Hatzfeld, review of *Journey to Beatrice*, by Charles S. Singleton, *Modern Language Journal*, vol. 43, no. 7 (Nov. 1959): 354-55.

final level of Mount Purgatory. This is significant because Dante (the author) is a Christian and is the author of the *Divine Comedy*, the "greatest Christian poem,"[10] and Virgil is a pagan. For the majority of this most Christian of Christian works, the protagonist Dante follows Virgil, a pagan, and calls him "master" and "lord." How can this be? How can a Christian follow a pagan and call him master and lord when there is one Master and Lord - Jesus Christ. Very telling is what the protagonist Dante says at the beginning of *Inferno* when he is in the Dark Wood after he is confronted by the three beasts who prevent him from climbing up the Mountain. Lost in the Dark Wood, Dante is met by Virgil. Stunned, he says:

> "Canst thou be Virgil? thou that fount of splendour
> Whence poured to wide a stream of lordly speech?"
> Said I, and bowed my awe-struck head in wonder;
> "O honour and light of poets all and each,
> Now let my great love stead me - the bent brow
> And long hours pondering all thy book can teach!
> Thou art my master, and my author thou,
> From thee alone I learned the in strain,

---

[10] *Encyclopedia Britannica*, "Dante," 1970.

> The noble style, that does me honour now
> (*Inferno,* 1.79-87).[11]

For Dante, "Virgil wasn't a normal man... [He] was a Roman poet, exalted and legitimized by the staying power of more than 13 centuries."[12] Hollander explains that in the poem, "Dante could not do without him [Virgil]. Virgil is the guide in Dante's poem because he served in that role in Dante's life."[13]

Like most cultured men, Dante believed that art, particularly poetry, had the power to persuade and therefore persuade his fellow man to seek Salvation. "A poet above all, he felt that only in poetry, which goes beyond the closed abstractions of a scientific treatise, would he be able to express fully his dream... of a spiritual and civil renewal of the whole of humanity."[14] More than Plato or Aristotle, Dante adored Virgil because Virgil was what Dante aspired to be like - a Roman poet, exalted and legitimized by a staying power that would last centuries. Virgil was proud to be an Italian. He believed in the glory of Rome. As evident in the *Aeneid,* Roman culture valued the team over the individual; unlike the

---

[11] Dante Alighieri, *The Divine Comedy I: Hell*, ed. and trans. with notes, by Dorothy L. Sayers (London: Penguin Books, 1949), 73.

[12] "Virgil's Role in the Divine Comedy." *Dante and Virgil: A Study of Poetry, Language and History.* (January 18, 2011). http://users.rcn.com/antos/dante/divine_com.html

[13] Robert Hollander, *Dante: A Life in Works* (New Haven: Yale University Press, 2001), 116.

Greeks, who held more esteem for the individual, as is evident in the journeys of one man in the *Odyssey*. I believe Dante saw truth in the Roman perspective and in his theology, he showed that, unlike the solitude of Hell, Heaven is a place of community.

Though Dante revered the author Virgil, he did not fashion the character Virgil as an ideal to be emulated. He fashioned Virgil flawed to show the limitations and weakness of Reason. For example, at the start of Canto IX, when Dante and Virgil wait for Divine assistance to enter the City of Dis, Dante and Virgil look at each other and notice the fear in the other:

> Seeing my face, and what a coward colour
> It turned when he came back, my guide was quick
> To put away his own unwonted pallor."

Dante explains that "So black the air was, and the fog so thick" to symbolize the ominous situation. Filled with anxiety awaiting for Divine assistance, Virgil cries out, "But oh! how long his coming seems to be!" (*Inferno* 9.1-9).[15] Virgil's anxiety at this moment symbolizes the weakness of Reason when reason is confronted with fear. Reason has the potential to crumble when things are uncertain; but, with the Light of Glory - Faith, Hope and Love - there

---

[14] *Encyclopedia Britannica*, "Dante," 1970.
[15] Dante Alighieri, *The Divine Comedy I: Hell*, 123.

is no fear.

Another example depicting Virgil's flawed nature is in Canto XII when Virgil taunts the Minotaur. Here, Virgil shouts,

> "... How now, hellion!
> Thinkst thou the Duke of Athens comes anew,
> That slew they in the upper world? Begone,
> Monster! not guided by thy sister's clue
> Has this man come; only to see and know
> Your punishments, he threads the circle through."
> Then as a bull pierced by the mortal blow
> Breaks loose, and cannot go straight, but reels in the ring
> Plunging wildly and staggering to and fro,
> I saw the Minotaur fall a-floundering,
> And my wary guide called: Run! run for the pass!
> Make good thy going now, while his rage has its fling"
> (*Inferno*, 12.16-27).[16]

Virgil shows no respect for his adversary and mocks him as "his rage has its fling." Reason can be cruel and unrelenting when left to its own devices. However, the Light of Glory brings peace, not anger.

An additional example is found in Canto XXI

---

[16] Dante Alighieri, *The Divine Comedy I: Hell*, 142-143.

when Virgil trusts the advice of Belzecue, the chief Demon, who directs Dante and Virgil to follow a path that he contests is safe. Later on in Canto XXIII, the Jovial Friar Catalano mocks Virgil because he listened to Belzecue who, as a demon, should never be trusted. Depicting Virgil's reaction to the news, Dante explains,

> My guide stood with bent head and downward look
> A while; then said: He gave us bad advice,
> Who spears the sinners yonder with his hook."
> And the Friar: "I heard the devil's iniquities
> Much canvassed at Bologna; among the rest
> 'Twas said, he was a liar and father of lies."
> My guide with raking steps strode off in haste,
> Troubled in his looks, and showing some small heat
> Of anger
> (*Inferno*, 23.139-147).[17]

This episode represents the insufficiency of Reason, which can fail without the light of Glory. It can be fooled. The representatives of evil know this and take advantage of Reason's weaknesses. The above examples represent the insufficiency of Reason working on its own without the light of Glory. As Ryan explains, "Supremely civilized though he may

---

[17] Dante Alighieri, *The Divine Comedy I: Hell*, 217.

be, Virgil is from the outset of the comedy a fatally flawed figure, his limitation serving to illustrate the plight of humankind when left to its own devices, without the benefit of Christ."[18]

Flawed, Virgil is, nonetheless, lovable. Sayers explains that "Virgil fills the first two books of the poem; and in making him so central and so lovable and in then rending him clean out of the story, Dante took a risk which only the very greatest of artists could venture or afford to take."[19] Dante was honest with himself and great artists are always true to themselves. He did not allow his affinity to Virgil overpower his plan to spread the Word as a Christian and prophet.

Virgil is Dante's guide through Hell and Purgatory and by better knowing Hell and Purgatory, we can better know Virgil and what he represents. In *Inferno*, Hell is made up of nine concentric circles descending below the earth. The levels and the departed represent the seven deadly sins with the deepest, most distant from God at the bottom - pride being the most severe sin. Satan is the most prideful - so in love with himself that he wanted to be like God and usurp God's power - and resides at the pit's bottom. In Dante's Hell, "surprisingly and revealingly, [there] contains very little of the ... meditations on death that communicate a contempt

---

[18] Ryan, "Dante Alighieri," 150.
[19] Dorothy L. Sayers, *Further Papers on Dante* (London: Methuen and Co., 1957), 59.

for life."[20] Rather, it focuses on sin and Virgil's warnings to Dante that as you see the damned sinners, so, too, will you be if you follow their paths. Hell is an allegory for the severity of sins that eat away at one's soul. "It is the condition to which the soul reduces itself by a stubborn determination to evil, and in which it suffers the torment of its own perversions."[21] Dante's Hell illustrates the ills that hinder one's journey to God. Virtues bring the individual closer to God, while sins distance the individual from God. In the individual, at first, sins are venial and seem harmless, like eating too many sweets or fibbing. But, then, they can grow and become habits - like gluttony or cheating, which direct the intellect and will away from God. Venial sins can become a gateway to vices and can corrupt the individual and twist his understanding of truth. This regression is allegorized and illustrated by the tortured souls in the narrative of the *Inferno*. During his journey through Hell, Dante recognizes the wrathful Filippo Agenti and apprehends the truth about sin, curses it and is reborn spiritually. Dante shouts at Filippo, "Accursed spirit, do thou remain and rot! / I know thee, filthy as thou art - I know." Proud and pleased, Virgil lays his arms about Dante's neck and kisses him saying, "Indignant soul, Blessed

---

[20] Ricardo J. Quinones, "Inferno," in *The Dante Encyclopedia*, ed. Lansing, Richard (New York: Garland Publishing, Inc., 2000), 511.
[21] Sayers, Introduction, *The Divine Comedy I: Hell,* 68.

is the womb that bare thee!" (*Inferno* 8.37-45).[22]

In *Purgatorio*, Purgatory is a mountain with seven levels, each corresponding to one of the seven deadly sins. The higher one climbs and overcomes each sin, the closer one will be to God. On each level, the souls of the departed "are purged successively of the taint of the seven deadly sins, and so made fit to ascend into the presence of God in Paradise."[23] They purge their sins by practicing the opposite virtues. They make themselves fit to enter Paradise through good habits, a theology not far from the Aristotelian philosophy which contests that "we are what we repeatedly do. Excellence, therefore, is not an act, but a habit" (Will Durant, *The Story of Philosophy*, 76). The souls in Purgatory move with urgency to reach Heaven. Purgatory is about the passage from time to eternity, the overcoming of sin, repentance, redemption and the hope of attaining Salvation. Like the souls in Purgatory, man living in the world must liberate his intellect and will from the shackles of sin which prevent him from reaching God.

Virgil is Dante's guide up the mountain, but is incapable of entering earthly paradise. As the light of Reason, Virgil is insufficient to journey further to God. He has traveled as far as he could and is elated when he reaches the top of the mountain with Dante and tells Dante,

---

[22] Dante Alighieri, *The Divine Comedy I: Hell*, 117.
[23] Sayers, Introduction, *The Divine Comedy I: Hell*, 69.

> See how the sun shines here upon thy head;
> See the green sward, the flowers, the boscages
> That from the soil's own virtue here are bred
> While those fair eyes are coming, bright with bliss,
> Whose tears sent me to thee, thou may'st prospect
> At large, or sit at ease to view all this.
> No word from me, no further sign expect;
> Free, upright, whole, thy will henceforth lays down
> Guidance that it were error to neglect,
> Whence o'er thyself I mitre thee and crown
> (*Purgatorio,* 27.133-142).[24]

Virgil cannot comprehend Dante's ultimate destination - the Beatific Vision of God Himself - and so he is overwhelmed with joy when he reaches his peak - the sight of earthly paradise. The Light of Reason can take us only so far and even at its highest, Reason cannot reach Faith's heights. So, protagonist Dante will see that which Virgil cannot by means of Faith, which is allegorized by Dante's next guide, Beatrice. Schnapp contests that,

> Virgil's role was defined as transitional from

---

[24] Dante Alighieri, *The Divine Comedy II: Purgatory*, ed. and trans. with notes, by Dorothy L. Sayers. (London: Penguin Books, 1955), 285.

the outset. His task was to guide his charge to another guide. [His] mission is completed at the mountain's summit, where Dante-pilgrim's will is pronounced 'free, upright and whole.' Until this juncture Virgil's guidance had been indispensable to the pilgrim's progress. Now it has reached its term, and Virgil can discern no further."[25]

Very interesting and insightful is Sayers's perspective on the relationship between Dante and Virgil in Purgatory. In one of my favorite observations, Sayers explains,

> Into this realm [Purgatory], Virgil could not go without Dante; he is still his companion but no longer in the strict sense his guide. Yet Dante needs him, since in the story, Virgil is his "contact" in the spirit-world, and lends him eyes to see those "secret things" which are hidden from mortal view.[26]

Virgil cannot go without Dante because Virgil does not have access to the realm of Purgatory by himself. Virgil resides in Limbo, the first circle of hell, where

---

[25] Jeffrey T. Schnapp, "Purgatorio," in *The Dante Encyclopedia,* ed. Richard Lansing (New York: Garland Publishing, Inc., 2000), 726.

[26] Dorothy L. Sayers, *Introductory Papers on Dante* (London: Methuen and Co., 1954), 108.

the unbaptized and virtuous pagans dwell. But, he is permitted to visit Purgatory because of Dante and Dante needs Virgil to see in the spirit-world. They need each other, which makes their bond stronger, which is why it is difficult to see Virgil go from the remainder of the narrative.

The author Dante honors and loves Virgil. However, Dante's destiny for Virgil is one in which he is trapped in Limbo forever, never to ascend to the heavens. As Sayers explains in *Further Papers on Dante*,

> The whole theme of the Comedy is that Virgil is fundamental, indispensable, and yet of himself inadequate. Man is inadequate. Natural Reason and Art, Natural Morality, Natural Religion, if without Grace, without Revelation, without Redemption, cannot at their best attain any higher state than Limbo.[27]

Pellegrini attests that Sayers "exhibits a keen sensitivity to the richness of meaning that attaches to Dante's Virgil, and all her Virgils do revolve about the central point of his exclusion from salvation."[28] Sayers attests that Reason is not enough for Salvation. She explains that "Virgil is the best of all that Man by

---

[27] Sayers, *Further Papers on Dante*, 60.
[28] Anthony L. Pellegrini, review of *Further Papers on Dante*, by Dorothy L. Sayers, *Speculum*, vol. 35, no. 1 (Jan. 1960): 143.

his own nature has and is; and it is not enough."[29] Crissman contests that Virgil "must have had a perfect will," which is "mastery of reason over the appetite."[30] And, still, he is inadequate to climb further.

Purgatory is a realm where philosophy cannot travel without theology. Without the help of theology, philosophy does not understand the degradation of sin. Philosophy recognizes the distinction between virtues and vices and can even persuade one to live a virtuous life. It has that potential - but it is unconvinced. Theology is convinced that a virtuous life is the only way to live because it brings one closer to God. Philosophy does not know God. If it did, it would be theology. Philosophy can be purified through theology and will reach its full potential by means of theology, but philosophy without theology lacks God's blessings. Until philosophy embraces theology, it remains in Limbo.

When Virgil and Dante reach earthly paradise, they meet Beatrice. However, she is mentioned during their journey heightening Dante's expectation to be reunited with her, his most loved. Reaching the second level of Mount Purgatory, Dante asks Virgil

---

[29] Sayers, *Further Papers on Dante*, 66.
[30] Charley Crissman, "The Tragedy of Virgil." (18 January 2011)
http://www.gmalivuk.com/otherstuff/otherpeople/charley_Tragedyvirgil.html

about the efficacy of payer. With an interim answer, Virgil says,

> These are deep waters; rest not there - reject
> Conclusion, till she show it thee who is
> Set as a light 'twixt truth and intellect -
> I know not if thou understandest this:
> I mean Beatrice; on this mount's high crest
> Thou shalt behold her, smiling and in bliss
> (*Purgatorio*, 6.43-48).[31]

Between truth and intellect, Beatrice is the next light in the movement toward God.

Beatrice as an Allegory for the Light of Faith

The character of Beatrice in Dante's *Divine Comedy* personifies the light of Faith and only with Faith can Dante journey through Heaven. Once Virgil has fulfilled his duty as guide to Dante, Beatrice takes over and leads Dante to the Empyrean where God dwells. Both Virgil and Beatrice serve as guides to Dante, but they are very different and represent different disciplines and institutions. Glazov explains that Virgil represents the light of Reason, Philosophy, the State, the Secular; while, Beatrice represents the light of Faith, Theology, the

---

[31] Dante Alighieri, *The Divine Comedy II: Purgatory*, 111.

Church, the Religious.[32] Though they are different they do not conflict with one another. In fact, as Dante intimates, there is a courteous relationship between the two guides and therefore, the two Lights. At the beginning of the *Divine Comedy*, Beatrice humbles herself and entreats Virgil's assistance to guide her friend Dante on his journey:

> 'O courteous Mantuan soul, whose skill in song
> Keeps green on earth a fame that shall not end
> While motion rolls the turning spheres along!
> A friend of mine, who is not Fortune's friend,
> Is hard beset upon the shadowy coast;
> Terrors and snares his fearful steps attend,
> Driving him back; yea, and I fear almost
> I have risen too late to help - for I was told
> Such news of him in Heaven - he's too far lost.
> But thou - go thou! Lift up thy voice of gold;
> Try every needful means to find and reach
> And free him, that my heart may rest consoled.
> Beatrice am I, who thy good speed beseech;
> Love that first moved me from the blissful place

---

[32] Gregory Glazov, "The Spiritual Journey in the Divine Comedy, Final Part." A Microsoft Office PowerPoint presentation. South Orange, New Jersey. 18 January 2011. Slide 10.

> Whither I'd fain return, now moves my speech
> (*Inferno*, 2.58-72).[33]

Beatrice knows she can rely on Virgil and that they must work together to lead Dante to the Beatific Vision of God. Their roles in the *Divine Comedy* are crystallized in verse form when Virgil tells Dante that,

> "So much as reason here distinguisheth
> I can unfold," said he; "thereafter, sound
> Beatrice's mind alone, for that needs faith"
> (Purgatorio, 18.46-48).[34]

Here, it is clear that Virgil represents the light of Reason and Beatrice the light of Faith. Unlike the light of Reason, the light of Faith is beyond human comprehension, yet it guides us nonetheless. Beyond the senses, Dante's journey with Beatrice is also beyond intelligence. Like Dante, we Christians seek the higher realm, which can only be reached by means of Faith. Singleton explains,

> … for all the "sense" experience which is had in this high sphere where Beatrice guides, the poet has made it clear beyond any doubt that this journey with her is one "surpassing the

---

[33] Dante Alighieri, *The Divine Comedy I: Hell*, 79-80.
[34] Dante Alighieri, *The Divine Comedy II: Purgatory*, 206.

human intelligence." To pass from Virgil's guidance to that of Beatrice means, when measured on the familiar pattern, to pass from journey by the first of three lights to journey by the second.[35]

Dante's Beatrice in the *Divine Comedy* is an extension of the historical Beatrice - his true life-love - who he celebrates in his earlier work, *Vita Nuova*. The light of Faith is the second of the three theological lights that were recognized during the Middle Ages. Saint Thomas Aquinas in his *Contra Gentiles* explains that "man's knowledge of divine things is threefold." Saint Thomas explains that after Reason, Faith is when,

> the divine truth which surpasses the human intelligence comes down to us by revelation, yet not as shown to him [man] that he may see it, but as expressed in words so that he may hear it."[36]

Dante met Beatrice only twice, but he loved her from a distance and his love for her remained constant throughout his life and will last unto the ages in his writings. As he writes in the *Vita Nuova,* "I hope to compose concerning her what has never been

---

[35] Charles S. Singleton, *Journey to Beatrice* (Baltimore: The John's Hopkins University Press, 1977), 25.
[36] Cited by Singleton, *Journey to Beatrice*, 23.

written in rhyme of any woman." Most scholars believe that Beatrice is Beatrice Portinari from Florence, the daughter of Folco Portinari, a wealthy banker. Biographical information is limited, but it appears that she and Dante mingled in the same social circle. She married - as did Dante - and she died young at the age of 24, but Dante's affections for her never ended. She was his muse, who inspired the *Vita Nuova* and influenced the *Divine Comedy*.

Vita Nuova means New Life. The work is composed of autobiographical detail and is unique because it is an anthology of poems that are linked by prose which comment on the poems. This literature was part of a new style of writing that blossomed within a circle of Tuscan poets. This new style was termed "stil novo," which means "new style" and it celebrated love. *Stil nova* was not sentimental, but saw love as an absolute ideal, even holy.

Both the *Vita Nuova* and the *Divine Comedy* are filled with symbolism. Very striking is the numerology in both works. It is important to mention this in order to better understand Dante as a poet and the mind behind the poetry, which will give us a deeper appreciation for his art and his illustration of Beatrice. He had a particular attraction to the number 3 and its multiple 9. In the *Vita Nova*, he says he met Beatrice for the first time at the age of 9 and a second time 9 years later at the age of 18 at the 9th hour of the day. Also, the *Divine Comedy* is composed of 3 volumes in which each volume is composed of 33 chapters (not including the introductory chapter in volume one which makes for 100 chapters in the set) and in the narrative, Dante is led by three 3 guides. This emphasis on 3 is clearly intentional. Some, such as Gilbert, have pointed out that *Paradiso* would have been shorter, but it appears that Dante added speeches to the character of Beatrice to complete 33 chapters in *Paradiso* to retain the symbolism and symmetry of the *Divine Comedy*.[37] Some contest that the number 3 honors the Holy Trinity and that the number 9 symbolizes perfection, specifically the perfection of Beatrice. What matters, here, is that Dante intentionally used symbolism to give his poetry deeper and deeper meaning. So, one may ask, "How much is the Beatrice of the *Vita Nova* and the *Divine Comedy* historically accurate and how much is she art?" Dante met Beatrice only twice, so he has little to tell us about her personally, but she was his muse and his feelings for her were very real. I contest that little about Beatrice is historically accurate and that both of the works are high art, but for different reasons. I believe the Beatrice of the *Vita Nuova* is true to Dante's heart. As Singleton explains, "the *Vita Nuova* is beyond any doubt the way of love and not the way of knowledge."[38] And, I believe the Beatrice of the *Divine Comedy* is true to Dante's

---

[37] Alan H. Gilbert, *Dante and His Comedy* (New York: New York University Press, 1963) 153.
[38] Charles S. Singleton, *An Essay on the Vita Nova* (Baltimore: The John's Hopkins University Press, 1977), 106.

mind in that he structures an allegorical universe where Faith is personified by the love of a beautiful woman. Furthermore, some have pointed out that Beatrice's name is poetically appropriate because it means one who beatifies or one who bestows blessedness. Some have questioned her historical existence, altogether. However, Ferrante suggests that "those who would deny her historicity, like those who reject her allegorical significance, deny the fullness of Dante's poetry."[39] What is important is to recognize the significance of Beatrice in Dante's life and how he was able to express theological truths through her as a character in his art.

In the *Vita Nuova,* Dante's love journey is made up of three parts. The first part describes Dante's encounter with Beatrice and his immediate enamorment of her. The second part describes his desire to establish contact with her that is not external, but internal. The third part is devoted to Dante's love for her on the intellectual level, which moves his love from the earthly to the divine. This last form of love compels "the poet to identify Beatrice with the glory of God once and for all."[40] Singleton explains that Dante's love is like that of a man,

---

[39] Joan M. Ferrante, "Beatrice," in *The Dante Encyclopedia*, ed. Richard Lansing (New York: Garland Publishing, Inc., 2000), 95.

[40] Diana Cavuoto Glenn, "Vita Nuova," in *The Dante Encyclopedia*, ed. Richard Lansing (New York: Garland Publishing, Inc., 2000), 877.

> whose love stretches out to Heaven from earth, [which] is precisely the situation of the mystic's love of God. It was an 'excess of the mind,' a 'stretching out of love.' When Augustine and Bonaventura speak of the journey to God, they mean it as a possibility in this life. It is for this reason especially that the pattern of the ascent of love in the *Vita Nuova* can so closely resemble the pattern of the mystic ascent to God."[41]

There is no mistaking Dante's intention to equate his love for Beatrice with the supernatural love of mystics. As I mentioned earlier, in the Middle Ages, the number three, in addition to representing the Holy Trinity, was often used to describe the degrees or levels of the mind and heart's ascent to God. Singleton explains,

> this itinerary of the mind to God, as Augustine had conceived it, began, at its first level, *outside* man. It turned *inward* at its second level or degree. And in its third and last stage, it rose *above* man.[42]

The three parts of the *Vita Nuova* convey this theology effectively. Saint Thomas Aquinas

---

[41] Singleton, *An Essay on the Vita Nuova*, 106.
[42] Singleton, *An Essay on the Vita Nuova*, 105-106.

describes the degrees or levels as three lights. Dante uses this same theology in the *Divine Comedy* in the form of three guides. These interpretations come from the same storehouse of theology that bloomed during that era.

Beatrice allegorically represents the middle light - the light of Faith - which descends from the heavens to meet every Christian wayfarer. Beatrice describes to Dante the celestialities of Heaven and all who call it home in a way that he can understand. She says to him,

> This way of speech best suits your apprehension,
> Which knows but to receive reports from sense
> And fit them for the intellect's attention.
> So Scripture stoops to your intelligence:
> It talks about God's 'hand' and 'feet', intending
> That you should draw a different inference.
> And so does holy Church, in pictures lending
> A human face to Michael, Gabriel,
> And him by whom old Tobit found amending
> (*Paradiso,* 4.37-48).[43]

Faith makes the indescribable ascertainable.

---

[43] Dante Alighieri, *The Divine Comedy III: Paradise,* ed. and trans. with notes, by Dorothy L. Sayers, Barbara Reynolds. (London: Penguin Books,1962) 82.

Similarly, so does Scripture and the Church. They describe God's universe in a way that makes it accessible to the human mind.

As Dante journeys from Hell to Heaven, the descriptions of each realm and the theology taught become more abstract. Just as in the narrative, so, too, is the reality of Heaven more enigmatic than the reality of Hell. As the poem moves forward, the more Psalm-like it becomes. For example, when Dante sees God's ineffable magnificence, he says,

> How weak are words, and how unfit to frame
> My concept - which lags after what was shown
> So far, 'twould flatter it to call it lame!
> Eternal light, that in Thyself alone
> Dwelling, alone dost know Thyself, and smile
> On Thy self-love, so knowing and so known!
> (*Paradiso,* 33.121-126).[44]

Ryan explains,

> … heaven is portrayed predominantly as an extended hymn to the joy experienced as the intellect expands its horizons through increasing knowledge of God and his ways and the will delights in the deeper knowledge

---

[44] Dante Alighieri, *The Divine Comedy III: Paradise,* 346.

thus gained.[45]

Few things bring me greater joy than when I am able to grasp bits of wisdom, grace, faith, revelation and theology - each personified by Beatrice - during my studies. Just as Dante cannot express in words God's magnificence, neither can he express Beatrice's radiance:

> Little by little out of sight withdrew,
> Whence I to Beatrice must needs transfer
> My gaze, for love, and lack of aught to view…
> … Beauty past knowledge was displayed to me -
> Not only ours: the joy of it complete
> Her Maker knows, I think, and only He.
> From this point on I must admit defeat
> Sounder than poet wrestling with his theme,
> Comic or tragic, e'er was doomed to meet;
> For her sweet smile remembered, as the beam
> Of sunlight blinds the weakest eyes that gaze,
> Bewilders all my wits and scatters them
> (*Paradiso*, 30.13-27).[46]

---

[45] Christopher Ryan, "Dante Alighieri," in *The Oxford Companion to Christian Thought,* ed. Adrian Hastings, (Oxford: Oxford University Press, 2000), 150.

[46] Dante Alighieri, *The Divine Comedy III: Paradise*, 318-319.

Dante intentionally embodied theology in the figure of Beatrice. His son Pietro pointed out of Beatrice that, "after she died, to enhance the fame of her name, he wanted her to be taken as an allegory and type of theology in this poem."[47] Singleton defines theology as "the science in which first principles are given, not by reason, but through faith and revealed truth."[48] Implying that Beatrice's wisdom is Theology, Virgil tells Dante to wait for Beatrice who will be able to answer his question about the religious phenomenon:

> Now, should my words thy hunger not remove,
> Beatrice shalt thou see, and she'll speak plain,
> This and all cravings else to rid thee of (*Purgatorio,* 15.76-78).[49]

As the light of Theology, Beatrice is the source for heavenly answers and as a master teacher to her student Dante, she tests him to see what he has learned during their journey together through Paradise. She herself does not ask him questions; rather, she compels Saint Peter to question Dante:

---

[47] Cited by Joan M. Ferrante, "Beatrice," in *The Dante Encyclopedia,* ed. Richard Lansing (New York: Garland Publishing, Inc., 2000), 91.
[48] Singleton, *Journey to Beatrice,* 23.
[49] Dante Alighieri, *The Divine Comedy II: Purgatory,* 183.

> "... Eternal light of that great man
> To whom Our Lord on earth bequeathed the keys
> Which to this wondrous joy admittance gain,
> Lightly and searchingly, as thou dost please,
> This person test and try concerning faith,
> By which thou once didst walk upon the seas.
> If love and hope and faith he truly hath
> Thou knowest, for thine eyes are fixed upon
> The centre which all visions mirroreth.
> Yet since this realm its citizens have won
> By the true faith, 'tis fitting he should seek
> To glorify it, answering thereon"
> (*Paradiso,* 24.36-45). [50]

Confident that he will pass, Beatrice looks on as Dante answers Saint Peter's questions about faith, hope and love.

Since *Inferno's* Canto two, when Beatrice entreats Virgil to guide her friend Dante during his journey through Hell and Purgatory, we have been waiting for Dante and Beatrice's reunion. Sayers explains that at this moment, the,

> literal and allegorical meanings are so closely and intimately fused that it is possible, and at the first reading inevitable, to take it throughout at the purely human level. It is

---

[50] Dante Alighieri, *The Divine Comedy III: Paradise*, 266.

> man and a woman meeting, after a long
> estrangement for which he is to blame; she is
> justly indignant, and he finds nothing to say
> for himself. She is the Sacrament of the Body,
> she is divine Theology, she is the vehicle of
> Grace, she is the Body of Christ in the Church
> - but all these identities are summed up in the
> single identity of her person:
>
> 'Look on us well; we are indeed, we are
> Beatrice...'
>
> Having said that, she has said everything.[51]

So true are Sayers's words. Little is left to say. Beatrice has said it all in one interjection. Once Beatrice has fulfilled her duty to Dante, she leads him to his third and final guide, Saint Bernard, who guides Dante to the Empyrean where God dwells to witness the unmediated vision of God Himself, granted through the gift of what is called the Beatific Vision.

Saint Bernard as an Allegory for the Light of Glory

Dante's third and final guide in the *Divine Comedy* is Saint Bernard. Historically, Saint Bernard was born in Burgundy in 1090. He entered the

---

[51] Dorothy Sayers, Introduction, *The Divine Comedy II: Purgatory,* by Dante Alighieri. ed. and trans. with notes, by Dorothy L. Sayers. (London: Penguin Books, 1949), 27.

Cistercian order at the age of 22 and within a few years he was the founding abbot of Clairvaux. He was a "passionately eloquent spokesman for institutional and intellectual orthodoxy of the staunchest kind" and "probably the most influential individual figure in the twelfth-century church."[52]

In the *Divine Comedy*, Saint Bernard appears in only the final 3 cantos of the entire 100 canto poem. He appears far less than Virgil or Beatrice, yet he is just as symbolically important. Neither Virgil nor Beatrice can lead Dante to the unmediated vision of God. This honor is reserved for a guide of higher esteem, a saint by the name Bernard.

Allegorically, Saint Bernard represents the light of Glory and only with the light of Glory can Dante behold God's Glory. Dante refers to Saint Bernard as "that contemplative soul"[53] teaching us that through contemplation and mysticism, the Christian can encounter God. In practical terms, contemplation coupled with mysticism is prayer. Saint Bernard's chief duty as Dante's guide is to intercede for him and pray to the Virgin Mother for the Grace needed to behold God. With humility and adoration, Saint Bernard pleads,

---

[52] Steven Botterill, "Bernard, St," in *The Dante Encyclopedia*, ed. Richard Lansing (New York: Garland Publishing, Inc., 2000), 99.
[53] Dante Alighieri, *The Divine Comedy III: Paradise*, 334.

> O Virgin Mother, Daughter of thy Son...
>
> This man, who witnessed from the deepest pit
> Of all the universe, up to this height,
> The souls' lives one by one, doeth now entreat
> That thou, by grace, may grant to him such might
> That higher yet in vision he may rise
> Towards the final source of bliss and light
> (*Paradiso*, 33.1-27).[54]

So, too, must the Christian wayfarer pray - with humility and adoration - if he seeks God, which Saint Thomas calls "patria" meaning home because it is in God that the soul is at home.

Saint Bernard is a representative for all the saints. Each one represents the light of Glory. Christians can be filled with Faith, but the saints are not normal Christians because they are filled with God's Glory. They are blessed with the gift of Beatific Vision to witness the unmediated vision of God Himself. It is a gift reserved for them because of their devotion to God. The protagonist Dante is allowed to see what the saints see because a saint is his guide.

The saints dwell in God's unmitigated love. Furthest from the saints and God's love is Satan who resides at the bottom of Hell's pit. He is frozen to his

---

[54] Dante Alighieri, *The Divine Comedy III: Paradise*, 343-344.

waist in ice. Hell is the coldest place in the universe, so cold that the condemned - isolated from each other and alone - cannot move or speak. The exception is Satan who beats his bat-like wings keeping Hell and all the condemned forever frozen. Heaven is the opposite. It is at the highest of highests where space and time do not exist. It is a bright comforting euphoric community. God dwells in the Empyrean with the angels and saints who sit on the petals of a snow-white rose. God's everlasting love is everywhere and in everything. What is better than love? Nothing. It is free, yet the most valuable thing in the universe. This is the reason why Dante wrote the poem, so we would journey toward God's light, warmth and love. Satan's torture is not the darkness or cold. It is the madness and insanity that drowns him because he will never again see God. He will never again be comforted by Him or be a part of His love. There is no place worse than Hell because it is a place without God.

Conclusion

In this paper, we have investigated the *Divine Comedy's* allegorical nature, specifically Dante's three guides who represent the three lights that guide humankind to God. The light of Reason personified by Virgil, the light of Faith personified by Beatrice and the light of Glory personified by Saint Bernard lead to the Supreme Light that is God. Each of the minor lights is a radiance or reflection of the Greater Light. By witnessing God's Supreme Light, Dante is "transformed." He explains,

> That light doth so transform a man's whole bent
> That never to another sight or thought
> Would he surrender, with his own consent;
> For everything the will has ever sought
> Is gathered there, and there is every quest
> Made perfect, which apart from it falls short (*Paradiso*, 33.100-105).[55]

So, too, are the experiences of the saints in our world. The saints in this world devote their lives to God because nothing else compares to Him. All else is superfluous in comparison to God, who alone is worthy of adoration and adulation. Every Christian in this world is called to become a saint. Dante's encounter with God is meant to be the goal for every Christian, but each Christian must seek it and journey toward it in order to experience it.

---

[55] Dante Alighieri, *The Divine Comedy III: Paradise*, 346.

Bibliography

Bloom, Harold, ed. *Dante's Divine Comedy*. New York: Chelsea House Publishers, 1987.

Botterill, Steven. "Bernard, St." In *The Dante Encyclopedia*, ed. Richard Lansing, 99-100. New York: Garland Publishing, Inc., 2000.

Crissman, Charley. "The Tragedy of Virgil." (18 January 2011). http://www.gmalivuk.com/otherstuff/otherpeople/charley_Tragedyvirgil.html

Dante Alighieri. *The Divine Comedy I: Hell*, ed. and trans. with notes, by Dorothy L. Sayers. London: Penguin Books, 1949.

_____. *The Divine Comedy II: Purgatory*, ed. and trans. with notes, by Dorothy L. Sayers. London: Penguin Books, 1955.

_____. *The Divine Comedy III: Paradise*, ed. and trans. with notes, by Dorothy L. Sayers, Barbara Reynolds. London: Penguin Books, 1962.

_____. *La Vita Nuova*, ed. and trans. with notes, by Barbara Reynolds. London: Penguin Books, 1969.

Ferrante, Joan M. "Beatrice." In *The Dante Encyclopedia*, ed. Richard Lansing, 89-95. New York: Garland Publishing, Inc., 2000.

Gilbert, Allan H. *Dante and His Comedy*. New York: New York University Press, 1963.

Glazov, Gregory. "The Spiritual Journey in Dante's Vita Nuova." A Microsoft Office PowerPoint presentation. South Orange, New Jersey. 18 January 2011.

_____. "The Spiritual Journey in the Divine Comedy." A Microsoft Office PowerPoint presentation. South Orange, New Jersey. 18 January 2011.

_____. "The Spiritual Journey in the Divine Comedy Part II: The Three Lights." A Microsoft Office PowerPoint presentation. South Orange, New Jersey. 18 January 2011.

_____. "The Spiritual Journey in Dante's Divine Comedy, Final Part." A Microsoft Office PowerPoint presentation. South Orange, New Jersey. 18 January 2011.

Glenn, Diana Cavuoto. "Vita Nuova." In *The Dante Encyclopedia*, ed. Richard Lansing, 874-878.

New York: Garland Publishing, Inc., 2000.

Hatzfeld, Helmut. Review of *Journey to Beatrice*, by Charles S. Singleton. *Modern Language Journal*, vol. 43, no. 7 (Nov. 1959): 354-55.

Hollander, Robert. *Dante: A Life in Works*. New Haven: Yale University Press, 2001.

_____. "Dante's Virgil: A Light That Failed." 1989. *Lectura Dantis: Online*. (18 January 2011). http://www.brown.edu/Departments/Italian_Studies/LD/numbers/04/hollander.html

_____. "Virgil." In *The Dante Encyclopedia*, ed. Richard Lansing, 862-865. New York: Garland Publishing, Inc., 2000.

Pellegrini, Anthony L. Review of *Further Papers on Dante*, by Dorothy L. Sayers. *Speculum*, vol. 35, no. 1 (Jan. 1960): 142-44.

Quinones, Ricardo J. *Dante Alighieri*. New York: Twayne Publishers, 1998.

Reynolds, Barbara. Introduction. *The Divine Comedy III: Paradise.* by Dante Alighieri. ed. and trans. with notes, by Dorothy L. Sayers, Barbara Reynolds. London: Penguin Books,

1962. 17-51.

Ryan, Christopher. "Dante Alighieri." In *The Oxford companion to Christian Thought,* ed. Adrian Hastings, 149-151. Oxford: Oxford University Press, 2000.

Sayers, Dorothy L. Introduction. *The Divine Comedy I: Hell.* by Dante Alighieri. ed. and trans. with notes, by Dorothy L. Sayers. London: Penguin Books, 1949. 9-69.

_____. Introduction. *The Divine Comedy II: Purgatory.* by Dante Alighieri. ed. and trans. with notes, by Dorothy L. Sayers. London: Penguin Books, 1955. 9-71.

_____. *Further Papers on Dante.* London: Methuen and Co., 1957.

_____. *Introductory Papers on Dante.* London: Methuen and Co., 1954.

Schnapp, Jeffrey T. "Purgatorio." In *The Dante Encyclopedia*, ed. Richard Lansing, 723-728. New York: Garland Publishing, Inc., 2000.

Singleton, Charles S. *Journey to Beatrice.* Baltimore: The John's Hopkins University Press, 1977.

_____. *An Essay on the Vita Nova.* Baltimore: The John's Hopkins University Press, 1977.

"Virgil's Role in the Divine Comedy." *Dante and Virgil: A Study of Poetry, Language and History.* (18 January 2011). http://users.rcn.com/antos/dante/divine_com.html

HIERARCHY OF TRUTHS

JAMES THOMAS ANGELIDIS

Copyright 2016 James Thomas Angelidis.
All rights reserved.
(Edited 2017)

The following is my graduate school paper about the expression, "hierarchy of truths," which reached a mass audience in Catholic Vatican Council II's decree on Christian ecumenism.

On November 21, 1964, Vatican Council II promulgated a special decree on ecumenism, *Unitatis redintegratio*. It noted that among the various Christian denominations there exist differences concerning doctrine, discipline and church structure; however, the decree emphasized that these present-day divisions contradict Christ's will and it emphasized the unifying elements of the Christian denominations. At the Council, observers attended representing the Orthodox churches, various Protestant denominations, the Anglican Church and members of the World Council of Churches. They had access to all the documents given to the Council Fathers and were present at all of the general sessions. Although, they were not allowed to speak or vote during the Council, their presence furthered the Council's ecumenical mission.[56] Congar asserts that the Decree on Ecumenism "ranks among the great documents of Christian history."[57] The expression "hierarchy of truths" thundered in the document and has echoed since it was penned almost fifty years ago and it has tremendous potential for ecumenism among Christians. Reamonin declared it as, "one of the great insights of Vatican II."[58] Cullman proclaimed the hierarchy of truths passage "the most revolutionary" of all 16 Vatican II documents.[59] This paper will be an investigation into the expression, "hierarchy of truths."

The Decree on Ecumenism states,

> In ecumenical dialogue, Catholic theologians standing fast by the teaching of the Church and investigating the divine mysteries with the

---

[56] M. Browne, E. Duff, J. Ford, V. Lafontaine, "Ecumenical Movement," in *New Catholic Encyclopedia*, 2nd ed., ed. Berard Marthaler, (Washington: Gale, 2003), 74-75.

[57] Yves Congar, *Diversity and Communion* (Mystic: Twenty-Third Publications, 1985), 126.

[58] Vincent Twomey, "'Hierarchy' of Truths," *The Furrow*, vol. 42, no. 9 (September, 1991): 500.

[59] Tom Stransky, "Hierarchy of Truths," in *Dictionary of the Ecumenical Movement,* ed. Nicholas Lossky (Geneva: WCC Publications, 2002), 519.

> separated brethren must proceed with love for the truth, with charity, and with humility. When comparing doctrines with one another, they should remember that in Catholic doctrine there exists a "hierarchy" of truths, since they vary in their relation to the fundamental Christian faith. Thus, the way will be opened by which through fraternal rivalry all will be stirred to a deeper understanding and a clearer presentation of the unfathomable riches of Christ.[60]

Though the expression "hierarchy of truths" received its greatest attention during Vatican II, it was originated in 1963 in a speech by Archbishop Andrea Pangrazio of Gorizia, Italy. In the speech, he explains that God's divine dynamism can change the course of history and that "God can make possible that desired union of separate Christianities which today still seems impossible. This will be possible, however, only if all Christians will be obedient to inspirations of divine grace."[61] He explains there are common elements among the Christian denominations, but to list them would be to pile them up in quantitative fashion. He believes we "should point to the *center*,

---

[60] Decree on Ecumenism, *Unitatis reintegratio*. Vatican II, November 21, 1964 (2.11).
[61] Andre Pangrazio, "The Mystery of the History of the Church," in *Council Speeches of Vatican II*, ed. H. Kung, Y. Congar & D. O'Hanlon (New York: Paulist Press, 1964), 190.

to which all these elements are related, and without which they cannot be explained. This bond and center is Christ himself, whom all Christians acknowledge as Lord of the Church."[62] Because there is unity and diversity among Christians, it is very important "to pay close attention to the *hierarchical order* of revealed truths which express the mystery of Christ."[63] The expression "hierarchy of truths" has appeared in many sources since Pangrazio first introduced it in 1963. Some will be referred to below.

The Catholic Church has not created an official rank or list of the hierarchy of truths because, as Cardinal Ratzinger explained, "What the term hierarchy of truths seeks to express is that the faith of the Church is... an organic whole in which every individual element obtains its meaning from being seen from within its proper place within the whole."[64] According to the *Catechism of the Catholic Church*, the center of this organic whole is the mystery of the Most Holy Trinity:

> It is the mystery of God in himself. It is therefore the source of all the other mysteries

---

[62] Pangrazio, "The Mystery of the History of the Church," 190-191.

[63] Pangrazio, "The Mystery of the History of the Church," 191.

[64] Christopher O'Donnell, "Hierarchy of Truths," in *Ecclesia: A Theological Encyclopedia of the Church*. ed. Michael Glazier (Collegeville: Liturgical Press, 1996) 195-196.

> of faith, the light that enlightens them. It is the most fundamental and essential teaching in the "hierarchy of the truths of faith."[56] The whole history of salvation is identical with the history of the way and the means by which the one true God, Father, Son and Holy Spirit, reveals himself to men "and reconciles and unites with himself those who turn away from sin"[65]

Congar was an early champion for ecumenism and the theology behind "hierarchy of truths." He explains, "Catholic doctrine is organized rather like a tree, the smallest branches of which are connected to the trunk by the others... Everything is attached to one foundation (a trunk), which is the mystery of Christ the savior, presupposing the mystery of the triunity of God."[66] The centrality of Christ "is not opposed to the trinitarian view; it is through the Incarnation of the Eternal son, his life, death and Resurrection, that the Father is revealed and the Spirit is given. Therefore, catechesis, to be trinitarian, has to be Christocentric."[67] More comprehensively, the *General Catechetical Directory* explains that the hierarchy of truths:

---

[65] *Catechism of the Catholic Church*, 234.
[66] Congar, *Diversity and Communion*, 128.
[67] Joseph Ratzinger. Christoph Schonborn, *Introduction to the Catechism of the Catholic Church* (San Francisco: Ignatius Press, 1994), 44-45.

> may be grouped under four basic heads: the mystery of God the Father, the Son, and the Holy Spirit, Creator of all things; the mystery of Christ the incarnate Word, who was born of the Virgin Mary, and who suffered, died, and rose for our salvation; the mystery of the Holy Spirit, who is present in the Church, sanctifying it and guiding it until the glorious coming of Christ, our Savior and Judge; and the mystery of the Church, which is Christ's Mystical Body, in which the Virgin Mary holds the preeminent place.[68]

This teaching is most visible in The Nicene-Constantinopolitan Creed of 381, which is central and fundamental to the Catholic Faith and must be accepted for ecumenism.

The Catholic Church teaches that all doctrinal teachings of the Church are true and that no truth is dispensable. "From a purely intellectual and logical point of view, any true statement of whatever kind is equal to another true statement. The character of truth is an absolute, which as such and in a formal way, cannot be either more or less true. From this point of view there can be no degrees in truth."[69]

---

[68] Sacred Congregation for the Clergy, *General Catechetical Directory*, 1971 (43).

[69] Congar, *Diversity and Communion*, 129.

However, Pangrazio explains that "although all the truths revealed by divine faith are to be believed with the same divine faith and all those elements which make up the Church must be kept with equal fidelity, not all of them are of equal importance."[70] In the hierarchy, no truths "pertain to faith itself less than others, but rather that some truths are based on others as of higher priority, and are illumined by them."[71] For example, the doctrine that Mary is the Mother God is unimaginable without understanding the doctrine that Jesus is both true God and true man. This latter doctrine about Jesus is higher in the hierarchy of truths and it illumines the teaching about Mary. Similarly, the doctrine of the two natures of Christ illumines the doctrine on the human and divine wills of Christ; the former doctrine has a higher priority in the hierarchy of truths.[72] The importance of each truth depends on how close it is to the Church's most fundamental teaching, "which is the mystery of Christ the savior, presupposing the mystery of the triunity of God."[73] Therefore, "grace has more importance than sin, sanctifying grace more than actual grace, the resurrection of Christ more than

---

[70] Pangrazio, "The Mystery of the History of the Church," 191.

[71] Sacred Congregation for the Clergy, *General Catechetical Directory*, 1971 (43).

[72] Douglas Bushman, "Understanding the Hierarchy of Truths." January 2000, available from http://www.ignatiusinsight.com/features2005/dbushman_hiertruths_sept05.asp. Internet; accessed 15 March 2013.

his childhood, the mystical aspect of the church more than its juridical; the church's liturgy more than private devotions."[74] The central truths "which all other truths are ordered consists of those basic truths, each of which evokes the others and cannot be reduced to some other."[75] The criteria to establish a hierarchy of truths comes from "Scripture, tradition, creeds, the Fathers, liturgy, official Church teaching and [the sense of faith]."[76] "Many of the most central truths of the faith, Christians are already one."[77]

All Christian statements "are either statements strictly concerned with Christ or derivative from such statements; in each case there are various grades... logically speaking, the hierarchy of truths is not a matter of demoting some truths, but rather concerns more carefully identifying the exact content of faith statements."[78] Some truths are less important, but no truth can be subtracted. As explained in the *Introduction to the Catechism of the Catholic Church*, "the 'hierarchy of truth' does not mean 'a principle of subtraction,' as if faith could be reduced to some 'essentials' whereas the 'rest' is left free or even

---

[73] Congar, *Diversity and Communion*, 128.

[74] Stransky, "Hierarchy of Truths," 519.

[75] William Henn, "The Hierarchy of Truths Twenty Years Later," *Theological Studies*, no. 48 (1987): 464.

[76] Henn, "The Hierarchy of Truths Twenty Years Later," 462.

[77] Henn, "The Hierarchy of Truths Twenty Years Later," 468.

[78] Henn, "The Hierarchy of Truths Twenty Years Later," 449.

dismissed as not significant. The 'hierarchy of truth' … is a principle of organic structure. It should not be confused with the degrees of certainty; it simply means that the different truths of faith are 'organized' around a center."[79] There is an interconnectedness and interdependence of the different truths: "the highest does not stand without the lowest though it is possible and necessary to distinguish between them."[80] The purpose of the hierarchy of truths is "not to separate non-negotiable fundamental articles from optional non-fundamental articles of faith. Rather it interprets and brings perspective into the whole body of truths."[81] No truths can be can be isolated because they are a part of a harmonious whole. "As in a piece of music, one wrong note can mar the whole. So too the truths of Faith and those of morals form a symphonic whole whose expression is liturgy, worship of God."[82] "They support one another, illuminate one another, complement one another. The principle of the hierarchy of truths is not meant to violate in any way the deposit of revelation."[83] Furthermore, Congar believes that "no truth contradicts another truth. If there appears to be

---

[79] Ratzinger, *Introduction to the Catechism of the Catholic Church*, 42.

[80] Twomey, "'Hierarchy' of Truths," 502.

[81] Henn, "The Hierarchy of Truths Twenty Years Later," 443.

[82] Twomey, "'Hierarchy' of Truths," 503.

such a contradiction, there has been some misunderstanding. This triumph of the consistency of truth allows for... an exuberant acceptance of the true affirmations of other Christian Churches, of world religions and of humanity in general."[84]

Cardona believes that faith is necessary for recognizing truths and their order. He asserts, as summarized by Henn, that,

> revealed truth is never a deduction from what is known through reason. Rather, it is known through an obedient faith to the authority of God. [Cardona] then relates the truth known in faith to truth as such. Truth is always in a way secondary to reality, insofar as it signifies the intellect's adequation to reality. As such, truth does not admit of being "more" or "less." One either knows reality or one does not. In considering any order among the truths, it is important to realize that one must accept the *totality* of what God reveals and that one must do so because of the authority of God who reveals.[85]

---

[83] William Henn, *The Hierarchy of Truths According to Yves Congar*. (Rome: Editrice Pontificia Universita Gregoriana, 1987), 209.

[84] Henn, *The Hierarchy of Truths According to Yves Congar*, 210.

[85] Henn, "The Hierarchy of Truths Twenty Years Later," 456.

Therefore, faith in God and what He reveals is essential to understanding the order of truths.

Though the expression "hierarchy of truths" was brought to the world's attention at Vatican II, the theology behind it is not completely new. In the Old Testament, prophets and rabbis were known to provide summaries or "cores" of the Law. For example, Hillel famously taught, "What is hateful to you, do not do to your neighbor; that is the whole Torah, while the rest is commentary thereof." Similarly, when Jesus was asked, "Teacher, which is the great commandment in the law?" he answered, "You shall love the Lord your God with all your heart, and with all your soul, and with all your mind. This is the great and first commandment. And a second is like it, you shall love your neighbor as yourself. On these two commandments depend all the law and the prophets."[86] Both Hillel and Jesus focused on the weightier matters and created a hierarchy of truths in their teachings.[87] We see in the New Testament, further latent forms of a hierarchy of truths in the words of the Apostle Paul: "So faith, hope, love abide, these three; but the greatest of these is love."[88] In addition, "For I delivered to you as of first importance what I also received, that Christ died

---

[86] Matthew 22:36-40, RSV.

[87] William McFadden, "Hierarchy of Truths" in *The Modern Catholic, Encyclopedia*, ed. Michael Glazier (Collegeville: Liturgical Press, 1994), 360.

[88] 1 Corinthians 13:13, RSV.

for our sins in accordance with the scriptures, that he was buried, that he was raised on the third day in accordance with the scriptures, and that he appeared to Cephas, then to the twelve."[89] In the fourteenth century, in William of Ockham's *Dialogus adversus haereticos*, an anonymous author writes, "The only truths that are to be considered Catholic and necessary to salvation are explicitly or implicitly stated in the cannon of the Bible... All other truths... are not to be held as Catholic, even if they are stated in the writings of the Fathers or the definitions of the supreme pontiffs, and even if they are believed by all the faithful. To assent to them... is not necessary to salvation."[90] Here, as the author stresses, a hierarchy of truths can only be derived from the Bible. Not all may accept his theology, but it is further evidence of a hierarchy of truths in the making. In the sixteenth century, Luther, grasping the relationship between scripture and what is apostolic, asserts that "the apostolic element in scripture is what speaks of Christ, my saviour. The criterion of apostolic authenticity is '*to preach and convey Christ.*' Whatever does not teach Christ is not apostolic, though it come from Peter or Paul; by contrast whatever preaches Christ is apostolic, even if it comes from Judas, from Annas, from Pilate or from

---

[89] 1 Corinthians 15:3-5, RSV.
[90] George Tavard, "'Hierarchia Veritatum' A Preliminary Investigation." *Theological Studies*, no.32 (1971): 286.

Herod."[91] Here, Luther has developed a criterion to decipher what is valuable. It is an example of what is the core in his faith. The idea of a hierarchy of truths is there in Luther's words, which makes dialogue possible. Later on in the sixteenth century, Calvin said, "For all the heads of true doctrine are not in the same position. Some are so necessary to be known, that all must hold them to be fixed and undoubted as the proper essentials for religion: for instance that God is one, that Christ is God, and the Son of God, that our salvation depends on the mercy of God, and the like. Others again, which are the subject of controversy among the churches, do not destroy the unity of the faith."[92] Almost 500 years before Vatican II, the theology of a hierarchy of truths is evident in Calvin's teachings. Like the Protestant theologians, the Orthodox theologians have a sense of a hierarchy of truths. As Congar explains, "Orthodoxy spontaneously re-attaches to their center all the elements of revelation, following the genius of the Fathers of the Church... Everything - including the most concrete details of life - is always rooted in the trinitarian center and illumined by it."[93] Congar also explains, "The East takes its stand on the Fathers and the Ecumenical Councils, which have stated the

---

[91] Congar, *Diversity and Communion*, 128.
[92] Henn, *The Hierarchy of Truths According to Yves Congar*, 174.
[93] Henn, *The Hierarchy of Truths According to Yves Congar*, 175.

essentials."[94] The fundamentals of Orthodox theology come from the Church Fathers and first seven Ecumenical Councils, fundamentals that are shared by Catholics and most Protestants.

The above examples show that, throughout history, attempts have been made to form a hierarchy of truths in the Christian denominations. With the rise of the ecumenical movement in the past century, the Vatican II Fathers were called to follow the above examples and focus on the weightier matters for the sake of fruitful dialogue. The workings of a hierarchy of truths have come from the past and will continue into the future. As Congar explains, faith in God,

> is drawn out into certain content, in affirmations and judgments, into which it becomes diversified. It is diversified in time, which has an effect on its formulation ("Christ will come," "Christ has come"); it is diversified into various articles or dogmas which are worked out over the course of time: those of the creed, those of the councils, those which have been possible to add already or those which will be added in the future"[95]

---

[94] Henn, *The Hierarchy of Truths According to Yves Congar*, 176.

[95] Henn, *The Hierarchy of Truths According to Yves Congar*, 169.

The Catholic Church has taken the first step toward ecumenism. Henn explains that "from a kind but one-sided call to return home, the Catholic Church moved to recognition of elements of salvation in other Churches. With the hierarchy of truths doctrine, the Catholic Church took another step forward and recognized an order within its own teachings, placing Christ at the foundation. This was an important move toward a better perspective. The hierarchy of truths should function as a hermeneutical principle. However, one should expect from this teaching not a quick unity but rather a growth in mutual understanding about the agreements and differences between Christians."[96] The hierarchy of truths is "an invitation and stimulus to further thought on the focus of faith."[97]

Congar is very important in the effort for ecumenism. He devoted his life to it. As he says, "The very idea of diversity compatible with communion, or of the necessary but sufficient minimum of common doctrine to be held if unity is to be preserved, is in fact the object of all my research."[98] In his theology, he makes a distinction between the perspective of the object known and the

---

[96] Henn, *The Hierarchy of Truths According to Yves Congar*, 217.

[97] Denis Carroll, "'Hierarchia Veritatum': A Theological and Pastoral Insight of the Second Vatican Council," *Irish Theological Quarterly*, no. 44 (1977): 129

[98] Henn, *The Hierarchy of Truths According to Yves Congar*, 198.

perspective of the knowing subject. The objects known are directly related to the foundation, core, nucleus, heart of the Christianity, "which is the mystery of Christ the savior, presupposing the mystery of the triunity of God."[99] All truths rely on this foundation. Suppositions that do not rely on this foundation are not truths and they can be seen in schools of indifferentism, bad liberalism and radical pluralism.[100] He believes that "the hierarchy of truths is not a 'creation' of the knower. The order among truths is not imposed by the subject but the reality." Revelation is God's self-manifestation and "revelation allows the believer to know reality from the perspective of God." Order is derived from that which is revealed by God who "alone is absolute truth." One can only know certain aspects of God's truth. "God's view is the final court of appeals. This view is imparted to us to some degree in revelation."[101]

In Congar's theology, the perspective of the knowing subject is just as critical as the perspective of the object known in deciphering a hierarchy of truths. The perspective of the knowing subject must be investigated through a historical lens. Any method that does not must be rejected. The study of the

---

[99] Congar, *Diversity and Communion*, 128.
[100] Henn, *The Hierarchy of Truths According to Yves Congar*, 209.
[101] Henn, *The Hierarchy of Truths According to Yves Congar*, 202.

historicity of the knowing subject can also be referred to as hermeneutics. "The hierarchy of truths might thus serve as a hermeneutical principle for appropriating historically the Christian tradition and for guiding contemporary subjects in their expression of that tradition."[102] The hierarchy of truths positively assesses diversity and unity in the knowing subjects. Mere pluralism is not the answer because unity is also desired. Neither is mere unity the answer because that would undermine legitimate pluralism. "Legitimate pluralism contributes to a fuller grasp of the truth."[103] Significantly, the hierarchy of truths is fundamentally integrated with the magisterium. "The hierarchy of truths helps make evident one of the reasons why an authoritative teaching office is needed - i.e. to determine with the help of the Holy Spirit what the central truths of the faith are." The magisterium "provides guidance on both more central and less central matters." It is essential in determining what qualifies as a truth. The magisterium's teachings make evident that there is a hierarchy of truths. It helps the faithful contemplate scripture and tradition to make discernible what God reveals to the individual and the community as a whole.[104]

---

[102] Henn, *The Hierarchy of Truths According to Yves Congar*, 210.

[103] Henn, *The Hierarchy of Truths According to Yves Congar*, 210.

[104] Henn, *The Hierarchy of Truths According to Yves Congar*, 211.

The perspective of the object known and the perspective of the knowing subject are both necessary to define truths. As Henn explains,

> Object and subject correlate. Neither are able to be taken out of the act of knowing in faith the truths God has revealed. One would expect, therefore, that the hierarchy of truths from the perspective of the object is conditioned by the hierarchy of truths from the perspective of the subject, and vice versa. Thus, the hierarchy obtaining among the truths is knowable only by the adequate subject of those truths, the Church guided by the Holy Spirit. Conversely, there are more important and less important elements in subjective expressions of the faith precisely because there is an objective hierarchy among the truths of revelation.[105]

Congar believes that in the past, the object known was the focus, while in the modern era, the knowing subject is the focus. However, because of Congar and through the hierarchy of truths, it is evident that both object and subject work together.

Truths in Catholic doctrine tend to fall into two categories: those on our final goal and those as a means to salvation. This theology was presented in

---

[105] Henn, *The Hierarchy of Truths According to Yves Congar*, 197.

Archbishop Pangrazio's 1963 speech. In the speech, he explains:

> Some truths are *on the level of our final goal*, such as the mystery of the Blessed Trinity, the Incarnation and Redemption, God's love and mercy toward sinful humanity, eternal life in the perfect kingdom of God, and others.
>
> Other truths are *on the level of means toward salvation*, such as that there are seven sacraments, truths concerning the hierarchical structure of the Church, the apostolic succession, and others. These truths concern the means which are given by Christ to the Church for her pilgrim journey here on earth; when this journey comes to an end, so also do these means.
>
> Now doctrinal differences among Christians have less to do with these primary truths on the level of our final goal, and deal mostly with truths on the level of means, which are certainly subordinate to those other primary truths.
>
> But we can say that the unity of Christians consists in a common faith and belief in those truths which concern our final goal.[106]

---

[106] Pangrazio, "The Mystery of the History of the Church," 191-192.

Taravad explains that the truths pertaining to our final goal will last in heaven, while the truths pertaining to the means of our salvation will disappear with present world.[107] Leeming believes that for fruitful ecumenical dialogue, Christians should pay more attention to the truths regarding the final goal of which there is already a sense of unity. Of secondary concern should be truths pertaining to the means of salvation, which divide the various Christian churches.[108]

There is a clear and rational reason for diversity among Christians and the churches, according to Congar. He explains that human beings have a limited perception of what is truth. It is developed in the mind. Only the Father, Son and Holy Spirit can perceive supernatural truth perfectly. Here on earth, supernatural truth is subject to historicity, which imposes limits on it. Therefore, naturally, supernatural truth is subject to differences in the perception and expression between different churches or even in different periods in one church. "In these expressions we necessarily find particular elements of culture, language and vocabulary, and of common philosophy. Thus a human element of interpretation, systematization and expression is

---

[107] Tavard, "'Hierarchia Veritatum' A Preliminary Investigation," 281.
[108] Tavard, "'Hierarchia Veritatum' A Preliminary Investigation," 283.

combined with the perception of faith which may become dogma." The differences of dogma show that there are different forms of a hierarchy of truths materializing from the objective supernatural form.[109] This is in line with Saint Thomas's "God-centered view of revelation which identifies religious truth ultimately with the outlook of God, never fully graspable by us and therefore calling for modesty in our truth claims and acceptance of legitimate diversity."[110]

Each of the Christian Churches should create a hierarchy of truths and as they do, it is expected that results will have some differences, but this should be no cause for alarm. As Cullman explains, as summarized by Henn, "Just as the Holy Spirit is the source of diverse charisms, so too is the Holy Spirit the source of various accentuations and perspectives in the understanding of the faith on the part of the various Churches. Uniformity is a sin against the Holy Spirit who always works by diversifying." Diversity is only a problem when there is no common ground. The task is to establish a foundation, so the churches can take a closer look at the differences and see how they relate to the foundation and each other. Differences are fine as long as all accept the foundation. "The differences between the hierarchies of truths expressed by the various Churches need not

---

[109] Congar, *Diversity and Communion*, 130.
[110] Henn, *The Hierarchy of Truths According to Yves Congar*, 230.

be divisive but can be complementary." Dialogue is essential and the various Churches can learn from each other; however, it is important to not isolate any doctrine. "Doctrines isolated from the whole tend to usurp the place for fundamental truths. The result is often heresy."[111]

Even if there is direct opposition between two Churches regarding a particular truth, ecumenism should still be pursued. Cullman points out Apostle Paul's advice about the question of eating food sacrificed to idols[112]:

> I know and am persuaded in the Lord Jesus that nothing is unclean in itself; but it is unclean for anyone who thinks it unclean. If your brother is being injured by what you eat, you are no longer walking in love. Do not let what you eat cause the ruin of one for whom Christ died. So do not let your good be spoken of as evil. For the kingdom of God is not food and drink but righteousness and peace and joy in the Holy Spirit; he who thus serves Christ is acceptable to God and approved by men.[113]

---

[111] Henn, *The Hierarchy of Truths According to Yves Congar*, 232.

[112] Henn, "The Hierarchy of Truths Twenty Years Later," 465.

[113] Romans 14:14-18, RSV.

Here, it is clear that Paul wants to unite his brethren and tries to persuade them to focus on the higher truth in the faith to live in "righteousness and peace and joy in the Holy Spirit" and not harm each other on a lesser truth about unclean foods. Cullmann believes that though one should not yield in proclaiming Christian truths, "there is no unity without some concessions"[114] and that "not only a variety of perspectives but even some opposition about less fundamental truths should be tolerated with love."[115]

Much of Vatican II was about the Catholic Church applying its teachings to a new era. The Council stood on the Church's past theology and applied it to the modern world. It was about renewal. It respected the past, while looking to the future. The hierarchy of truths is a perfect example of this dynamism. In the past, Jesus and Paul taught a hierarchy of truths and then Vatican II reaffirmed its importance for our age. The hierarchy of truths is a powerful tool to produce fruitful ecumenical dialogue. Although it has not fully matured, it has immense potential for ecumenism. Through it, Christians will see that we have more in common than not. All who believe in the Father, Son and Holy Spirit are already one. Our beliefs in the means of salvation must not supersede our beliefs on our final

---

[114] Henn, *The Hierarchy of Truths According to Yves Congar*, 234.

[115] Henn, *The Hierarchy of Truths According to Yves Congar*, 232.

goal. Should differences in methods of fasting separate Christians? I think not. Does believing that Jesus is "the way, and the truth, and the life" unite Christians?[116] Indeed, it does. Though there may be diversity in our Christian community, we are all Christians. Diversity must not divide us. We must look beyond it, if not embrace it. I believe ecumenism is near. In 2001, Pope John Paul II sorrowfully apologized on behalf of the Catholic Church to Ecumenical Patriarch Bartholomew I of Constantinople for the sacking of Constantinople in 1204 by Catholic Crusaders. The sack of Constantinople has been seen as the final act of the East-West Schism; however, Pope John Paul II's apology can be the beginning of ecumenism between the Catholic Church and the Orthodox Church. Furthermore, about a month ago, Ecumenical Patriarch Bartholomew I celebrated and attended Pope Francis's Inauguration as the leader of the Catholic Church. If an 800 year old rift between the Catholic Church and the Orthodox Church can be mended, there is hope for ecumenism for all the Christian Churches. We must set aside our differences and focus on the weightier matters. We must not allow our worldly agendas prevent us from attaining our heavenly goals. We have great things in common and I see this more clearly than ever before

---

[116] John 14:6, RSV.

because of my investigation into the expression, "hierarchy of truths."

Works Cited

Browne, M, E. Duff, J. Ford, V. Lafontaine. "Ecumenical Movement." In *New Catholic Encyclopedia, 2nd ed.* ed. Berard Marthaler, 74-75. Washington: Gale, 2003.

Bushman, Douglas. "Understanding the Hierarchy of Truths." January 2000. Available from http://www.ignatiusinsight.com/features2005/dbushman_hiertruths_sept05.asp. Internet; accessed 15 March 2013.

Carroll, Denis. "'Hierarchia Veritatum': A Theological and Pastoral Insight of the Second Vatican Council." *Irish Theological Quarterly*, no. 44 (1977): 125-133.

Catechism of the Catholic Church. New York: Doubleday, 1995 (234).

Congar, Yves. *Diversity and Communion*. Mystic: Twenty-Third Publications, 1985.

Decree on Ecumenism, *Unitatis reintegratio*. Vatican II, November 21, 1964 (2.11). http://www.vatican.va/archive/hist_councils/ii_vatican_council/documents/vat-ii_decree_19641121_unitatis-redintegratio_en.html.

Ford, J.T. "Hierarchy of Truths." In *New Catholic Encyclopedia, 2nd ed*. ed. Berard Marthaler, 822. Washington: Gale, 2003.

Henn, William. *The Hierarchy of Truths According to Yves Congar*. Rome: Editrice Pontificia Universita Gregoriana, 1987.

Henn, William. "The Hierarchy of Truths Twenty Years Later." *Theological Studies*, no. 48 (1987): 439-471.

McFadden, William. "Hierarchy of Truths." In *The Modern Catholic Encyclopedia*, ed. Michael Glazier, 360. Collegeville: Liturgical Press, 1994.

O'Donnell, Christopher. "Hierarchy of Truths." In *Ecclesia: A Theological Encyclopedia of the Church.* ed. Michael Glazier, 195-196, Collegeville: Liturgical Press, 1996.

Pangrazio, Andre. "The Mystery of the History of the Church." In *Council Speeches of Vatican II*, ed. H. Kung, Y. Congar & D. O'Hanlon, 188-92. New York: Paulist Press, 1964.

Ratzinger, Joseph, Christoph Schonborn. *Introduction to the Catechism of the Catholic*

Church. San Francisco: Ignatius Press, 1994.

Sacred Congregation for the Clergy, *General Catechetical Directory*, 1971 (43). http://www.papalencyclicals.net/Paul06/gencatdi.htm.

Stransky, Tom. "Hierarchy of Truths." In *Dictionary of the Ecumenical Movement,* ed. Nicholas Lossky, 519. Geneva: WCC Publications, 2002.

Tavard, George. "'Hierarchia Veritatum' A Preliminary Investigation." *Theological Studies*, no.32 (1971): 278-289.

Twomey, Vincent. "'Hierarchy' of Truths." *The Furrow*, vol. 42, no. 9 (September, 1991): 500-504.

A THEOLOGICAL MEMOIR
an article about my journey through the six great world religions' sacred scriptures

DANTE'S DIVINE COMEDY
my graduate school paper about the allegorical nature of Dante's Divine Comedy - a trilogy about Hell, Purgatory and Heaven

HIERARCHY OF TRUTHS
my graduate school paper about the expression, "hierarchy of truths," which reached a mass audience in Catholic Vatican Council II's decree on Christian ecumenism

IN THE NAME OF SALVATION

Three Theological Treatises

James Thomas Angelidis

IN THE NAME OF SALVATION

Three Theological Treatises

James Thomas Angelidis

IN THE NAME OF SALVATION

THREE THEOLOGICAL TREATISES

ONE: THE SUPREME TRANSFORMATION - WATER INTO WINE

TWO: AGAPE INTO ETERNITY

THREE: THE MESSIAH JESUS

JAMES THOMAS ANGELIDIS

jtangelidis.com

Copyright 2016 James Thomas Angelidis.
All rights reserved.
(Edited 2017)

TREATISE ONE

THE SUPREME TRANSFORMATION – WATER INTO WINE

JAMES THOMAS ANGELIDIS

Copyright 2016 James Thomas Angelidis.
All rights reserved.
(Edited 2017)

Introduction

The Bible is the most translated book in the world. It is widely accepted that the second most translated book in the world is the Tao Te Ching. Both books teach truths to the ready reader and if they are examined together, we can find evidence of Christ's impact on the world as the Son of God. He transformed the world as only the Son of God could have. Beyond the most profound influence of any man, He transformed the natural rhythm of the cosmos. This celestial transformation was foreshadowed by His first sign of transforming water into wine. In this treatise, through the Tao Te Ching and relevant sections of the Bible, we will examine our Lord's first sign of transforming water into wine and the truth it exposes about His impact on the cosmos. I believe if we can better understand the Tao as taught in the Tao Te Ching, we will be able to better see the magnitude, magnificence and majesty of Christ. In writing this treatise, I hope to help my fellow Christians better understand our Lord through knowledge of the Tao and to help non-Christians, through the Spirit of Truth, begin to believe that Christ is the Son of the Most High God.

The Tao Te Ching

The Tao Te Ching is the principal text of Taoism - an ancient Chinese philosophy that became one of the world's great religions. Probably a compilation of wisdom and insight from many sages, the Tao Te Ching began to take shape as far back as the seventh century before Christ, but most likely did not reach its final form until the mid-third century before Christ. However, tradition ascribes the authorship of the text to Lao Tzu, a seemingly legendary figure who is said to have been a contemporary of Confucius during the early sixth century before our Lord.

With 81 short poem-like chapters, the text is primarily concerned with the Tao and Te. Taoism adopted its name from the Tao, which translates into English as "Way," as in the way the cosmos operates. It is the primal life force that sustains the harmony and natural rhythm of the universe. It is the ineffable reality of the universe. From before the beginning of time, it is the mysterious source of Heaven and earth and the fountain of life for all life in the universe. Te translates into English as "Virtue," as in the virtue characteristic of one who abides by the Tao. It is the manifestation or power of the Tao in one who acts in accordance with the Tao. Ching means "classic work," so the Tao Te Ching neatly, yet roughly translates into "The Classic Work of the Way and its Virtue."

It is important to note that as I explicate the Tao Te Ching, there is no single definitive English translation of the text. There are, actually, over 100 translations of the text in English. Ancient Chinese does not translate easily into English, so there can be variation in translation. Jonathan Star explains that, "The nature of ancient Chinese is one reason why this scripture, for thousand of years, has 'baffled all inquiry.' Ancient Chinese is a conceptual language; it is unlike English and other Western languages, which are perceptual. Western languages are rooted in grammar that frames events in real time, identifies subject and object, clarifies relationships, and establishes temporal sequences. Ancient Chinese is based on pictorial representations, without grammar. Characters symbolize concepts that can be interpreted as singular or plural; as a noun, a verb, or an adjective; as happening in the past, present, or future. Therefore, when translating from Chinese to English, the Chinese characters must be framed within a perceptual context to be understood" (Jonathan Star, Tao Te Ching, 3 [see pages 3-7 for examples]). There are many who have made great efforts to bring the Tao Te Ching from the East to the West. Each translator interprets the text with his or her own understanding of the text to try to bring out the true meaning of the text. In English, I have discovered three solid translations that I believe do the text justice: the Stephen Addiss and Stanley Lombardo translation, the Gia-Fu Feng and Jane English translation, and the John C.H. Wu translation. These translations differ, but their essences are the same. I have used my discernment to use the three translations together and write about the Tao in the light of Christ to enlighten people about Christ.

The Tao and Water

The Tao is unfamiliar to many people, so I have explicated it below to the best of my abilities. It is important to understand what the Tao is and how it functions in order to appreciate and comprehend the magnitude of Christ, to understand who our Lord is and what He did as the Son of God.

In the Tao Te Ching, Chapter 21 provides an insightful description of the Tao:

> Now what is the Tao?
> It is Something elusive and evasive.
> Evasive and elusive!
> And yet it contains within Itself a Form.
> Elusive and evasive!
> And yet it contains within itself a substance
> Shadowy and dim!
> And yet It contains within Itself a Core of Vitality.
> The Core of Vitality is very real,
> It contains within Itself an unfailing Sincerity.
> Throughout the ages Its Name has been preserved
> In order to recall the Beginning of all things.

> How do I know the ways of all things at the Beginning?
> By what is within me (Wu).

For peoples in the West, the teachings in the Tao Te Ching are enigmatic and difficult to comprehend. Though I was born and raised in the West and have never visited the East, I have devoted myself to the great world religions' sacred scriptures and through studying them and my experiences as a man in the world, I feel confident that I have a firm grasp of the lessons to be learned in the Tao Te Ching. Nonetheless, the first two lines of the text illustrate the difficulty in conveying the meaning of and discussing the Tao:

> Tao can be talked about, but not the Eternal Tao
> Names can be named, but not
> the Eternal Name (Wu, 1).

The nature of the Tao is described throughout the text, but I believe Chapter 25 provides the most comprehensive and acute description:

> Something unformed and complete
> Before heaven and earth were born,
> Solitary and silent,

> Stands alone and unchanging,
> Pervading all things without
> limit.
> It is like the mother of all under
> heaven,
> But I don't know its name -
> Better call it Tao.
> Better call it great.
> Great means passing on.
> Passing on means going far.
> Going far means returning.
> Therefore,
> Tao is great,
> And heaven,
> And earth,
> And humans,
> Four great things in the world.
> Aren't humans one of them?
> Humans follow earth
> Earth follows heaven
> Heaven follows Tao.
> Tao follows its own nature
> (Addiss).

Trying to understand the Tao can be difficult - whether one is from the East or the West, the North or the South - and I believe few attempt to do so. In Chapter 41, the Tao Te Ching teaches,

> When a wise scholar hears the Tao,

> He practices it diligently.
> When a mediocre scholar hears the Tao,
> He wavers between belief and unbelief.
> When a worthless scholar hears the Tao,
> He laughs boisterously at it.
> But if such a one does not laugh at it,
> The Tao would not be the Tao (Wu).

Upon reading this passage, I ask myself, "How many of us are wise scholars? How many of us have read about the Tao? How many of us are able to recognize the Tao?" And, I tell myself, "Few." Though I am certain there are great men and women who have not formally studied the Tao, who are unread, yet who are close to the Tao, I believe most people waver between belief and unbelief and many laugh. I believe few people devote themselves to the Tao and try to understand and live in union with it. In writing this treatise, I hope to awaken people to the Tao, to feed their hunger for something more in life and for God.

Water is a clear Taoist symbol and is used in the Tao Te Ching as a metaphor for the Tao. The Tao is ineffable and difficult to comprehend, yet water is compared with it to make it accessible to the human mind. There are a handful of metaphors in the Tao Te Ching that are used to pin down the elusive nature of the Tao, but water is chief among them as it is used to indicate the highest good. Chapter 8 is the principal chapter that elaborates on the metaphor of water.

In Chapter 8, we learn,

> The highest form of goodness is like water (Wu).

Tao is the highest good. More virtuous than virtue, Tao permeates the world and is made manifest in the form of Te in people who follow the Tao. It is beyond all other forms of goodness and is of the highest value. In chapter 38, we learn,

> Failing Tao, man resorts to Virtue.
> Failing Virtue, man resorts to humanity.
> Failing humanity, man resorts to morality.
> Failing morality, man resorts to ceremony.
> [And] ceremony is the merest husk of faith and loyalty (Wu).

Chapter 16 also illustrates the superior value of the Tao:

> Mind opening leads to compassion,
> Compassion leads to nobility,
> Nobility to heavenliness,
> Heavenliness to Tao (Addiss).

The highest good is the power of the Tao in the world and in people. The Tao behaves like water and I believe if we keep the image of flowing water in our minds, we can see the metaphor's truth in Chapter 73:

Heaven's Tao does not contend
But prevails,
Does not speak
But responds,
Is not summoned
But arrives,
Is utterly still
But plans all actions (Addiss).

The Waters in the Jewish Scriptures

In the beginning when the Uncreated God Created, His Spirit moved "over the face of the waters" (Genesis 1:2). The ancient Taoists were aware that there was Something "unformed and complete before heaven and earth were born" that behaved like water and assigned it the name Tao (Addiss, 25).

On the second day of Creation, God said, "Let there be a firmament in the midst of the waters, and let it separate the waters from the waters" (Genesis 1:6). God called the firmament Heaven with waters above and below. As mentioned, the ancient Taoists understood that there is Something above Heaven that behaves like water. The Jews, as well, were aware of the waters above the heavens. As the Psalmist exclaims,

Praise the Lord!

> Praise the Lord from the heavens,
> praise him in the heights!
> 2 Praise him, all his angels,
> praise him, all his host!
> 3 Praise him, sun and moon,
> praise him, all you shining stars!
> 4 Praise him, you highest heavens,
> and you waters above the heavens!
> 5 Let them praise the name of the Lord!
> For he commanded and they were created.
> 6 And he established them for ever and ever;
> he fixed their bounds which cannot be
> passed (Psalm 148:1, RSV).

The ancient Taoists did not know God, but both Taoists and Jews were aware of the waters above the heavens.

Te and Water

Like the Tao, Te is described throughout the Tao Te Ching. Once we familiarize ourselves with the nature of the Tao, we will be in good shape to understand Te, which is the manifestation of the Tao in human action, reaction and, even, non-action. Those who are close to the Tao are filled with Te. Chapter 21 explains,

> Great Te appears flowing from Tao (Addiss).

The Tao Te Ching was written thousands of years ago to teach us how to come close to the Tao and be filled with Te. This lifestyle brings wellbeing to the person and to the cosmos. By abiding by the Tao and acquiring Te, we are able to benefit ourselves and humankind and maintain order and balance in the universe. This is possible by behaving like water, by conducting ourselves in harmony with the Tao, which behaves like water. In Chapter 8, we are taught to,

> Live in a good place.
> Keep your mind deep.
> Treat others well.
> Stand by your word.
> Make fair rules.
> Do the right thing.
> Work when its time.
> Only do not contend,
> And you will not go wrong (Addiss).

A person who can act accordingly - who is cautious, hesitant, polite, yielding, blank, open, and mixes freely (Addiss, 15) - who behaves like water is called a sage. He practices "wu-wei," which literally means non-action, in essence, not to strive, like water, which does not contend. Like the Tao, Te is unfamiliar to most in the West and is difficult to comprehend and, still further, to practice. The sage practices wu-wei and all things in the cosmos settle themselves and return to their natural state; harmony returns to the natural rhythm of the universe and all is restored, as it was meant to be. Wu-wei is not a form of apathy or recklessness. It means to take no unnatural action and to be one with the cosmos, with the Tao, which is "solitary and silent" (Addiss, 25). Understanding this, the world "moves without danger in safety and peace" (Addiss, 35).

Chapter 81 comprehensively and concisely expresses the water-like nature of the Tao in nature and in man:

> Heaven's Tao
> Benefits and does not harm.
> The Sage's Tao
> Acts and does not contend (Addiss).

Wu-wei - acting like water - is well described in chapter 63:

> Do the Non-Ado.
> Strive for the effortless.
> Savor the savorless
> Exalt the low.
> Multiply the few.
> Requite injury with kindness.
> Nip troubles in the bud.
> Sow the great in the small (Wu).

The above passage describes wu-wei on a personal level. Chapter 66, below, describes the sage's wu-wei and its impact on society:

> River and seas
> Can rule the hundred valleys.
> Because they are good at lying low
> They are lords of the valleys.
> Therefore those who would be above
> Must speak as if they are below.
> Those who would lead
> Must speak as if they are behind.
> In this way the sage dwells above
> And the people are not burdened.
> Dwells in front
> And they are not hindered.
> Therefore the whole world
> Is delighted and unwearied.
> Since the Sage does not contend
> No one can contend with the Sage (Addiss).

The sage is praiseworthy as benefactor to universe. Everyone who reads the Tao Te Ching is encouraged to follow the example of the sage, but I do not want my fellow Christians to get the wrong idea. As Christians, we are not meant to emulate the sage - we are meant to emulate Christ. Christ is not the sage. He is not a Taoist. He is the Son of God who mixes up the waters to bring up the poor. He had no desire to leave the world as it was. He came to the earth as an active agent to lift up the weak, the infirm, the poor and the afflicted.

In Chapter 8, we learn,

> Water knows how to benefit all things without striving with them.
> It stays in places loathed by all men.
> Therefore, it comes near to the Tao (Wu).

Of all things, water comes nearest to Tao. They share common qualities and behave in similar manners. Water is essential to life and is our body's most vital nutrient. It nourishes us like the Tao nourishes us. Even though it excels, it does not strive with anything because it voluntarily takes the lowest position, like the man of Tao. Most men seek fame, fortune and power and desire to be on top, but the man of Tao cultivates modesty and humility and chooses the low. Most men loathe the low, when,

> Truly, humility is the root from which greatness springs,
> And the high must be built upon the foundation of the low.
> That is why barons and princes style themselves 'The Helpless One,' 'The Little One,' 'The Worthless One.'
> Perhaps they too realize their dependence upon the lowly.

> Truly, too much honor means no honor
> (Wu, 39).

Even Christ, our Lord, acknowledging His humanity, humbles Himself at the title "Good Teacher," when He says "Why do you call me good? No one is good but God alone" (Mark 10:18). God humbled Himself and became man for us. No words can express His goodness, yet He corrects the rich man for calling Him good. This is the epitome of humility. This is what it means to come near to the Tao, like water.

Water into Wine

In the poorest countries, drinkable water is scarce and, in many cases, evident throughout history, it has been replaced by wine:

> Wine had a more practical reason in its beginning than the mere pleasure of drinking. Ancient peoples had little pure water to drink, and they learned that alcohol formed by fermentation protected fruit juice from spoiling. The people who drank this fermented juice did not get sick as often as those that drank the impure water. This reason for wine drinking continues down to our day. Many peoples, especially [in poorer countries,] use wine [diluted] instead of water

> for drinking (The World Book Encyclopedia, 1966, "Wine").

This truth gives us a key insight into our Lord's first sign that revealed He was the Son of God. He turned water into wine, literally, as expressed in the Gospel of John, but just as importantly, He did so in a figurative and celestial sense. The ancient Chinese sages likened the Tao to water and Christ turned the Tao into what can be best described as wine. There was a lack of pure water for the people to drink in that the Tao of the ancient Chinese sages was scarce. It could not help most people because the Tao's lofty esoteric principles were followed by few. So, Christ transformed the Tao into what resembles wine for all people, especially the poor, to quench their thirst, to nourish their souls. Truly, water was made wine. Truly, the Tao was transformed. Truly, Christ came into the world for the poor and afflicted.

In Chapter 23 of the Tao Te Ching, we learn: "those on the way become the way." Christ became the way. "I am the way, and the truth, and the life," He says. He is the new way. His incarnation, ministry, death, resurrection and ascension mark the beginning of a new time. "I make all things new," so His words read and so we have seen since his advent. Only the Son of God could have renewed the Tao.

Christ's first sign that manifested his glory took place at a wedding in Cana:

On the third day there was a marriage at Cana in Galilee, and the mother of Jesus was there; 2 Jesus also was invited to the marriage, with his disciples. 3 When the wine gave out, the mother of Jesus said to him, "They have no wine." 4 And Jesus said to her, "O woman, what have you to do with me? My hour has not yet come." 5 His mother said to the servants, "Do whatever he tells you." 6 Now six stone jars were standing there, for the Jewish rites of purification, each holding twenty or thirty gallons. 7 Jesus said to them, "Fill the jars with water." And they filled them up to the brim. 8 He said to them, "Now draw some out, and take it to the steward of the feast." So they took it. 9 When the steward of the feast tasted the water now become wine, and did not know where it came from (though the servants who had drawn the water knew), the steward of the feast called the bridegroom 10 and said to him, "Every man serves the good wine first; and when men have drunk freely, then the poor wine; but you have kept the good wine until now." 11 This, the first of his signs, Jesus did at Cana in Galilee, and manifested his glory; and his disciples believed in him (John 2:1, RSV).

There are few occasions that can be as joyous as a wedding. It is when two souls become one and it is a time to celebrate a new beginning and a new life. Our Lord chose such a celebration of new beginnings to begin His ministry and because of Him the way of the cosmos would begin new. Turning water into wine showed God's presence in our Lord. In a literal sense, I may not understand the sign, but I believe, I have faith. Skeptics may have doubts, but our Lord performed many signs that are beyond our limited human mind. And this should not be cause for alarm, for there are instances of holy men and women to this day who perform signs pointing to the glory of God that we may not understand. We must not be puffed up with pride and think that we know everything or vain and think too highly of ourselves. And, we should not give too much credit to our faculties of reasoning. Let us remember Plato and his allegory of the cave where men believed in shadows on the wall and how they were unable fathom the realities that were beyond those shadows with the limited scope of their knowledge.

However, if this sign was taken only literally, then we would miss an extremely significant, deep and important symbolic lesson, which is just as potent as the literal lesson. Christ turned water into wine to show us and make us understand the bigger picture. The plain sign of physically turning water into wine helps us to ascertain the celestial transformation of the Tao. Once we realize what our Lord did by transforming the Tao, the plain sign's symbolic meaning is clear and visible; and then we can see how the plain sign clarifies, supports and makes certain the deeper sign of transforming the Tao. The plain sign helps us to conceptualize the deeper sign and it sheds light on the deeper sign. It is an anticipation or prefiguring of the deeper sign. The plain sign teaches a lesson that paves the way for the deeper sign and makes the deeper sign discernible. The two phenomena parallel each other.

Second century Church theologian Melito of Sardis explains,

> Nothing, beloved, is spoken or made without an analogy and a sketch; for everything which is made and spoken has its analogy, what is spoken an analogy, what is made a prototype, so that whatever is made may be perceived through the prototype and whatever is spoken clarified by the illustration (*On Puscha*, 35 [SVS Press book, 46]).

Melito's theology is evident when our Lord transformed water into wine, which foreshadowed the transformation of the Tao. Most noticeable and most important is that Christ acts at the wedding during a time of tribulation - the lack of wine - which is an analogy or "preliminary sketch" of His action as the Savior of the world. Christ makes wine on the third day at the wedding. This sign foreshadowed His Resurrection from the dead on the third day, which was the beginning of the Messianic Wine. On the third day, He saves the wedding and on the third day, He saves the world. Christ's Mother foresees trouble as the wine gives out and notifies her son. "They have no wine," she alerts. He is reluctant to act because His "hour" had not yet come - the time when He was to fulfill His destiny as humankind's Savior from death defined by his glorious Passion and Resurrection. Nonetheless, He acts and so begins a new age for humankind with Christ as our Immortal Priest King.

Very telling are the steward's words about the quality of wine served at the wedding. He says, "Every man serves the good wine first; and when men have drunk freely, then the poor wine; but you have kept the good wine until now." His words are prophetic and poignant. The wine served first was inferior to Christ's wine, which was remarkable and exceptional. The wine served first reached an end just as the Jewish faith was to reach its final day. The Jewish nation proved to be unfruitful. As Prophet Isaiah professed,

> Let me sing for my beloved
>   a love song concerning his vineyard:
> My beloved had a vineyard
>   on a very fertile hill.
> 2 He digged it and cleared it of stones,
>   and planted it with choice vines;
> he built a watchtower in the midst of it,
>   and hewed out a wine vat in it;

and he looked for it to yield grapes,
    but it yielded wild grapes.
3 And now, O inhabitants of Jerusalem
    and men of Judah,
judge, I pray you, between me
    and my vineyard.
4 What more was there to do for my vineyard,
    that I have not done in it?
When I looked for it to yield grapes,
    why did it yield wild grapes?
5 And now I will tell you
    what I will do to my vineyard.
I will remove its hedge,
    and it shall be devoured;
I will break down its wall,
    and it shall be trampled down.
6 I will make it a waste;
    it shall not be pruned or hoed,
    and briers and thorns shall grow up;
I will also command the clouds
    that they rain no rain upon it.
7 For the vineyard of the Lord of hosts
    is the house of Israel,
and the men of Judah
    are his pleasant planting;
and he looked for justice,
    but behold, bloodshed;
for righteousness,
    but behold, a cry! (Isaiah 5:1, RSV).

The Jewish nation protests and pleads to God to save it. In Scripture, we hear,

> Thou didst bring a vine out of Egypt [when the Jews were slaves];
> thou didst drive out the nations and plant it.
> 9 Thou didst clear the ground for it;
> it took deep root and filled the land.
> 10 The mountains were covered with its shade,
> the mighty cedars with its branches;
> 11 it sent out its branches to the sea,
> and its shoots to the River.
> 12 Why then hast thou broken down its walls,
> so that all who pass along the way pluck its fruit?
> 13 The boar from the forest ravages it,
> and all that move in the field feed on it.
> 14 Turn again, O God of hosts!
> Look down from heaven, and see;
> have regard for this vine,
> 15   the stock which thy right hand planted.[b]
> 16 They have burned it with fire, they have cut it down;
> may they perish at the rebuke of thy countenance!
> 17 But let thy hand be upon the man of thy right hand,

> the son of man whom thou hast made strong for thyself!
> 18 Then we will never turn back from thee;
> give us life, and we will call on thy name!
> 19 Restore us, O Lord God of hosts!
> let thy face shine, that we may be saved!
> (Psalm 80:8, RSV).

Christ hears the cry and becomes the above son of man at the right hand of God who restores and saves God's people. Christ calls himself the true vine,

> "I am the true vine, and my Father is the vinedresser. 2 Every branch of mine that bears no fruit, he takes away, and every branch that does bear fruit he prunes, that it may bear more fruit. 3 You are already made clean by the word which I have spoken to you. 4 Abide in me, and I in you. As the branch cannot bear fruit by itself, unless it abides in the vine, neither can you, unless you abide in me. 5 I am the vine, you are the branches. He who abides in me, and I in him, he it is that bears much fruit, for apart from me you can do nothing. 6 If a man does not abide in me, he is cast forth as a branch and withers; and the branches are gathered, thrown into the fire and burned. 7 If you abide in me, and my words abide in you, ask whatever you will, and it shall be done for you. 8 By this my Father is

glorified, that you bear much fruit, and so prove to be my disciples. 9 As the Father has loved me, so have I loved you; abide in my love. 10 If you keep my commandments, you will abide in my love, just as I have kept my Father's commandments and abide in his love. 11 These things I have spoken to you, that my joy may be in you, and that your joy may be full. 12 "This is my commandment, that you love one another as I have loved you. 13 Greater love has no man than this, that a man lay down his life for his friends. 14 You are my friends if you do what I command you. 15 No longer do I call you servants,[a] for the servant[b] does not know what his master is doing; but I have called you friends, for all that I have heard from my Father I have made known to you. 16 You did not choose me, but I chose you and appointed you that you should go and bear fruit and that your fruit should abide; so that whatever you ask the Father in my name, he may give it to you. 17 This I command you, to love one another (John 15:1, RSV).

Christ is the Jewish nation's salvation. He is the only fruitful vine. The Jewish nation failed to produce fruit, so Christ stepped in and took action. The wine that Christ produced is extraordinary and is the awaited celebratory wine of the triumphant Messianic Age.

The massive amount of wine produced - six stone jars each holding twenty or thirty gallons - signifies that in the age of Christ there is enough wine for everybody (insight from Stanley D. Toussaint, "The Significance of the First Sign in John's Gospel," *Bibliotheca Sacra*, (Jan-Mar 1977): 49-51).

Christ's first sign is an "analogy" or "preliminary sketch" for the transformation of the Tao. He performed His first sign with water because it best characterized the Tao and the Taoist sages, too, identified water as the best expression of the Tao. Both Jewish Christ and the Taoists sages saw the Tao in the same way. I believe that there are universal truths and that religions often illustrate these truths with common metaphors, such as light, darkness and fire. So, when Christ transformed water into wine - symbolically announcing the impact He was going to have on the cosmos - He used the same expression as the Taoist sages and equated water with the Tao. For both Jewish Christ and the Taoist sages, the cosmos's natural rhythm was best described as "the waters above the heavens." It is a shared metaphor. Both Taoists and Christ observed a common truth. Such theology is also seen when Christ allegorizes his body with the temple (John 2:19). Christ calls his body a temple in the same way that Buddhists call the body a temple. It is a shared metaphor. There is shared theology among religions as well as in their metaphors.

The new wine in Christ's first sign represents the Messianic Age. Jewish Scripture often uses wine to describe the Messianic Age. From Prophet Joel, we learn,

> And in that day
> the mountains shall drip sweet wine,
>   and the hills shall flow with milk,
> and all the stream beds of Judah
>   shall flow with water (Joel 3:18, RSV).

The image of a vineyard and an abundance of wine marking the Messianic Age is clearly painted by Prophet Amos, in whom God speaks and declares,

> "Behold, the days are coming," says the Lord,
>   "when the plowman shall overtake the reaper
>   and the treader of grapes him who sows the seed;
> the mountains shall drip sweet wine,
>   and all the hills shall flow with it.
> 14 I will restore the fortunes of my people Israel,
>   and they shall rebuild the ruined cities and inhabit them;
> they shall plant vineyards and drink their wine,

> and they shall make gardens and eat their fruit (Amos 9:13, RSV).

The promise of the Messianic Age came to fruition with our Lord. This coming age was already present in Christ who performed signs trumpeting His arrival as the sovereign ruler of the Jewish nation. By transforming water into wine, He made Himself known and thereby begins a new age, with a new cosmic order in which Christ our Lord is King and God.

The Messianic Age began with Christ because of Christ. The workings of the Holy Spirit define the Messianic Age. Christ gave sight to the blind, healed the lame, cleansed the lepers and cast out demons. God had pity on us and sent His Incarnate Son to renew our fallen state. Action was necessary. The cosmic order which was once maintained by non-action, as prescribed by the ancient Chinese sages, was transformed by God through His Incarnate Son for the salvation of man. The selfless proactive action of Christ was the new Way, the new Tao. When Christ was on the Cross and His work on earth was complete, He gave up the Holy Spirit. Prior to His death, He told His disciples, "I tell you the truth: it is to your advantage that I go away, for if I do not go away, the Counselor [Holy Spirit] will not come to you; but if I go, I will send him to you" (John 16:7, RSV). This promise was fulfilled after Christ's crucifixion at Pentecost when the Holy Spirit entered the Apostles and they were given the power to perform God's signs in the name of Christ:

> When the day of Pentecost had come, they were all together in one place. 2 And suddenly a sound came from heaven like the rush of a mighty wind, and it filled all the house where they were sitting. 3 And there appeared to them tongues as of fire, distributed and resting on each one of them. 4 And they were all filled with the Holy Spirit and began to speak in other tongues, as the Spirit gave them utterance.
>
> … 12 And all were amazed and perplexed, saying to one another, "What does this mean?" 13 But others mocking said, "They are filled with new wine."
>
> 14 But Peter, standing with the eleven, lifted up his voice and addressed them, "Men of Judea and all who dwell in Jerusalem, let this be known to you, and give ear to my words. 15 For these men are not drunk, as you suppose, since it is only the third hour of the day; 16 but this is what was spoken by the prophet Joel:
>
> > 17 'And in the last days it shall be, God declares,
> > that I will pour out my Spirit upon all flesh,

> and your sons and your daughters shall prophesy,
> and your young men shall see visions,
> and your old men shall dream dreams;
> 18 yea, and on my menservants and my maidservants in those days
> I will pour out my Spirit; and they shall prophesy.
> 19 And I will show wonders in the heaven above
> and signs on the earth beneath, blood, and fire, and vapor of smoke;
> 20 the sun shall be turned into darkness
> and the moon into blood,
> before the day of the Lord comes, the great and manifest day.
> 21 And it shall be that whoever calls on the name of the Lord shall be saved' (Acts 2:1, RSV).

Most telling is how the onlookers believed that the disciples were "filled with new wine." Indeed, they were. They were filled with new wine - the wine of the Holy Spirit. They were not drunk from a liquid, but moved from within by the Holy Spirit, who is the essence of the Messianic Age. The new Tao of Christ had come upon the earth and was made manifest in the disciples at Pentecost.

APPROACHING THE KINGDOM - JTA

The new Tao of Christ and the Messianic Age was revealed by Christ when He preached the Sermon on the Mount. Most poignant are the Beatitudes, the Blessings:

> "Blessed are the poor in spirit, for theirs is the kingdom of heaven.
> 4 "Blessed are those who mourn, for they shall be comforted.
> 5 "Blessed are the meek, for they shall inherit the earth.
> 6 "Blessed are those who hunger and thirst for righteousness, for they shall be satisfied.
> 7 "Blessed are the merciful, for they shall obtain mercy.
> 8 "Blessed are the pure in heart, for they shall see God.
> 9 "Blessed are the peacemakers, for they shall be called sons of God.
> 10 "Blessed are those who are persecuted for righteousness' sake, for theirs is the kingdom of heaven.
> 11 "Blessed are you when men revile you and persecute you and utter all kinds of evil against you falsely on my account. 12 Rejoice and be glad, for your reward is great in heaven, for so men persecuted the prophets who were before you (Matthew 5:3, RSV).

In the Sermon on the Mount, Christ preached a new message, a revolutionary message that transformed the world. He preached the Gospel, the Good News, the coming of God's Kingdom of Heaven for all people - including the weak, the infirm, the poor and the afflicted. A taste of Heaven has come upon the earth for those who live by Christ's teachings. And Paradise - a place of bliss in God's Supreme Love - awaits those who repent for their sins and pray for mercy. Because of God's merciful Grace, eternal life awaits those who seek it and journey toward it.

Christ has unveiled the mysteries of Heaven and Hell. God has made Christ Judge, so justice and righteousness may prevail. Miracles - God's works - have manifested on earth. Saints have walked the earth performing signs and healing the sick.

Salvation is awarded to those who "love the Lord your God with all your heart, and with all your soul, and with all your mind" and those who "love your neighbor as yourself" (Matthew 22:37-39, RSV).

Love - specifically, agape love - is the key to God's Kingdom of Heaven and Paradise. The commandment to be filled with agape love is exemplified by Christ who suffered for us on the Cross. He paid the ultimate price and gave up His life because He loved us so much. As the Tao Te Ching teaches, "Extreme love exacts a great price" (Addiss, 44). Christ's agape love is the new way that forever changed the cosmos.

In this treatise, we have dug deep into invaluable treasures and have uncovered hidden truths. As the Son of God, Christ transformed water into wine at a wedding in Cana in Galilee. This sign foreshadowed and illustrated His transformation of the Tao - a feat that only the Son of God could have performed. The ancient Chinese sages used the term Tao to refer to the natural rhythm of the cosmos and they observed that it behaved like water. The Tao's lofty esoteric principles were followed by few. But, there was tribulation in the world and Christ came into the world to save all people, not just the few. He transformed the Tao into what resembles wine to save lowly humankind from its sins. With the supreme transformation of the Tao, Christ ushered in a new cosmic order and announced to the world His eminence as Lord, King and God.

TREATISE TWO

AGAPE INTO ETERNITY

JAMES THOMAS ANGELIDIS

Copyright 2016 James Thomas Angelidis.
All rights reserved.
(Edited 2017)

PART ONE

UNION WITH GOD

Hindu theology was fundamental as I worked out my understanding of God, the universe and us. The *Upanishads* and *Bhagavad-Gita* are the two most revered Hindu texts and were of principal importance during my quest for answers. They are the result of the human inquiry, but go beyond philosophy to become revelation. I wanted to know the meaning and goal of life, so I went to the literature that disclosed or at least, thought deeply about them. There are countless numbers of books that have passed the test of time, but few books have thrived as perennially as the *Upanishads* and *Bhagavad-Gita.* There are a couple of hundred Upanishads, but the first twenty or so are the most significant and they date back as far as 3000 years ago. The sages who authored them are some of the first to ponder human existence and to this very day, hundreds of millions of Hindus abide by their teachings. This attests to the strength of their claims. The *Bhagavad-Gita* stems from the *Upanishads* and seems to have begun to take form as far back as 2500 years ago. Hindus of all walks of life treasure the *Bhagavad-Gita* as a transformative masterpiece. It would be foolish to object to their teachings without examining them, so I encourage all to read them. You will be surprised with how refreshing they are.

The two most important words in the *Upanishads* and *Bhagavad-Gita* are Brahman and Atman. These are no ordinary words because their meanings cannot be confined to word definitions. Brahman is that "which cannot be expressed in words but by which the tongue speaks - know that to be Brahman… That which is not comprehended by the mind, but by which the mind comprehends - know that to be Brahman… That which is not seen by the eye but by which the eye sees - know that to be Brahman… That which is not heard by the ear but by which the ear hears - know that to be Brahman… That which is not drawn by the breath but by which the breath is drawn - know that to be Brahman (Kena, Upanishads, Signet Classic, 30). Nonetheless, the ancient Hindu sages explain that Brahman is the supreme infinite reality of the universe. It is the origin: "Brahman willed that it should be so, and brought forth out of himself the material cause of the universe; from this came the primal energy, and from the primal energy mind, from mind the subtle elements, from the subtle elements the many worlds, and from the acts performed by beings in the many worlds the chain of cause and effect - the reward and punishment of works" (Mundaka, Upanishads, 43). The "self-luminous, subtler than the subtlest, in whom exist all the worlds and all those that live therein - he is the imperishable Brahman. He is the principle of life. He is speech, and he is mind. He is real. He is immortal. Attain him, O my friend, the one goal to be attained! (Mundaka, Upanishads, 45).

Atman is the innermost reality of a person. "When we consider Brahman as lodged within the individual being, we call Him Atman" (Bhagavad-Gita, Signet Classic, 74). Atman is within and Brahman is without. Atman is Brahman and Brahman is all (Isha, Upanishads, 26) "This Atman, who understands all, who knows all, and whose glory is manifest in the universe, lives within the lotus of the heart, the bright throne of Brahman. By the pure in heart is he known. The Atman exists in man, within the lotus of the heart, and is the master of his life and of his body. With mind illumined by the power of meditation, the wise know him, the blissful, the immortal" (Mundaka, Upanishads, 46). "The Atman is ear of the ear, mind of the mind, speech of speech. He is also breath of the breathe, and eye of the eye. Having given up the false identification of the Atman with the senses and the mind, and knowing the Atman to be Brahman, the wise, on departing this life, become immortal" (Kena, Upanishads, 30).

Brahman is the universe's soul and Atman is the individual's soul and they are of the same essence and substance. Atman within is immortal, like Brahman without. Life's purpose is to release and free Atman, so it may become one with Brahman. When Atman becomes one with Brahman, the devotee transcends suffering and death and becomes immortal. It is like when a drop of water enters and becomes one with water. To become one with the immortal is to become immortal. "Let him worship Brahman as Brahman, and he will become Brahman" (Taittiriya, Upanishads, 59). "When can a man be said to have achieved union with Brahman? When his mind is under perfect control and freed from all desires, so that he becomes absorbed in the Atman, and nothing else" (Bhagavad-Gita, 66). The devotee's "mind is dead to the touch of the external: it is alive to the bliss of the Atman. Because his heart knows Brahman his happiness is forever" (Bhagavad-Gita, 60). The sages, "these great ones attain to immortality in this very life; and when their bodies fall away from them at death, they attain liberation" (Mundaka, Upanishads, 48). "The secret of immortality is to be found in purification of the heart, in meditation, in realization of the identity of the Atman within and the Brahman without. For immortality is union with God" (Katha, Upanishads, 13).

However, uniting Atman with Brahman takes effort because we are consumed by other concerns. The ancient Hindu sages understood that the world is filled with suffering and our suffering is caused by our worldly attachments and actions. We work for riches, fame, sex and power, but our actions are futile because those things fail to satisfy. "Thinking about-sense objects will attach you to sense-objects; grow attached, and you become addicted; thwart your addiction, it turns to anger; be angry, and you confuse your mind; confuse your mind, you forget the lesson of experience; forget experience, you lose discrimination; lose discrimination, and you miss life's only purpose" (Bhagavad-Gita, 42). "He who, brooding upon sense objects, comes to yearn for them, is born here and there, again and again, driven by his desire. But he who has realized the Atman, and thus satisfied all hunger, attains to liberation even in this life" (Mundaka, Upanishads, 48). Our actions have held Atman, within, hostage. You "must first control your senses, then kill this evil thing which obstructs discriminative knowledge and realization of the Atman (Bhagavad-Gita, 49). Through self-discipline, asceticism and mysticism, we can detach ourselves from worldly attachments, break free from the confines of the world and transcend suffering and death. The release, liberation and emancipation from suffering, the world and death is called Moksha.

    The relationship between Brahman and Atman reveals deep truths about the relationship between God and us. This Hindu theology is also sound Christian theology. The following verse is a part of the ancient Trisagion Prayer, which many Orthodox Christian's use daily:

> O heavenly King, O Comforter, the Spirit of truth, who art in all places and fillest all things; Treasury of good things and Giver of life: Come and dwell in us and cleanse us

> from every stain, and save our souls, O gracious Lord (*A Pocket Prayer Book for Orthodox Christians*, Antiochian Orthodox Christian Archdiocese of North America 1956, 5).

This simple, yet powerful prayer is an excellent representation of a shared theology between Hindus and Christians. I have recited this prayer twice a day - once in the morning and once at night - for nearly ten years. My journey through the great world religions' sacred scriptures began over ten years ago. The shared theology that I discovered had been with me for a while, but one night, as I was reciting the prayer, I made the connection between the prayer and the theology. That ordinary day turned into an extraordinary night because the theology I discovered was confirmed. It was crystallized in this prayer. I knew the theology was correct, but the prayer expressed it perfectly. The prayer's words are few, but its theology is eternal. The next day, I told a coworker who is a friend and later that day, I told my parents that I was able to describe the means to Heaven and immortality. I was talking so quickly that they encouraged me to breath. I could barely sleep for four days and I did not want to sleep. My eyes were as wide as the moon and my spirit ascended to the heavens. Peace filled my soul and I knew I had to express my discovery so others could understand it. In this work, I hope I have done so. I wish I was a better writer, communicator and teacher, but here, I have done my best. In a moment, I will illustrate how love - specifically, agape love - is important to this cosmic theology. As the theology has done for me, I believe it will bring hope, comfort and peace to many in our troubled world.

To make clear the prayer's theology, I have broken it down below:

- O heavenly King, O Comforter, the Spirit of truth, who art in all places and fillest all things [the definition of Brahman]

- Treasury of good things and Giver of life: Come and dwell in us [the definition Atman]

- and cleanse us from every stain, and save our souls [the definition of Moksha]

- O gracious Lord.

This is a prayer from a Christian to Almighty God, but it can easily be used by a Hindu to pray to Almighty Brahman. It reveals the relationship between God and us - the Creator and the created - and our deep desire for Salvation - the means to union with Him - which is only possible because of His Grace.

In the same way that Hindu's believe Atman is Brahman and Brahman is all, Christians believe Jesus is God and God is all. Hindu's believe Atman is true Brahman of true Brahman and Christians believe Jesus is true God of true God. In the same way that Hindus believe Atman is one essence and substance of Brahman who is the source all things, Christians believe Jesus is of one essence with God, by whom all things were made. In the same way that Hindus believe that Atman is the true self and the full potential of the individual known only by the pure in heart, the Apostle Paul says, "it is no longer I who live, but Christ who lives in me" (Galatians 2:20).

Hindu's believe union with Brahman is made possible through Moksha and Christians believe union with God is made possible through Salvation. The theology is similar, but not the same. Moksha leads to complete satisfaction, fullness and peace; while, Salvation leads to unmitigated bliss. Hindus believe that discriminative knowledge through self-discipline makes Moksha possible; while, Christians believe agape love makes Salvation possible. The difference between discriminative knowledge and agape love is the difference between satisfaction and bliss.

As I was studying the Christian Bible's New Testament, I discovered a powerful insight that struck me and deepened my understanding about God. That is, "God is agape" (1 John 4:8). Christianity is the only religion to make this claim. Here, we learn that not only does God have agape for us, He is Agape. In the next chapter, I will define agape in detail, but for now, it is enough to know that agape means love - the kind of love Jesus embodied.

Agape is crucial for union with God. There are many ways to get close to God, but only agape can unite us with God. God is the source of agape and God's Son Jesus brings God's agape to earth. Jesus is agape Incarnate and perfectly revealed agape to the world through his life, suffering and death. To become one with God, we must become one with the Son. Becoming one with the Son is the only way to become one with God because the Son fills us with agape and only those who are filled with agape can become one with God who is Agape. To be filled with agape, we have to be reborn in spirit with God's Son Jesus. We do not know agape or how to give agape until Jesus enters us. It begins with respect and recognition of his suffering. Consider his suffering and it will lead to empathy. Agape compelled him and his agape will fill you with agape. Then, you will understand that he was no ordinary man. He will transform your mind and heart. And, when you pay attention to his teachings, you will hear truth in his words. No man spoke like this man. No man died like this man. No man loved like this man. Reflect and embrace him and you will understand why Christians call him God's Suffering Servant, the Christ and God's Son.

Jesus's agape lives within us and God's agape lives all around us. The purpose of life is to unite the agape within us with the agape all around us - in the same way that a drop of water becomes one with water. Those who can - like the saints - attain immortality.

Like the Hindu sages who wrote the Upanishads, Jesus believed that oneness with God is the Ultimate. In prayer, he asks his Father, "I do not pray for these [his disciples] only, but also for those who believe in me through their word, that they may all be one; even as thou, Father, art in me, and I in thee, that they also may be in us, so that the world may believe that thou hast sent me. The glory which thou hast given me I have given to them, that they may be one even as we are one, I in them and thou in me, that they may become perfectly one" (John 17:20). This way, Jesus explains, "the world may know that thou hast sent me and hast loved them even as thou hast loved me." Jesus wants the world to know about the love he and his Father have for each other and that the Father loves those who follow Jesus as much as He loves Jesus.

Jesus tells us, "As the Father has loved me, so have I loved you; abide in my love" (John 15:9). The agape Jesus has with his Father he wants us to have with him. He wants us to have the same relationship with him as he has with his Father. God and Jesus's relationship is no ordinary relationship because they are not ordinary. They are perfect and their agape is perfect. There is no agape more sublime or glorious than the agape between the Father and the Son. An agape of the highest order from "before the foundation of the world" (John 17:24). Jesus invites us to be a part of their agape. Could anything be better? Who would not want to join God and His Son and their agape? At the nadir of human history, when Jesus was sacrificed, their agape remained irrepressible and undying. Like at the highest of highests, at the lowest of lowests, their love is perfection. Through them we are saved. "For God so loved the world that He gave his only Son, that whoever believes in him should not perish but have eternal life" (John 3:16). Because of their love for each other and us, the angels sing, "Hallelujah, Hallelujah, Hallelujah! Glory to You O God!" Their agape for each other conquered death and Jesus wants us to abide in that same agape with him, so we, too, can conquer death.

Jesus tells us, "If you keep my commandments, you will abide in my love, just as I have kept my Father's commandments and abide in his love" (John 15:10). Keeping Jesus's commandments means embodying agape as he does. If my master was an ordinary man and he told me that he would love me if I kept his commandments, I would be skeptical, even apprehensive. His commandments may be outrageous. However, Jesus does not command us with rules or laws. He works on what is within us. Jesus's commandments have to do with agape: "You shall love the Lord your God with all your heart, and with all your soul, and with all your mind. This is the great and first commandment. And a second is like it, You shall love your neighbor as yourself" (Matthew 22:37). Loving God and neighbor will move us to bring Heaven to earth. A time and place when and where, "the mountains shall drip sweet wine, and the hills shall flow with milk, and all the stream beds of Judah shall flow with water" (Joel 3:18). Jesus even tells us, "Love your enemies and pray for those who persecute you... For if you love those who love you, what reward have you? Do not even the tax collectors do the same? And if you salute only your brethren, what more are you doing than others? Do not even the Gentiles do the same?" (Matthew 5:44).

By keeping Jesus's commandments, we will abide in his love, just as he has kept his Father's commandments and abides in His love. To "abide in" means to remain or dwell in. To abide in agape is to dwell in a state, place or being that is agape. When Jesus abides in God's agape, he dwells in God's agape and is one with God. Jesus invites us to dwell in his agape just as he dwells in God's agape. Agape unites God and Jesus and agape unites Jesus and us. How comforting is that? Irresistible, indeed, to know that agape is the only thing necessary to unite us with God and Jesus. Agape is all you need.

There is a special relationship among the Father, the Son and us. Jesus tells us, "I am in my Father, and you in me, and I in you" (John 14:20b). We who keeps Jesus's commandments of agape are in Jesus and because Jesus is in the Father we, too, are in the Father. Jesus also tells us that he is in us. We who are filled with agape like Jesus have Jesus in us. As Apostle Paul said, "it is no longer I who live, but Christ who lives in me" (Galatians 2:20).

Through agape, we can be one with Jesus and because Jesus is "Light of Light, true God of true God," we can be one with God. Because of Jesus, we can be in God and God in us. Thus, we are one with God. Jesus, who is inside us, is the same essence as God, who is greater than the universe. This relationship is identical to the Hindu theology that the Atman inside of us is the same essence as Brahman, who is greater than the universe.

In prayer, Jesus asks his Father, "the love with which thou hast loved me may be in them, and I in them" (John 17:26). This agape from God and Jesus that Jesus prays for us to have inside of us is like the Hindu Atman. Hindus teach that Atman "lives within the lotus of the heart, the bright throne of Brahman" (Mundaka, Upanishads, 46). Similarly, God who is greater than the universe has a place in our hearts. There is a place for Almighty God in our hearts, if we let him in.

Jesus tells us, "If a man loves me, he will keep my word, and my Father will love him, and we will come to him and make our home with him" (John 14:23). If we love Jesus, God will love us and we will live in agape with God and Jesus forever together in their home in Heaven - a place where the King is known as a Comforter and rules with his Spirit and speaks Truth.

Jesus tells us, "These things I have spoken to you, that my joy may be in you, and that your joy may be full" (John 15:11). And, he tells us, "The word which you hear is not mine but the Father's who sent me" (John 14:24b).

The author of 1 John speaks to us saying, "Beloved, let us love [agape] one another; for love is of God, and he who loves is born of God and knows God. He who does not love does not know God; for God is love. In this love of God was made manifest among us, that God sent his only Son into the world, so that we might live through him. In this is love, not that we loved God but that he loved us and sent his Son to be the expiation for our sins. Beloved, if God so loved us, we also ought to love one another. No man has ever seen God; if we love one another, God abides in us and his love is perfected in us. By this we know that we abide in him and he in us, because he has given us of his own Spirit. And we have seen and testify that the Father has sent his Son as the Savior of the world. Whoever confesses that Jesus is the Son of God, God abides in him, and he in God. So we know and believe the love God has for us. God is love, and he who abides in love abides in God, and God abides in him. In this is love perfected with us, that we may have confidence for the day of judgment, because as he is so are we in this world. There is no fear in love, but perfect love casts out fear. For fear has to do with punishment, and he who fears is not perfected in love. We love, because he first loved us. If any one says, "I love God," and hates his brother, he is a liar; for he who does not love his brother whom he has seen, cannot love God whom he has not seen. And this commandment we have from him, that he who loves God should love his brother also (1 John 4:7).

In Hinduism, when a devotee's Atman is one with Brahman, the devotee is perfect and is destined for immortality. Similarly, in Christianity, when a Christian "confesses that Jesus is the Son of God, God abides in him, and he in God." If God is in the Christian and the Christian is in God, the Christian is one with God. This union with God is life's goal because it means immortality. Furthermore, "God is love, and he who abides in love abides in God, and God abides in him." God is agape and the Christian who dwells in agape dwells in God and God dwells in him. "In this is love perfected with us." Such a one who is united with God through agape is destined for immortality. The agape we share with God must be shared with one another. "[If] we love one another, God abides in us and his love is perfected in us. By this we know that we abide in him and he in us, because he has given us of his own Spirit." Those who do not have agape in them should fear the day of judgement. One who rejects agape has rejected God. Therefore, Salvation would be meaningless and impossible. However, we must not be quick to judge each other. We do not know what is in another's heart, if one has made a home for God in one's soul. Only God knows and He will judge us according to our agape.

PART TWO

DEFINING AGAPE LOVE

The ancient Greeks identified four forms of love that we experience in life: storge, philia, eros, agape. Before Jesus, the term agape was rarely used because it was so general. The other terms for love had specific meanings - storge refers to love for family, philia refers to love for friends, eros refers to love for a romantic partner - which allowed one to express more clearly what one wanted to say. Christians adopted the general term agape and revolutionized it to indicate Jesus and Christians' unique love. After Jesus, when people heard the term agape, they understood it meant Christian love (Kreeft, *The God Who Loves You*, 50).

Jesus defines agape because in his life and death, he expresses its meaning in totality. In life, Jesus taught us how to have agape: "love the Lord your God with all your heart, and with all your soul, and with all your mind [and] love your neighbor as yourself" (Matthew 22:37). And, in death, Jesus showed us how to have agape: "By this we know love, that he [Jesus] laid down his life for us; and we ought to lay down our lives for the brethren" (1 John 3:16). Jesus's message and death are the perfect expressions of agape.

    Agape is the essence of our relationship with God. His agape is a gift to us because He does not need to love us. We are blessed that He has agape for us and that He considers us. Just as He did not need to create Creation, He does not need to give us the gift of agape. However, just as He created light and earth and man and saw that they were good, He showers us with agape and sees that it is good. God created us because He wanted to and He gives us His gift of agape because He wants to. Furthermore, God created just so He could share agape with Creation. God has agape for everything He made, but He does not have agape for everything in the same way. We are special because God made us in His image and likeness and He has so much agape for us that He wants for us what He wants for Himself, which is to live in agape. That was the intention of our existence. We were made to live in Paradise in forever-present agape and though it is now lost, we are, nonetheless, meant to return to Paradise in forever-present agape.

    God needs nothing. He has everything. But, there is one thing He desires: our agape. He has given us free will and we can chose Him or not and when a person chooses God, nothing brings God greater happiness. How sweet it is to know that we can make God happy! All was not for nothing. The

Divine Plan has come to fruition. The made has returned to his Maker. God desires for us to have agape for Him in return because He knows the agape shared between He and us will bring us joy, which we know to be true from the testimonies of the saints.

God's agape is evident throughout human history. However, many may say that, at times, God has acted with vengeance and not agape. Many may say that if Jesus was, in fact, His Son, Jesus's sacrifice was the epitome of God's terrible acts. Many may say that Christians are crazy to believe that a God who sacrifices His only Son loves His Son. But, we Christians are not crazy, "For God so loved the world that he gave his only Son, that whoever believes in him [God's Son] should not perish but have eternal life" (John 3:16). God tells me, "Believe in my Son who I love because His death is not the end. His sacrifice was for you because I love you. I love you so much that my Son and I paid the ultimate price with His death. So, do not let Our act of love be in vain. Do not turn away from it. Look at my Son. Believe in Him and we will be together forever in agape." A Christian must have faith in this to be a Christian and if you do, you will see God's agape in everything and everywhere. The sacrifice is real and that is why saints cry with joy - something many may not understand, but which the saints know to be more real than life itself because it arises from deep within their souls - because no love is greater than the agape of God and His Son.

I know God by what I have learned in Scripture and the Church and what is corroborated deep inside my soul. God's agape is real, but many question Him because of tragedies like the 2004 South Asian tsunami and the 2012 Sandy Hook elementary school massacre. Scripture teaches us,

> For my thoughts are not your thoughts,
>   neither are your ways my ways, says the Lord.
> 9 For as the heavens are higher than the earth,
>   so are my ways higher than your ways
>   and my thoughts than your thoughts (Isaiah 55:8).

I trust Scripture and believe what it tells me. I may not know why certain things happen. Many things are beyond me. God's ways are higher than my ways, but I trust God. I believe in His agape and His Son Jesus's agape. When Jesus tells me, "in my Father's house are many rooms," and that he must die and go to his Father to prepare a place for those who follow him, I believe him (John 14:2). I believe in Paradise and that there are rooms for those who follow Jesus in God's house in Paradise.

There have been moments when I have asked myself, "Why do good people suffer misfortune? Where is God when there is pain?" In Scripture, there is a parable about how God gave the homeless Lazarus - whose sores were licked by stray dogs -

relief and eternal peace after death in Paradise. I believe God is good and just and that righteousness will prevail, even if it must be after death. As I dig deep, I hear Jesus cry out to me and to those suffering in this life in this world, "I know your pain!" because he took the form of a human being in flesh and experienced the peak of human suffering by being nailed to a cross for hours and left to die - a torture reserved for criminals, not something we would imagine for the Sinless One. And, to those who have lost loved ones in their lives, to parents who have lost their children (perhaps, life's greatest ill), God cries out to them, "I know your pain!" because His only Son was tortured and killed. Understanding this about Jesus the Christ and God the Father, I find comfort because I know I am not alone. If God and His Son experienced pain, we are not immune to it either.

I believe God never leaves us, even when we think He has. This sentiment is illustrated in one of my favorite poems, *Footprints in the Sand*. In it, a man has a dream about his life with God of which is represented by two sets of footprints on a beach. He notices that during his most difficult times, there is only one set and so questions God's presence. The poem ends with God comforting and reassuring the man that when he saw only one set of footprints on the beach, it was not that God was not by his side, but rather that God was carrying him.

Agape has no motive, other than to give love. It is altruistic and gives without consideration for itself - even in danger. It is resilient and strong, but is gentle. It is gracious. It does not measure or contend. It loves without bias, impartially, disinterestedly and, therefore, is limitless in its love. It loves everyone without reservation. It is unconditional. Its love is absolute. It is the purest of the loves. It does not go wrong because it makes no judgments. It simply loves. It does so without reward because it is its own reward. The more it gives, the more it enjoys. It loves to love. Who can resist such love? For how long can one deny such love? It is free and the most valuable thing in the universe. To deny it to the end is self-destruction because there is no love in the beloved who cannot open himself up to it. Without love, there is no living because to love is to live. To not love only leads to death. Agape is tall, but does not look down on the beloved; rather, it picks the beloved up.

Agape is everlasting because it comes from God. The other forms of love promise to be everlasting and when they are at their peaks, it is easy to believe them, but they do not follow through. My family's storge, my friends' philia and my girlfriends' eros deeply affected me and bettered my life, but the feelings I shared with them were confined by time and space and eventually faded. The power of agape endures. Even when it feels weak because God seems distant, I know it is there because I know God will never leave me. It is faith, but it is not blind faith. I trust Scripture, the Church and the testimonies of the saints who encourage me to stay strong and be patient because God is near. My storge for my family, my philia for my friends and my eros for the girls in my life have faded in time, but my agape for them has not. My agape for them remains in me. It is my moments of agape with them that make me smile during the day and help me sleep soundly at night.

The agape I share with them is everlasting because its source is God. God gives us His agape, which we must reciprocate and also share with our neighbor. Even when we behave unlovable, agape remains. Differences and disagreements may tarnish storge, philia and eros, but they will not tarnish agape. Agape is so pure that it does not get dirty.

Agape is unlike the other loves because it is not an emotion - it is an action. Storge, philia and eros are manifested by feelings and become emotions; while, agape is manifested by the will and becomes an action. When our agape is directed toward God, it is a response to and reciprocation of His agape. This is not rooted in a feeling. It is us accepting Him as our Maker. We are His and there is no better way to express our agape for him than to obey His commandments. We express our agape for Jesus in the same way. As Jesus tells us, "He who has my commandments and keeps them, he it is who loves me" (John 14:21). Agape begins with a choice, but it only becomes real if we follow through with action.

It is a love to live by and is not sentimental or romantic.

Agape is not an emotion like happiness. Though its aim is not happiness, if we have agape for God, we will be happy. If we work for happiness and not God, we will never find happiness. If we want happiness, we must not seek happiness, but God who will give us happiness. God knows our agape. There is no fooling Him and He gives happiness to those who love Him for Himself and not to those who seek after what He can give them. Agape is choosing God above all other things. No bond or love is stronger because it is the made returning to his Maker.

When our agape is directed to our neighbors, we are loving God. By loving that which our Maker made, we show our love for our Maker. Out of love for God, we must love our neighbor, who God loves. Jesus calls us brethren: "Truly, I say to you, as you did it to one of the least of these my brethren, you did it to me" (Matthew 25:40). We must follow Jesus's example and love one another: "even as I have loved you, that you also love one another. By this all men will know that you are my disciples, if you have love for one another." (John 13:34). Because of our agape for each other, we are Christians. Agape defines true Christians. Christianity was formed to spread agape. When used correctly, it is the religion of agape. Though storge, philia and eros are noble, agape is divine.

Agape is an activity because God is active. It is alive because God is alive. I have a connection to and relationship with God through the agape. We communicate through agape. Our agape is between the two of us alone together with no one else. It is personal and intimate. God is always awake; He never sleeps and it is up to us to be alert and reciprocate with agape and make the effort to continue the relationship.

Agape and faith are the New Testament's dominant themes and they have a unique relationship. Each has the ability to lead to the other. Through faith in Jesus, one comes to realize the power of agape. Jesus's self-sacrificial death is the ultimate expression of agape. If one has faith in Jesus, one cannot help to follow Jesus's lead and practice agape. Once a believer begins to emulate his Lord by practicing agape - as every believer should - he will become a more fervent believer and a more devoted servant. Faith in Jesus leads to acts of agape. The other direction of the relationship is also true: agape leads to faith. As one begins to practice agape with his neighbor, he will realize the truth of Jesus's message of agape. The more he practices agape, the closer he will be to Jesus. Agape can take one to the threshold of faith and if one continues to follow the path of agape and recognizes the reality of agape's transformative power, his immersion into faith in God and Jesus is not far.

The agape we experience with God is not unlike the eros we experience with a beloved. Both are euphoric and transcendent. Both are unmistakable and transformative. Both take us to places unseen and rise in us feelings never before felt. There is no earthly feeling as powerful as eros, but agape is heavenly. And, still further, the agape we experience with God on earth is only a taste of the unmitigated, fully revealed and eternal agape that we will experience with God in Heaven.

> "Greater love [agape] has no man than this, that a man lay down his life for his friends"
> - Jesus
> (John 15:13)

Jesus's Passion is the most well documented, detailed and thorough period described in all four Gospels: Matthew, Mark, Luke, John. The term "passion" that is used when we refer to Jesus's Passion does not have the same definition as the term that we use in ordinary daily dialogue. In ordinary daily dialogue, the term passion refers to zeal, love and devotion for person, place, thing or idea. It is true that Jesus was filled with passion, but that is not why we say the Passion of the Christ. The word "passion" comes from a Greek word meaning "to suffer." To suffer means to go through pain, to hurt, to feel close to death, but many not understand the glory of suffering. Suffering brings us closer to Jesus who suffered. With suffering, we have the honor of emulating Jesus - God's only begotten Son - who suffered because of his agape for us. He lowered himself to reach us, so when we die, we can be elevated to be with him.

The Christian Church celebrates Jesus's Passion during Holy Week, which begins with Palm Sunday. For Christians, it is one of the most joyful days of the year, preceded by only Easter and Christmas. It commemorates Jesus's triumphal entry into Jerusalem trumpeting his arrival as our King, Savior and God. He enters the city sitting on a donkey announcing that he is the king that Jerusalem had been waiting for. Prophet Zechariah prophesied;

> Rejoice greatly, O daughter of Zion!
> Shout aloud, O daughter of Jerusalem!
> Lo, your king comes to you;
> triumphant and victorious is he,
> humble and riding on an ass,
> on a colt the foal of an ass (Zechariah 9:9).

The crowd that greeted Jesus glorified him shouting, "Hosanna! Blessed is he who comes in the name of the Lord! Blessed is the kingdom of our father David that is coming! Hosanna in the highest!" (Mark 11:9b). They spread palm tree branches on the ground and hailed him as their King. In the past, on the day before Palm Sunday, I have gone to church and joined fellow Christians to make palm leaf crosses. We split palm leaves into thin strips and then folded them into crosses, which would be handed to the church parishioners the next day on Palm Sunday. I would keep the cross I received all year - sometimes more than a year - because I felt its holy power would bless me.

    For Christians, Palm Sunday is a day to celebrate, but the days following Palm Sunday are sad because we know that our King will soon be killed. Jesus is better than a political king who can gain territory or peace for his subjects in this world. He is our King and Priest who can save us from death and give us eternal life. Most did not understand this at first. Not even Jesus's disciples were fully aware of his eternal power. Not until Jesus rose from the dead and appeared to his disciples, did they fully understand his power. Truly, his kingship is not of this world. Jesus's reign is in the Kingdom of God and not in a kingdom of man.

    Holy Week builds momentum as it approaches Great Friday, which, for Christians, is the most solemn and poignant day of the year. It is the definitive moment of Jesus's Passion and agape. Even on the Cross, he has agape for those who are killing him crying, "Father, forgive them; for they know not what they do" (Luke 23:34). He was killed like a guilty criminal, but the Cross is a symbol of victory. Our reasoning minds tell us the way Jesus died is a curse and a disgrace; however, over two billion people wear the Cross around their necks with pride because Jesus was killed on the Cross for us because of his agape for us. Easter may be the most sublime and reverent day of the year because it is a day of hope and promise that there is eternal life with God in Heaven and that one day our bodies will resurrect. However, we love Jesus not for what he can give us, but because of his incomprehensible agape for us. His self-sacrificial death defines agape and he is worthy of adoration and adulation. The Cross is a sign of victory because on it, Jesus completed his mission for our salvation. Not even death could stop Jesus from fulfilling his mission. In fact, death made it possible. Dying for us is why he came into the world.

Only through Jesus's suffering can we understand his kingship. As Prophet Isaiah prophesied for God,

> I [God] will divide him a portion with the great,
>   and he shall divide the spoil with the strong;
> because he poured out his soul to death,
>   and was numbered with the transgressors
> (Isaiah 53:12).
>
> Behold, my servant [God's servant] shall prosper,
>   he shall be exalted and lifted up,
>   and shall be very high.
> 14 As many were astonished at him[b]—

> his appearance was so marred, beyond human semblance,
> and his form beyond that of the sons of men—
> 15 so shall he startle[c] many nations;
> kings shall shut their mouths because of him;
> for that which has not been told them they shall see,
> and that which they have not heard they shall understand (Isaiah 52:13).

This world's kings may be baffled by Jesus - Isaiah's prophesied Suffering Servant of God - and his resurrection and the miracles worked in his name by the Holy Spirit, but for Christians, they are as real as Heaven.

Jesus knew what he was getting into and the suffering that was ahead of him. This makes his agape more compelling than if he did not know because most people, if they knew, would have run. As Prophet Isaiah prophesied,

> He was oppressed, and he was afflicted,
> yet he opened not his mouth;
> like a lamb that is led to the slaughter,
> and like a sheep that before its shearers is dumb,
> so he opened not his mouth (Isaiah 53:7).

There are a few times when the Gospels say that Jesus prophesied his own death and how it would happen. For example, Jesus told his disciples,

> "Behold, we are going up to Jerusalem, and everything that is written of the Son of man by the prophets will be accomplished. 32 For he will be delivered to the Gentiles, and will be mocked and shamefully treated and spit upon; 33 they will scourge him and kill him, and on the third day he will rise" (Luke 18:31b).

Even in agony, Jesus's faith in God his Father remained steadfast. In Gethsemane in anticipation of his "cup" of suffering and death, he "prayed more earnestly; and his sweat became like great drops of blood falling down upon the ground" (Luke 22:44). To God, he prayed, "Abba, Father, all things are possible to thee; remove this cup from me; yet not what I will, but what thou wilt" (Mark 14:36). He was obedient to God's will and submitted to God's power. He was God's perfect servant and a son who adored his Father.

When Jesus was questioned about who he was, even if it meant suffering, he fearlessly told the truth:

> The high priest then questioned Jesus about his disciples and his teaching. 20 Jesus answered him, "I have spoken openly to the

world; I have always taught in synagogues and in the temple, where all Jews come together; I have said nothing secretly. 21 Why do you ask me? Ask those who have heard me, what I said to them; they know what I said." 22 When he had said this, one of the officers standing by struck Jesus with his hand, saying, "Is that how you answer the high priest?" 23 Jesus answered him, "If I have spoken wrongly, bear witness to the wrong; but if I have spoken rightly, why do you strike me?" (John 18:19).

Still further:

> Now the chief priests and the whole council sought false testimony against Jesus that they might put him to death, 60 but they found none, though many false witnesses came forward. At last two came forward 61 and said, "This fellow said, 'I am able to destroy the temple of God, and to build it in three days.'" 62 And the high priest stood up and said, "Have you no answer to make? What is it that these men testify against you?" 63 But Jesus was silent. And the high priest said to him, "I adjure you by the living God, tell us if you are the Christ, the Son of God." 64 Jesus said to him, "You have said so. But I tell you, hereafter you will see the Son of man seated at

> the right hand of Power, and coming on the clouds of heaven." 65 Then the high priest tore his robes, and said, "He has uttered blasphemy. Why do we still need witnesses? You have now heard his blasphemy. 66 What is your judgment?" They answered, "He deserves death." 67 Then they spat in his face, and struck him; and some slapped him, 68 saying, "Prophesy to us, you Christ! Who is it that struck you?" (Matthew 26:59).

Jesus, my King, not only experienced physical pain for us, but was also belittled, mocked and disgraced for us:

> Then the soldiers of the governor took Jesus into the praetorium, and they gathered the whole battalion before him. 28 And they stripped him and put a scarlet robe upon him, 29 and plaiting a crown of thorns they put it on his head, and put a reed in his right hand. And kneeling before him they mocked him, saying, "Hail, King of the Jews!" 30 And they spat upon him, and took the reed and struck him on the head. 31 And when they had mocked him, they stripped him of the robe, and put his own clothes on him, and led him away to crucify him (Matthew 27:27).

My King is the Son of the Most High, yet he was stepped on like dirt. He suffered many things for me. The soldiers spat on him. How could they spit on my King? He lowered himself for me. Who am I am? I am little and he is great. A devoted servant would lay down his life for his king, but my King laid down his life for his servants. What have we done to deserve such grace? How can we repay him? The only way I know how to repay him is to emulate him. We must be willing to sacrifice ourselves for him and the brethren. They treated him less than a human being when in reality he was God. It makes no sense, but if you listen to his words, you will see he did it out of agape. He was disgraced, but that is why I glorify him.

    The climax of Jesus's Passion is his crucifixion - an incomprehensible suffering where the sentenced one dies slowly. With his limbs nailed to and his body hanging from a wood, Jesus cried with a loud voice, "My God, my God, why hast thou forsaken me?" (Mark 15:34 and Matthew 27:46). It would be hard to find greater suffering - suffering so great that the Son of God is praying for mercy. However, Jesus never curses God or His authority. Knowing he was innocent and was sentenced unjustly to death, Jesus never separates himself from God. On the Cross, with a loud voice, Jesus cries out, "'Father, into thy hands I commit my spirit!' And having said this he breathed his last" (Luke 23:46). It was finished. Triumph. Jesus accomplished what he was meant to do. To his very end, he was a messenger of the truth and fulfilled his mission for the forgiveness of our sins, so we can have eternal life.

Jesus is often referred to as the Good Shepherd - a glorious, edifying and sweet title. In the Old Testament, Psalm 23 refers to the Lord as a shepherd:

A Psalm of David.

The Lord is my shepherd, I shall not want;
2   he makes me lie down in green pastures.
He leads me beside still waters;[a]
3   he restores my soul.[b]
He leads me in paths of righteousness[c]
    for his name's sake.
4 Even though I walk through the valley of the shadow of death,[d]
    I fear no evil;
for thou art with me;
    thy rod and thy staff,
    they comfort me.
5 Thou preparest a table before me
    in the presence of my enemies;
thou anointest my head with oil,
    my cup overflows.
6 Surely[e] goodness and mercy[f] shall follow me
    all the days of my life;

and I shall dwell in the house of the Lord
> for ever.

This title is also used in the in the New Testament. Jesus tells us,

> I am the good shepherd. The good shepherd lays down his life for the sheep. 12 He who is a hireling and not a shepherd, whose own the sheep are not, sees the wolf coming and leaves the sheep and flees; and the wolf snatches them and scatters them. 13 He flees because he is a hireling and cares nothing for the sheep. 14 I am the good shepherd; I know my own and my own know me, 15 as the Father knows me and I know the Father; and I lay down my life for the sheep. 16 And I have other sheep, that are not of this fold; I must bring them also, and they will heed my voice. So there shall be one flock, one shepherd. 17 For this reason the Father loves me, because I lay down my life, that I may take it again. 18 No one takes it from me, but I lay it down of my own accord. I have power to lay it down, and I have power to take it again; this charge I have received from my Father" (John 10:11).

Jesus is the Good Shepherd because he lay down his life for us, his flock. He lay down his life everyone, including those who have not yet heard his voice.

Not one of us unimportant. He is trying to save us all.

Another important Psalm to meditate is Psalm 22, which is often referred to as the Passion Psalm. When you read it, try to hear Jesus's suffering and agony when he prays in Gethsemane and when he is hanging on the Cross. You will see Jesus's humanity as his suffers as a man, but you will also see his confidence in God as God's Son. He has nowhere to go. God is all he has. He trusts in God who gives him strength before he falls apart. Jesus endured to show us we have the power to endure and that we must endure.

In Isaiah, God's Suffering Servant prophecy explains that "he bore the sin of many, and made intercession for the transgressors" (53:12c). We are the transgressors - the sinners in this world - and are far from God, but Jesus interceded for us, so we can have a way to unite with God. Sinful man has no way of entering Heaven and uniting with God on his own. We are unworthy of God because we have rejected Him, as did our parents Adam and Eve, and have no way of making amends with Him. God and His Son Jesus knew this and made a plan to save us from our wicked ways that lead to hell, so we can be with God forever in Heaven. The plan was for perfect Jesus to die for us. He was the only worthy sacrifice to God to redeem sinful man. It hurts God and Jesus for Jesus to be tortured and killed, but they did so willingly to retain justice in a God centered universe.

God's Justice required punishment for sin and Jesus took our place.

> Surely he has borne our griefs[d]
>   and carried our sorrows;[e]
> yet we esteemed him stricken,
>   smitten by God, and afflicted.
> 5 But he was wounded for our transgressions,
>   he was bruised for our iniquities;
> upon him was the chastisement that made us whole,
>   and with his stripes we are healed (Isaiah 53:4).

Only perfect Jesus was a satisfactory substitution for humankind. "The LORD has laid on him the iniquity of us all" (Isaiah 53:6). He satisfied the debt due to God for human sin. "He makes himself an offering for sin" (Isaiah 53:10). His blood was "poured out for many for the forgiveness of sins" (Matthew 26:28). We dishonor God, as did our parents Adam and Eve, with our sin of disobedience. Jesus makes reconciliation possible between God and us. He was perfectly obedient to God's will to the very end of his life. His obedience mends the rift of our disobedience. This is known as atonement, which refers to our redemption and salvation. "By his knowledge shall the righteous one, my servant, make many to be accounted righteous" (Isaiah 53:11).
Through Jesus, we are saved and we must accept

Jesus as our Savior to be put right with God. If we do, we will live forever in Paradise with God and Jesus.

I did not fabricate the meaning of agape. The teachings about agape that I have highlighted in this work are the result of studying about, praying to and following Jesus. I humble myself under my Teacher and Master Jesus the Christ who is "the only-begotten Son of God, begotten of the Father before all ages, Light of Light, true God of true God, begotten, not made, of one essence with the Father, by whom all things were made" (The Creed). Unlike Jesus, we are not begotten children of God. We are made by God and if we are true to ourselves, we understand that we are made by Jesus the Christ, who is true God of true God. We who have learned from, worship and abide in Christ are made by him. For, "it is no longer I who live, but Christ who lives in me" (Galatians 2:20).

This work is meant to be a painting in words of the means to union with God. This way people can see the big picture, so there is no longer fear - only hope, comfort and peace - about eternity. The 3000 year old thriving Hindu theology of Brahman, Atman and Moksha is the image and Jesus is the way. I have not focused on Jesus's miracles or resurrection to illustrate his unique position as God's only begotten Son who makes eternal life possible. I have focused on his agape, which if embraced and emulated, will unite one with God who is Agape. Implicit in the theology is the Holy Spirit who, too, is Agape.

TREATISE THREE

THE MESSIAH JESUS

JAMES THOMAS ANGELIDIS

Copyright 2016 James Thomas Angelidis.
All rights reserved.
(Edited 2017)

> "Hosanna! Blessed is he who comes in the name of the Lord! Blessed is the kingdom of our father David that is coming! Hosanna in the highest!"
> (Mark 11:9b).

INTRODUCTION

The title Messiah comes from the Hebrew word "mashiach," which means "anointed one." In Jewish tradition, it was used to refer to priests and kings who were anointed with holy oil to consecrate their positions and signify God's blessing. However, in the Jewish theology about the end of days, it has greater significance because it refers to the Messiah who will usher in God's Kingdom. The Greek term for the title Messiah is Christ. Jesus's followers identify Jesus as the Christ. They are known as Christians. In the following treatise, I will display Old Testament passages about the Messiah and God's Kingdom of Heaven and how Jesus makes the prophecies reality. My goal is to strengthen my fellow Christians' faith and show Jews that Jesus is the One.

Some people deny Jesus even existed. But, the indisputable truth that Jesus was not a fictional character is that he had disciples who died for him. Even when tortured, these men never let go. They had a single mind with the same mission to travel the world preaching the good news of Jesus. They were peaceful martyrs and their devotion to Jesus cannot be denied. To those who do not believe in Jesus's disciples, it is because of the hardness of their hearts. One must have to work hard to not believe in them. To reject their conviction, acts, martyrdoms and existences is pure madness.

Jesus was a Jew of the highest level. He knew the Hebrew Scriptures inside and out, from beginning to end. He knew the Hebrew Scriptures so well that he could quote them. Some people may question if what is ascribed to Jesus in the Gospels are his authentic words. The words may or may not be verbatim, but I have no doubt that the words are a reflection of his words. The Gospel of Mark is estimated to be written about 30-35 years after Jesus was crucified, only a generation after Jesus lived. Why is it harder to believe that the words ascribed to Jesus are based on his own words than are words fabricated by the Gospel writers? Said differently, why is it easier to believe that the words are the Gospel writers' words and not based on Jesus's words?

Jewish sage and scholar Hillel the Elder was born about 100 years before Jesus. He is quoted saying, "That which is hateful to you, do not do to your neighbor. That is the whole Torah; the rest is commentary. Go and study it." As an erudite Jew, Jesus knew of Hillel and his teachings. However, Jesus revolutionized Hillel's worldly proverb and made it divine by replacing hate with love. Jesus says, "So whatever you wish that men would do to you, do so to them; for this is the law and the prophets" (Matthew 7:12). Elsewhere, Jesus says, "You shall love your neighbor as yourself" (Matthew 22:39).

Jesus applied Old Testament imagery to his teachings and also used it to illustrate his role as the Messiah. In the Old Testament, Israel is described as God's Vine:

> Psalm 80:8 (RSV)
> Prayer for Israel's Restoration
> To the choirmaster: according to Lilies. A Testimony of Asaph. A Psalm.
> 8 Thou didst bring a vine out of Egypt [when the Jews were slaves];
>   thou didst drive out the nations and plant it.
> 9 Thou didst clear the ground for it;
>   it took deep root and filled the land.
> 10 The mountains were covered with its shade,
>   the mighty cedars with its branches;
> 11 it sent out its branches to the sea,
>   and its shoots to the River.
> 12 Why then hast thou broken down its walls,
>   so that all who pass along the way pluck its fruit?
> 13 The boar from the forest ravages it,
>   and all that move in the field feed on it.

14 Turn again, O God of hosts!
   Look down from heaven, and see;
have regard for this vine,
15   the stock which thy right hand planted.[b]
16 They have burned it with fire, they have cut it down;
   may they perish at the rebuke of thy countenance!
17 But let thy hand be upon the man of thy right hand,
   the son of man whom thou hast made strong for thyself!
18 Then we will never turn back from thee;
   give us life, and we will call on thy name!
19 Restore us, O LORD God of hosts!
   let thy face shine, that we may be saved!

Jesus identifies himself as the above son of man who sits at the right hand of God. He calls himself the True Vine with his faithful as the branches that bear fruit and that God is the Vinedresser:

John 15:1 (RSV)
Jesus the True Vine
15 "I am the true vine, and my Father is the vinedresser. 2 Every branch of mine that bears no fruit, he takes away, and every branch that does bear fruit he prunes, that it may bear more fruit. 3 You are already made clean by

the word which I have spoken to you. 4 Abide in me, and I in you. As the branch cannot bear fruit by itself, unless it abides in the vine, neither can you, unless you abide in me. 5 I am the vine, you are the branches. He who abides in me, and I in him, he it is that bears much fruit, for apart from me you can do nothing. 6 If a man does not abide in me, he is cast forth as a branch and withers; and the branches are gathered, thrown into the fire and burned. 7 If you abide in me, and my words abide in you, ask whatever you will, and it shall be done for you. 8 By this my Father is glorified, that you bear much fruit, and so prove to be my disciples. 9 As the Father has loved me, so have I loved you; abide in my love. 10 If you keep my commandments, you will abide in my love, just as I have kept my Father's commandments and abide in his love. 11 These things I have spoken to you, that my joy may be in you, and that your joy may be full. 12 "This is my commandment, that you love one another as I have loved you.13 Greater love has no man than this, that a man lay down his life for his friends. 14 You are my friends if you do what I command you. 15 No longer do I call you servants,[a] for the servant[b] does not know what his master is doing; but I have called you friends, for all that I have heard from my Father I have made known to you. 16 You did not choose me, but I chose you and appointed you that you should go and bear fruit and that your fruit should abide; so that whatever you ask the Father in my name, he may give it to you. 17 This I command you, to love one another.

Similarly, Jesus was aware of the Old Testament imagery of God as Shepherd who tends to His people, His flock:

Ezekiel 34:1 (RSV)
Israel's False Shepherds
34 The word of the LORD came to me: 2 "Son of man, prophesy against the shepherds of Israel, prophesy, and say to them, even to the shepherds, Thus says the Lord GOD: Ho, shepherds of Israel who have been feeding yourselves! Should not shepherds feed the sheep? 3 You eat the fat, you clothe yourselves with the wool, you slaughter the fatlings; but you do not feed the sheep. 4 The weak you have not strengthened, the sick you have not healed, the crippled you have not bound up, the strayed you have not brought back, the lost you have not sought, and with force and harshness you have ruled them. 5 So they were scattered, because there was no shepherd; and they became food for all the wild beasts. 6 My sheep were scattered, they

wandered over all the mountains and on every high hill; my sheep were scattered over all the face of the earth, with none to search or seek for them.

7 "Therefore, you shepherds, hear the word of the LORD: 8 As I live, says the Lord GOD, because my sheep have become a prey, and my sheep have become food for all the wild beasts, since there was no shepherd; and because my shepherds have not searched for my sheep, but the shepherds have fed themselves, and have not fed my sheep; 9 therefore, you shepherds, hear the word of the LORD: 10 Thus says the Lord GOD, Behold, I am against the shepherds; and I will require my sheep at their hand, and put a stop to their feeding the sheep; no longer shall the shepherds feed themselves. I will rescue my sheep from their mouths, that they may not be food for them.

God, the True Shepherd

11 "For thus says the Lord GOD: Behold, I, I myself will search for my sheep, and will seek them out. 12 As a shepherd seeks out his flock when some of his sheep[a] have been scattered abroad, so will I seek out my sheep; and I will rescue them from all places where they have been scattered on a day of clouds and thick darkness. 13 And I will bring them

out from the peoples, and gather them from the countries, and will bring them into their own land; and I will feed them on the mountains of Israel, by the fountains, and in all the inhabited places of the country. 14 I will feed them with good pasture, and upon the mountain heights of Israel shall be their pasture; there they shall lie down in good grazing land, and on fat pasture they shall feed on the mountains of Israel. 15 I myself will be the shepherd of my sheep, and I will make them lie down, says the Lord GOD. 16 I will seek the lost, and I will bring back the strayed, and I will bind up the crippled, and I will strengthen the weak, and the fat and the strong I will watch over;[b] I will feed them in justice. 17 "As for you, my flock, thus says the Lord GOD: Behold, I judge between sheep and sheep, rams and he-goats. 18 Is it not enough for you to feed on the good pasture, that you must tread down with your feet the rest of your pasture; and to drink of clear water, that you must foul the rest with your feet? 19 And must my sheep eat what you have trodden with your feet, and drink what you have fouled with your feet? 20 "Therefore, thus says the Lord GOD to them: Behold, I, I myself will judge between the fat sheep and the lean sheep. 21 Because you push with side and shoulder, and thrust at all the weak with your horns, till you have scattered them abroad, 22 I will save my flock, they shall no longer be a prey; and I will judge between sheep and sheep. 23 And I will set up over them one shepherd, my servant David, and he shall feed them: he shall feed them and be their shepherd. 24 And I, the LORD, will be their God, and my servant David shall be prince among them; I, the LORD, have spoken. 25 "I will make with them a covenant of peace and banish wild beasts from the land, so that they may dwell securely in the wilderness and sleep in the woods.26 And I will make them and the places round about my hill a blessing; and I will send down the showers in their season; they shall be showers of blessing.27 And the trees of the field shall yield their fruit, and the earth shall yield its increase, and they shall be secure in their land; and they shall know that I am the LORD, when I break the bars of their yoke, and deliver them from the hand of those who enslaved them. 28 They shall no more be a prey to the nations, nor shall the beasts of the land devour them; they shall dwell securely, and none shall make them afraid. 29 And I will provide for them prosperous[c] plantations so that they shall no more be consumed with hunger in the land, and no longer suffer the reproach of the nations. 30

And they shall know that I, the LORD their God, am with them, and that they, the house of Israel, are my people, says the Lord GOD. 31 And you are my sheep, the sheep of my pasture,[d] and I am your God, says the Lord GOD."

As Jesus does with the Old Testament vine imagery, he uses the shepherd imagery to describe himself. He takes the shepherd imagery a step further and declares that he is the Good Shepherd who lays down his life for God's flock:

John 10:1 (RSV)
Jesus the Good Shepherd
10 "Truly, truly, I say to you, he who does not enter the sheepfold by the door but climbs in by another way, that man is a thief and a robber; 2 but he who enters by the door is the shepherd of the sheep. 3 To him the gatekeeper opens; the sheep hear his voice, and he calls his own sheep by name and leads them out. 4 When he has brought out all his own, he goes before them, and the sheep follow him, for they know his voice. 5 A stranger they will not follow, but they will flee from him, for they do not know the voice of strangers." 6 This figure Jesus used with them, but they did not understand what he was saying to them. 7 So Jesus again said to them,

"Truly, truly, I say to you, I am the door of the sheep. 8 All who came before me are thieves and robbers; but the sheep did not heed them. 9 I am the door; if any one enters by me, he will be saved, and will go in and out and find pasture. 10 The thief comes only to steal and kill and destroy; I came that they may have life, and have it abundantly. 11 I am the good shepherd. The good shepherd lays down his life for the sheep. 12 He who is a hireling and not a shepherd, whose own the sheep are not, sees the wolf coming and leaves the sheep and flees; and the wolf snatches them and scatters them. 13 He flees because he is a hireling and cares nothing for the sheep. 14 I am the good shepherd; I know my own and my own know me, 15 as the Father knows me and I know the Father; and I lay down my life for the sheep. 16 And I have other sheep, that are not of this fold; I must bring them also, and they will heed my voice. So there shall be one flock, one shepherd.17 For this reason the Father loves me, because I lay down my life, that I may take it again. 18 No one takes it from me, but I lay it down of my own accord. I have power to lay it down, and I have power to take it again; this charge I have received from my Father."

JESUS

Below are the Old Testament prophecies that specify Jesus as the Messiah.

> Isaiah 7:10 (RSV)
> Isaiah Gives Ahaz the Sign of Immanuel
> 10 Again the LORD spoke to Ahaz, 11 "Ask a sign of the LORD your God; let it be deep as Sheol or high as heaven." 12 But Ahaz said, "I will not ask, and I will not put the LORD to the test." 13 And he said, "Hear then, O house of David! Is it too little for you to weary men, that you weary my God also? 14 Therefore the Lord himself will give you a sign. Behold, a young woman [or virgin] shall conceive and bear[c] a son, and shall call his name Imman'u-el [meaning, God is with us] 15 He shall eat curds and honey when he knows how to refuse the evil and choose the good. 16 For before the child knows how to refuse the evil and choose the good, the land before whose two kings you are in dread will be deserted. 17 The LORD will bring upon you and upon your people and upon your father's house such days as have not come since the day that E'phraim departed from Judah—the king of Assyria."

As we learn in Matthew and Luke, the Virgin Mother Mary gave birth to Jesus, who is God.

> Micah 5:2 (RSV)
> The Ruler from Bethlehem
> 2 [c] But you, O Bethlehem Eph'rathah,
>   who are little to be among the clans of Judah,
> from you shall come forth for me
>   one who is to be ruler in Israel,
> whose origin is from of old,
>   from ancient days.
> 3 Therefore he shall give them up until the time
>   when she who is in travail has brought forth;
> then the rest of his brethren shall return
>   to the people of Israel.
> 4 And he shall stand and feed his flock in the strength of the LORD,
>   in the majesty of the name of the LORD his God.
> And they shall dwell secure, for now he shall be great
>   to the ends of the earth.

As we learn in Matthew, Jesus was born in Bethlehem.

> Isaiah 61:1 (RSV)
> The Good News of Deliverance

61 The Spirit of the Lord GOD is upon me,
   because the LORD has anointed me
to bring good tidings to the afflicted;[a]
   he has sent me to bind up the brokenhearted,
to proclaim liberty to the captives,
   and the opening of the prison[b] to those
who are bound;
2 to proclaim the year of the LORD's favor,
   and the day of vengeance of our God;
   to comfort all who mourn;
3 to grant to those who mourn in Zion—
   to give them a garland instead of ashes,
the oil of gladness instead of mourning,
   the mantle of praise instead of a faint spirit;
that they may be called oaks of righteousness,
   the planting of the LORD, that he may be
glorified.

As we learn in Luke, Jesus recites part of this passage in a Nazarene synagogue on the Sabbath day announcing to the congregation that he is the Messiah.

Zechariah 9:9 (RSV)
The Coming Ruler of God's People
9 Rejoice greatly, O daughter of Zion!
   Shout aloud, O daughter of Jerusalem!
Lo, your king comes to you;
   triumphant and victorious is he,
humble and riding on an ass,

> on a colt the foal of an ass.
> 10 I will cut off the chariot from E′phraim
>   and the war horse from Jerusalem;
> and the battle bow shall be cut off,
>   and he shall command peace to the nations;
> his dominion shall be from sea to sea,
>   and from the River to the ends of the earth.

As we learn in Matthew, during Palm Sunday, Jesus is greeted by the crowds as their king, humble and riding on an ass.

> Isaiah 9:1 (RSV)
> The Righteous Reign of the Coming King
> 9 [a] But there will be no gloom for her that was in anguish. In the former time he brought into contempt the land of Zeb′ulun and the land of Naph′tali, but in the latter time he will make glorious the way of the sea, the land beyond the Jordan, Galilee of the nations.
> 2 [b] The people who walked in darkness
>   have seen a great light;
> those who dwelt in a land of deep darkness,
>   on them has light shined.
> 3 Thou hast multiplied the nation,
>   thou hast increased its joy;
> they rejoice before thee
>   as with joy at the harvest,
>   as men rejoice when they divide the spoil.
> 4 For the yoke of his burden,

and the staff for his shoulder,
the rod of his oppressor,
thou hast broken as on the day of Mid′ian.
5 For every boot of the tramping warrior in battle tumult
and every garment rolled in blood
will be burned as fuel for the fire.
6 For to us a child is born,
to us a son is given;
and the government will be upon his shoulder,
and his name will be called
"Wonderful Counselor, Mighty God,
Everlasting Father, Prince of Peace."
7 Of the increase of his government and of peace
there will be no end,
upon the throne of David, and over his kingdom,
to establish it, and to uphold it
with justice and with righteousness
from this time forth and for evermore.
The zeal of the LORD of hosts will do this.

Jesus is none other than the Wonderful Counselor, Mighty God, Everlasting Father, Prince of Peace.

Psalm 72:1 (RSV)
Prayer for Guidance and Support for the King
A Psalm of Solomon.
72 Give the king thy justice, O God,

and thy righteousness to the royal son!
2 May he judge thy people with righteousness,
  and thy poor with justice!
3 Let the mountains bear prosperity for the people,
  and the hills, in righteousness!
4 May he defend the cause of the poor of the people,
  give deliverance to the needy,
  and crush the oppressor!
5 May he live[a] while the sun endures,
  and as long as the moon, throughout all generations!
6 May he be like rain that falls on the mown grass,
  like showers that water the earth!
7 In his days may righteousness flourish,
  and peace abound, till the moon be no more!
8 May he have dominion from sea to sea,
  and from the River to the ends of the earth!
9 May his foes[b] bow down before him,
  and his enemies lick the dust!
10 May the kings of Tarshish and of the isles
   render him tribute,
may the kings of Sheba and Seba bring gifts!
11 May all kings fall down before him,
   all nations serve him!
12 For he delivers the needy when he calls,
   the poor and him who has no helper.
13 He has pity on the weak and the needy,

and saves the lives of the needy.
14 From oppression and violence he redeems their life;
and precious is their blood in his sight.

Jesus is the Messiah King.

Isaiah 11:1 (RSV)
The Peaceful Kingdom
11 There shall come forth a shoot from the stump of Jesse,
and a branch shall grow out of his roots.
2 And the Spirit of the LORD shall rest upon him,
the spirit of wisdom and understanding,
the spirit of counsel and might,
the spirit of knowledge and the fear of the LORD.
3 And his delight shall be in the fear of the LORD.
He shall not judge by what his eyes see,
or decide by what his ears hear;
4 but with righteousness he shall judge the poor,
and decide with equity for the meek of the earth;
and he shall smite the earth with the rod of his mouth,
and with the breath of his lips he shall slay the wicked.

5 Righteousness shall be the girdle of his waist,
  and faithfulness the girdle of his loins.

Again, Jesus fulfills the role as the Messiah King.

Psalm 22:1 (RSV)
Plea for Deliverance from Suffering and Hostility
To the choirmaster: according to The Hind of the Dawn. A Psalm of David.
22 My God, my God, why hast thou forsaken me?
  Why art thou so far from helping me, from the words of my groaning?
2 O my God, I cry by day, but thou dost not answer;
  and by night, but find no rest.
3 Yet thou art holy,
  enthroned on the praises of Israel.
4 In thee our fathers trusted;
  they trusted, and thou didst deliver them.
5 To thee they cried, and were saved;
  in thee they trusted, and were not disappointed.
6 But I am a worm, and no man;
  scorned by men, and despised by the people.
7 All who see me mock at me,
  they make mouths at me, they wag their heads;

8 "He committed his cause to the LORD; let him deliver him,
>   let him rescue him, for he delights in him!"

9 Yet thou art he who took me from the womb;
>   thou didst keep me safe upon my mother's breasts.

10 Upon thee was I cast from my birth,
>   and since my mother bore me thou hast been my God.

11 Be not far from me,
>   for trouble is near
>   and there is none to help.

12 Many bulls encompass me,
>   strong bulls of Bashan surround me;

13 they open wide their mouths at me,
>   like a ravening and roaring lion.

14 I am poured out like water,
>   and all my bones are out of joint;

my heart is like wax,
>   it is melted within my breast;

15 my strength is dried up like a potsherd,
>   and my tongue cleaves to my jaws;
>   thou dost lay me in the dust of death.

16 Yea, dogs are round about me;
>   a company of evildoers encircle me;
>   they have pierced[a] my hands and feet—

17 I can count all my bones—
>   they stare and gloat over me;

18 they divide my garments among them,

and for my raiment they cast lots.
19 But thou, O LORD, be not far off!
O thou my help, hasten to my aid!
20 Deliver my soul from the sword,
my life[b] from the power of the dog!
21 Save me from the mouth of the lion,
my afflicted soul[c] from the horns of the wild oxen!
22 I will tell of thy name to my brethren;
in the midst of the congregation I will praise thee:
23 You who fear the LORD, praise him!
all you sons of Jacob, glorify him,
and stand in awe of him, all you sons of Israel!
24 For he has not despised or abhorred
the affliction of the afflicted;
and he has not hid his face from him,
but has heard, when he cried to him.
25 From thee comes my praise in the great congregation;
my vows I will pay before those who fear him.
26 The afflicted[d] shall eat and be satisfied;
those who seek him shall praise the LORD!
May your hearts live for ever!
27 All the ends of the earth shall remember
and turn to the LORD;
and all the families of the nations
shall worship before him.[e]

28 For dominion belongs to the LORD,
   and he rules over the nations.
29 Yea, to him[f] shall all the proud of the earth bow down;
   before him shall bow all who go down to the dust,
   and he who cannot keep himself alive.
30 Posterity shall serve him;
   men shall tell of the Lord to the coming generation,
31 and proclaim his deliverance to a people yet unborn,
   that he has wrought it.

As we learn in Matthew, Jesus quotes part of this Psalm when he is dying on the Cross.

GOD'S SERVANT

The Jewish nation sees itself as God's Chosen Servant. During moments of ecstasy and affliction it is obedient to God's will. It never questions God's plan and accepts its fate. On the Cross, Jesus represents the nobility and affliction of the Jewish nation. He becomes God's Chosen Servant. He is the perfect Jew and represents everything a Jew should be. Below are two passages from Isaiah that talk about God's Chosen Servant. In them, the Jewish nation sees itself and Christians see Jesus.

Isaiah 42:1 (RSV)
The Servant, a Light to the Nations
42 Behold my servant, whom I uphold,
   my chosen, in whom my soul delights;
I have put my Spirit upon him,
   he will bring forth justice to the nations.
2 He will not cry or lift up his voice,
   or make it heard in the street;
3 a bruised reed he will not break,
   and a dimly burning wick he will not quench;
   he will faithfully bring forth justice.
4 He will not fail[a] or be discouraged[b]
   till he has established justice in the earth;
   and the coastlands wait for his law.

Isaiah 52:13-53:12 (RSV)
The Suffering Servant
13 Behold, my servant shall prosper,
   he shall be exalted and lifted up,
   and shall be very high.
14 As many were astonished at him[b]—
   his appearance was so marred, beyond human semblance,
   and his form beyond that of the sons of men—
15 so shall he startle[c] many nations;
   kings shall shut their mouths because of him;

for that which has not been told them they shall see,
   and that which they have not heard they shall understand.

53 Who has believed what we have heard?
   And to whom has the arm of the LORD been revealed?
2 For he grew up before him like a young plant,
   and like a root out of dry ground;
he had no form or comeliness that we should look at him,
   and no beauty that we should desire him.
3 He was despised and rejected[d] by men;
   a man of sorrows,[e] and acquainted with grief;[f]
and as one from whom men hide their faces
   he was despised, and we esteemed him not.
4 Surely he has borne our griefs[g]
   and carried our sorrows;[h]
yet we esteemed him stricken,
   smitten by God, and afflicted.
5 But he was wounded for our transgressions,
   he was bruised for our iniquities;
upon him was the chastisement that made us whole,
   and with his stripes we are healed.
6 All we like sheep have gone astray;
   we have turned every one to his own way;

and the LORD has laid on him
   the iniquity of us all.
7 He was oppressed, and he was afflicted,
   yet he opened not his mouth;
like a lamb that is led to the slaughter,
   and like a sheep that before its shearers is dumb,
   so he opened not his mouth.
8 By oppression and judgment he was taken away;
   and as for his generation, who considered
that he was cut off out of the land of the living,
   stricken for the transgression of my people?
9 And they made his grave with the wicked
   and with a rich man in his death,
although he had done no violence,
   and there was no deceit in his mouth.
10 Yet it was the will of the LORD to bruise him;
   he has put him to grief;[i]
when he makes himself[j] an offering for sin,
   he shall see his offspring, he shall prolong his days;
the will of the LORD shall prosper in his hand;
11   he shall see the fruit of the travail of his soul and be satisfied;
by his knowledge shall the righteous one, my servant,
   make many to be accounted righteous;

and he shall bear their iniquities.
12 Therefore I will divide him a portion with the great,
and he shall divide the spoil with the strong; because he poured out his soul to death,
and was numbered with the transgressors; yet he bore the sin of many,
and made intercession for the transgressors.

As the Messiah, Jesus is the embodiment of Israel. He is Israel personified. He is the culmination of Israel, its fulfillment and everything it was meant to be.

A NEW COVENANT OF THE HEART

Jeremiah 31:31 (RSV)
A New Covenant
31 "Behold, the days are coming, says the LORD, when I will make a new covenant with the house of Israel and the house of Judah, 32 not like the covenant which I made with their fathers when I took them by the hand to bring them out of the land of Egypt, my covenant which they broke, though I was their husband, says the LORD. 33 But this is the covenant which I will make with the house of Israel after those days, says the LORD: I will put my law within them, and I will write it upon their

hearts; and I will be their God, and they shall be my people. 34 And no longer shall each man teach his neighbor and each his brother, saying, 'Know the LORD,' for they shall all know me, from the least of them to the greatest, says the LORD; for I will forgive their iniquity, and I will remember their sin no more."

Jesus gave us this new covenant written upon our hearts. He fulfilled this promise and taught us with his words and showed us with his death the meaning of love. The two great commandments are to "love the Lord your God with all your heart, and with all your soul, and with all your mind" and to "love your neighbor as yourself. On these two commandments depend all the law and the prophets" (Matthew 22.36) and they cannot be practiced unless they are written upon one's heart.

JESUS'S RESURRECTION

After Jesus's crucifixion and death, Jesus's body was laid in a new rock tomb secured by a great stone. On the third day, when the women visited the tomb, they did not find his body. Then, he appeared to them and his disciples breathing, speaking, walking and even eating in flesh and bones. His resurrection was prophesied in the Old Testament. So, too, was his role as our Savior from Death.

> In Psalm 16:8 (RSV), King David prophesied,
> 8 I keep the Lord always before me;
>   because he is at my right hand, I shall not be moved.
> 9 Therefore my heart is glad, and my soul rejoices;
>   my body also dwells secure.
> 10 For thou dost not give me up to Sheol,
>   or let thy godly one see the Pit.
> 11 Thou dost show me the path of life;
>   in thy presence there is fulness of joy,
>   in thy right hand are pleasures for evermore.
>
> In Job 19:25 (RSV), Job declares,
> 25 For I know that my Redeemer[b] lives,
>   and at last he will stand upon the earth;[c]
> 26 and after my skin has been thus destroyed,
>   then from[d] my flesh I shall see God,[e]
> 27 whom I shall see on my side,[f]
>   and my eyes shall behold, and not another.

In the television news documentary The Search for Jesus (2000), Peter Jennings reports his findings on Jesus, including the historical integrity of Jesus's Resurrection.

Meyer: "One of the things I believe that early Christians did is they took the model of the mystery religions, they took that story and retold that story as the story of Jesus."

Jennings: "But the mystery religions and their gods lost all credibility centuries ago. Not so with the resurrection of Jesus. His followers stuck to their story even though they were persecuted. And, as we know the Jesus movement grew and flourished. Which is why some eminent scholars believe there was indeed a resurrection."

Wright: "I simply cannot explain why Christianity began without it. I have already said, there were many other messianic or would be messianic movements around in the first century. Routinely, they ended with the violent death of the founder. After that, what happens? The followers either all get killed, as well, or if they are any of them left, they have a choice: they either quite the revolution or they find themselves another messiah. We have example of people doing both. If Jesus had died and stayed dead, they would either have given up the movement or they would have found another messiah. Something extraordinary happened which convinced them that Jesus was the Messiah."

Jennings: "And, over 300 hundred years after Jesus's execution, Christianity was the official religion of the Roman Empire. 2000 years later, Christians from all over the world venerate the place in Jerusalem where it is said Jesus rose from his tomb."

Fredriksen: "I know in their own terms what they saw was the raised Jesus. That's what they say and that all the historic evidence we have afterwards attests to their conviction that that's what they saw. I'm not saying that they really did see the raised Jesus. I wasn't there. I don't know what they saw, but I do know, as a historian, that they must have seen something."

Jennings: "And, even the most skeptical of scholars and historians agree on this: In his brief life, Jesus of Nazareth probably met and spoke with no more than a few thousand people. He wrote nothing. He commanded no great army. And, he spent most of his time with the poor and the outcast. But, he had a vision for a just world, which was so vivid and which moved him so powerfully that he was willing to die for it. And, after his death, his vision somehow transformed the world. Miraculous."

- Peter Jennings, Anchor of ABC's World News Tonight.
- Marvin Meyer, Author "Magic and Ritual in the Ancient World."
- Reverend N.T. Wright, Canon Theologian of Westminster Abbey.
- Paula Fredriksen, Boston University.

MESSIANIC WINE IN GOD'S KINGDOM OF HEAVEN

If Jesus can rise from the dead, he can also perform signs revealing his divinity. If he can resurrect from the dead, he can transform the natural rhythm of the cosmos. Through the Messiah's blood, the natural rhythm of the cosmos no longer behaves like water and takes on qualities of wine. Jesus performed many signs revealing his divinity that are irrational, but they all point to the glory of God. They are not imaginary. They are as real as God's Kingdom of Heaven. Below are the Old Testament passages that describe God's Kingdom of Heaven, which at the moment on this earth takes on qualities of wine.

Isaiah 55:1 (RSV)
An Invitation to Abundant Life

55 "Ho, every one who thirsts,
   come to the waters;
and he who has no money,
   come, buy and eat!
Come, buy wine and milk
   without money and without price.
2 Why do you spend your money for that which is not bread,
   and your labor for that which does not satisfy?
Hearken diligently to me, and eat what is good,
   and delight yourselves in fatness.
3 Incline your ear, and come to me;
   hear, that your soul may live;
and I will make with you an everlasting covenant,
   my steadfast, sure love for David.
4 Behold, I made him a witness to the peoples,
   a leader and commander for the peoples.
5 Behold, you shall call nations that you know not,
   and nations that knew you not shall run to you,
because of the LORD your God, and of the Holy One of Israel,
   for he has glorified you.
6 "Seek the LORD while he may be found,
   call upon him while he is near;
7 let the wicked forsake his way,

and the unrighteous man his thoughts;
let him return to the LORD, that he may have mercy on him,
and to our God, for he will abundantly pardon.

8 For my thoughts are not your thoughts,
neither are your ways my ways, says the LORD.

9 For as the heavens are higher than the earth,
so are my ways higher than your ways
and my thoughts than your thoughts.

10 "For as the rain and the snow come down from heaven,
and return not thither but water the earth, making it bring forth and sprout,
giving seed to the sower and bread to the eater,

11 so shall my word be that goes forth from my mouth;
it shall not return to me empty,
but it shall accomplish that which I purpose,
and prosper in the thing for which I sent it.

12 "For you shall go out in joy,
and be led forth in peace;
the mountains and the hills before you
shall break forth into singing,
and all the trees of the field shall clap their hands.

13 Instead of the thorn shall come up the cypress;

instead of the brier shall come up the myrtle;
and it shall be to the LORD for a memorial,
for an everlasting sign which shall not be cut off."

Jeremiah 31:7 (RSV)
The Joyful Return of the Exiles
7 For thus says the LORD:
"Sing aloud with gladness for Jacob,
and raise shouts for the chief of the nations;
proclaim, give praise, and say,
'The LORD has saved his people,
the remnant of Israel.'
8 Behold, I will bring them from the north country,
and gather them from the farthest parts of the earth,
among them the blind and the lame,
the woman with child and her who is in travail, together;
a great company, they shall return here.
9 With weeping they shall come,
and with consolations[e] I will lead them back,
I will make them walk by brooks of water,
in a straight path in which they shall not stumble;
for I am a father to Israel,
and E′phraim is my first-born.
10 "Hear the word of the LORD, O nations,

and declare it in the coastlands afar off;
say, 'He who scattered Israel will gather him,
 and will keep him as a shepherd keeps his flock.'
11 For the LORD has ransomed Jacob,
 and has redeemed him from hands too strong for him.
12 They shall come and sing aloud on the height of Zion,
 and they shall be radiant over the goodness of the LORD,
over the grain, the wine, and the oil,
 and over the young of the flock and the herd;
their life shall be like a watered garden,
 and they shall languish no more.
13 Then shall the maidens rejoice in the dance,
 and the young men and the old shall be merry.
I will turn their mourning into joy,
 I will comfort them, and give them gladness for sorrow.
14 I will feast the soul of the priests with abundance,
 and my people shall be satisfied with my goodness,
        says the LORD."

Micah 4:1 (RSV)

Peace and Security through Obedience
4 It shall come to pass in the latter days
   that the mountain of the house of the LORD
shall be established as the highest of the mountains,
   and shall be raised up above the hills;
and peoples shall flow to it,
2   and many nations shall come, and say:
"Come, let us go up to the mountain of the LORD,
   to the house of the God of Jacob;
that he may teach us his ways
   and we may walk in his paths."
For out of Zion shall go forth the law,
   and the word of the LORD from Jerusalem.
3 He shall judge between many peoples,
   and shall decide for strong nations afar off;
and they shall beat their swords into plowshares,
   and their spears into pruning hooks;
nation shall not lift up sword against nation,
   neither shall they learn war any more;
4 but they shall sit every man under his vine and under his fig tree,
   and none shall make them afraid;
   for the mouth of the LORD of hosts has spoken.
5 For all the peoples walk
   each in the name of its god,

but we will walk in the name of the LORD our God
> for ever and ever.

Micah 4:6 (RSV)
Restoration Promised after Exile
6 In that day, says the LORD,
> I will assemble the lame
and gather those who have been driven away,
> and those whom I have afflicted;
7 and the lame I will make the remnant;
> and those who were cast off, a strong nation;
and the LORD will reign over them in Mount Zion
> from this time forth and for evermore.
8 And you, O tower of the flock,
> hill of the daughter of Zion,
to you shall it come,
> the former dominion shall come,
> the kingdom of the daughter of Jerusalem.
9 Now why do you cry aloud?
> Is there no king in you?
Has your counselor perished,
> that pangs have seized you like a woman in travail?
10 Writhe and groan,[a] O daughter of Zion,
> like a woman in travail;
for now you shall go forth from the city
> and dwell in the open country;
> you shall go to Babylon.

There you shall be rescued,
>   there the LORD will redeem you
>   from the hand of your enemies.
11 Now many nations
>   are assembled against you,
saying, "Let her be profaned,
>   and let our eyes gaze upon Zion."
12 But they do not know
>   the thoughts of the LORD,
they do not understand his plan,
>   that he has gathered them as sheaves to the threshing floor.
13 Arise and thresh,
>   O daughter of Zion,
for I will make your horn iron
>   and your hoofs bronze;
you shall beat in pieces many peoples,
>   and shall[b] devote their gain to the LORD,
>   their wealth to the Lord of the whole earth.

Isaiah 25:6 (RSV)
Praise for Deliverance from Oppression
6 On this mountain the LORD of hosts will make for all peoples a feast of fat things, a feast of wine on the lees, of fat things full of marrow, of wine on the lees well refined. 7 And he will destroy on this mountain the covering that is cast over all peoples, the veil that is spread over all nations. 8 He will swallow up death for ever, and the Lord GOD

will wipe away tears from all faces, and the reproach of his people he will take away from all the earth; for the LORD has spoken. 9 It will be said on that day, "Lo, this is our God; we have waited for him, that he might save us. This is the LORD; we have waited for him; let us be glad and rejoice in his salvation."

Amos 9:11 (RSV)
The Restoration of David's Kingdom
11 "In that day I will raise up
   the booth of David that is fallen
and repair its breaches,
   and raise up its ruins,
   and rebuild it as in the days of old;
12 that they may possess the remnant of Edom
   and all the nations who are called by my name,"
   says the LORD who does this.
13 "Behold, the days are coming," says the LORD,
   "when the plowman shall overtake the reaper
   and the treader of grapes him who sows the seed;
the mountains shall drip sweet wine,
   and all the hills shall flow with it.
14 I will restore the fortunes of my people Israel,

> and they shall rebuild the ruined cities and inhabit them;
> they shall plant vineyards and drink their wine,
>> and they shall make gardens and eat their fruit.
> 15 I will plant them upon their land,
>> and they shall never again be plucked up
>> out of the land which I have given them,"
>>> says the LORD your God.

Joel 3:17 (RSV)
The Glorious Future of Judah
17 "So you shall know that I am the LORD your God,
> who dwell in Zion, my holy mountain.
And Jerusalem shall be holy
> and strangers shall never again pass through it.
18 "And in that day
the mountains shall drip sweet wine,
> and the hills shall flow with milk,
and all the stream beds of Judah
> shall flow with water;
and a fountain shall come forth from the house of the LORD
> and water the valley of Shittim.
19 "Egypt shall become a desolation
> and Edom a desolate wilderness,
for the violence done to the people of Judah,

>   because they have shed innocent blood in
> their land.
> 20 But Judah shall be inhabited for ever,
>   and Jerusalem to all generations.
> 21 I will avenge their blood, and I will not
> clear the guilty,[c]
>   for the LORD dwells in Zion."

God's Kingdom of Heaven has begun. It is here. It is among us, but it is reserved for those who are faithful and devoted to Jesus, for those who live by his two great commandments to "love the Lord your God with all your heart, and with all your soul, and with all your mind" and to "love your neighbor as yourself. On these two commandments depend all the law and the prophets" (Matthew 22:36).

JESUS'S SECOND COMING

If we recognize Jesus as the Messiah and follow and emulate him, we will be saved from death and enter God's Kingdom of Heaven and be rewarded with Resurrection. If we do not, death is our end. At Jesus's Second Coming, he will be the Righteous Judge and the living must be able to recognize him, so, like those in God's Kingdom of Heaven, their souls and bodies will not perish. Jesus's physical appearance will not indicate his status; rather, we will know him by his speech, actions and soul. This is only possible if we read the New Testament. Below are the Old Testament passages that describe Jesus's Second Coming.

>Zephaniah 2:1 (RSV)
>Judgment on Israel's Enemies
>2 Come together and hold assembly,
>O shameless nation,
>2 before you are driven away
>   like the drifting chaff,[a]
>before there comes upon you
>   the fierce anger of the LORD,
>before there comes upon you
>   the day of the wrath of the LORD.
>3 Seek the LORD, all you humble of the land,
>   who do his commands;
>seek righteousness, seek humility;
>   perhaps you may be hidden
>   on the day of the wrath of the LORD.
>
>Isaiah 27:1 (RSV)
>Israel's Redemption
>27 In that day the LORD with his hard and great and strong sword will punish Levi′athan the fleeing serpent, Levi′athan the twisting serpent, and he will slay the dragon that is in the sea.
>2 In that day:
>"A pleasant vineyard, sing of it!
>3   I, the LORD, am its keeper;

every moment I water it.
Lest any one harm it,
   I guard it night and day;
4   I have no wrath.
Would that I had thorns and briers to battle!
   I would set out against them,
   I would burn them up together.
5 Or let them lay hold of my protection,
   let them make peace with me,
   let them make peace with me."
6 In days to come[a] Jacob shall take root,
   Israel shall blossom and put forth shoots,
   and fill the whole world with fruit.
7 Has he smitten them as he smote those who smote them?

   Or have they been slain as their slayers were slain?

8 Measure by measure,[b] by exile thou didst contend with them;

Psalm 110:1 (RSV)
Assurance of Victory for God's Priest-King
A Psalm of David.
110 The LORD says to my lord:
"Sit at my right hand,
till I make your enemies your footstool."
2 The LORD sends forth from Zion
   your mighty scepter.
   Rule in the midst of your foes!
3 Your people will offer themselves freely

> on the day you lead your host
> upon the holy mountains.[a]
> From the womb of the morning
> like dew your youth[b] will come to you.
> 4 The LORD has sworn
> and will not change his mind,
> "You are a priest for ever
> after the order of Melchiz′edek."
> 5 The Lord is at your right hand;
> he will shatter kings on the day of his wrath.
> 6 He will execute judgment among the nations,
> filling them with corpses;
> he will shatter chiefs[c]
> over the wide earth.
> 7 He will drink from the brook by the way;
> therefore he will lift up his head.

OUR RESURRECTION

Our Resurrection is illustrated in the below Old Testament passages. The Resurrection is not the product of imagination; rather, it is made possible through our love for God and Jesus.

> Ezekiel 37:1 (RSV)
> The Valley of Dry Bones
> 37 The hand of the LORD was upon me, and he brought me out by the Spirit of the LORD,

and set me down in the midst of the valley;[a] it was full of bones. 2 And he led me round among them; and behold, there were very many upon the valley;[b] and lo, they were very dry. 3 And he said to me, "Son of man, can these bones live?" And I answered, "O Lord GOD, thou knowest." 4 Again he said to me, "Prophesy to these bones, and say to them, O dry bones, hear the word of the LORD. 5 Thus says the Lord GOD to these bones: Behold, I will cause breath[c] to enter you, and you shall live. 6 And I will lay sinews upon you, and will cause flesh to come upon you, and cover you with skin, and put breath[d] in you, and you shall live; and you shall know that I am the LORD." 7 So I prophesied as I was commanded; and as I prophesied, there was a noise, and behold, a rattling; and the bones came together, bone to its bone. 8 And as I looked, there were sinews on them, and flesh had come upon them, and skin had covered them; but there was no breath in them. 9 Then he said to me, "Prophesy to the breath, prophesy, son of man, and say to the breath,[e] Thus says the Lord GOD: Come from the four winds, O breath,[f] and breathe upon these slain, that they may live." 10 So I prophesied as he commanded me, and the breath came into them, and they lived, and stood upon their feet, an exceedingly great host. 11 Then he said to me, "Son of man, these bones are the whole house of Israel. Behold, they say, 'Our bones are dried up, and our hope is lost; we are clean cut off.' 12 Therefore prophesy, and say to them, Thus says the Lord GOD: Behold, I will open your graves, and raise you from your graves, O my people; and I will bring you home into the land of Israel. 13 And you shall know that I am the LORD, when I open your graves, and raise you from your graves, O my people. 14 And I will put my Spirit within you, and you shall live, and I will place you in your own land; then you shall know that I, the LORD, have spoken, and I have done it, says the LORD."

Hosea 13:14 (RSV)
14 Shall I ransom them from the power of Sheol?
　Shall I redeem them from Death?
O Death, where[a] are your plagues?
　O Sheol, where[b] is your destruction?
　Compassion is hid from my eyes.

Here, our Lord taunts Death revealing His will for our Resurrection.

Isaiah 26:19 (RSV)
Judah's Song of Victory

19 Thy dead shall live, their bodies[c] shall rise.

   O dwellers in the dust, awake and sing for joy!
For thy dew is a dew of light,
   and on the land of the shades thou wilt let it fall.

Daniel 12:1 (RSV)
The Resurrection of the Dead
12 "At that time shall arise Michael, the great prince who has charge of your people. And there shall be a time of trouble, such as never has been since there was a nation till that time; but at that time your people shall be delivered, every one whose name shall be found written in the book. 2 And many of those who sleep in the dust of the earth shall awake, some to everlasting life, and some to shame and everlasting contempt. 3 And those who are wise shall shine like the brightness of the firmament; and those who turn many to righteousness, like the stars for ever and ever. 4 But you, Daniel, shut up the words, and seal the book, until the time of the end. Many shall run to and fro, and knowledge shall increase."

"every scribe who has been trained for the kingdom of heaven is like a householder who brings out of his treasure what is new and what is old."
- Jesus Christ (Matthew 13.52)

THE SUPREME TRANSFORMATION - WATER INTO WINE

In the following treatise, I examine Christ's first miracle - transforming water into wine, which took place at a wedding in Cana in Galilee. This sign foreshadowed and illustrated his transformation of the natural rhythm of the cosmos. Ancient Chinese sages used the term Tao to refer to the natural rhythm of the cosmos and they observed that it behaved like water. The Tao's lofty esoteric principles were followed by few. But, there was tribulation in the world and Christ came into the world to save all people, not just the few. He transformed the Tao into what resembles wine to save lowly mankind from its sins. I believe if we can better understand the Tao, we will be able to better see the magnitude, magnificence and majesty of Christ. In writing this treatise, I hope to help my fellow Christians better understand our Lord through knowledge of the Tao and to help non-Christians, through the Spirit of Truth, begin to believe that Christ is the Son of the Most High God.

AGAPE INTO ETERNITY

The following treatise is meant to be a painting in words of the means to union with God. This way people can see the big picture, so there is no longer fear - only hope, comfort and peace - about eternity. The 3000 year old thriving Hindu theology of Brahman, Atman and Moksha is the image and Jesus is the way. I have not focused on Jesus's miracles or resurrection to illustrate his unique position as God's only begotten Son who makes eternal life possible. I have focused on his agape, which if embraced and emulated, will unite one with God who is Agape. Implicit in the theology is the Holy Spirit who, too, is Agape.

THE MESSIAH JESUS

The title Messiah comes for the Hebrew word "mashiach," which means "anointed one." In Jewish tradition, it was used to refer to priests and kings who were anointed with holy oil to consecrate their positions and signify God's blessing. However, in the Jewish theology about the end of days, it has greater significance because it refers to the Messiah who will usher in God's Kingdom. The Greek term for the title Messiah is Christ. Jesus's followers identify Jesus as the Christ. They are known as Christians. In the following treatise, I display Old Testament passages about the Messiah and God's Kingdom of Heaven and how Jesus makes the prophecies reality. My goal is to strengthen my fellow Christians' faith and show Jews that Jesus is the One.

LETTERS

God's Supreme Love

What is the supreme love?
There are many ways to love,
but there is only one supreme love.
It is this...
that God - the Infinite, Almighty and Everlasting -
becomes man to die for us.
He humbles and condescends Himself
as one of us, a finite human being,
in the person of Jesus of Nazareth born of Mary.
This alone is sublime
that Great God would choose to make Himself little -
an event we celebrate on Christmas.
But, then, in still deeper sublimity,
the Creator, who created us and all things,
decides, in His Most High Wisdom,
to sacrifice Himself for His creation.
He briefly enters the world
with the sole purpose of dying for us
to die in incomprehensible suffering
to be tortured on
and nailed to
a wood cross,
so we could have life
to atone for our sins
to retain justice for righteousness in His universe
for us to choose and receive Him or not
to save us from our ends

so we can join Him in Eternity.
God's selfless self-sacrificial death
is agape love.
No one loves us more than God.
It is an event we Christians worship on Great Friday.
This single, pivotal, supreme love
transformed our cosmos, our universe.
His parables are truth.
His prophecies have come to fruition.
Many have reaped the fruits of His love
without giving Him His due credit
when they should and must
for their own Salvation.
Our Easter.
How do we repay God
for this Divine act of Grace
that we do not merit
and are unworthy of?
How can we thank Him?
It is impossible.
But we must try.

- James Thomas Angelidis (2017)

God's Mother - The Theotokos

Who is the Theotokos
and what is her power?
God had a mother
and we call her the Theotokos.
She gave birth to Him,
raised, nurtured and loved Him.
She lives in all women
in this living world
because all women are compelled
to nurture and raise our children
to be living Christs.
Regardless of race, nationality or creed,
all women want to raise men -
strong and real men.
And, there was only one true and perfect man -
Jesus, who is
"Wonderful Counselor, Mighty God,
Everlasting Father, Prince of Peace" (Isaiah 9:6)
born of Mary, who is
Theotokos.
No other man comes close,
but the women try.
They never stop,
constantly working,
trying to help their men
and raise the children.
And, they do it together, selflessly,

looking out for each other
for a better world.
They are one.
The Theotokos lives in them.
They are our mothers
and God's handmaids.
No man would dare lust after
God's Mother.
And, so, no man should lust after
her heirs and inheritors.
Keep the Theotokos in mind and near to you
and with her light
you can wipe out
lust's corrosive and corruptive power
and be what you are meant to be
which is a child of God.
Push out, overcome, destroy and replace lust
with agape for God and His Mother.

- James Thomas Angelidis (2017)

O, Saint Augustine

O, Saint Augustine, my dearest friend.
You opened my eyes and taught me about
the heavenly City of God,
which is in this present world
commingled and entangled with
the earthly City of Man.
In the Holy City, God's angels serve with love
for the Almighty,
even with contempt for self.
For the sacrifice acceptable to God is a broken spirit,
a broken and contrite heart.
The Founder of the City of God
has inspired me with a love
which has made me covet its citizenship.
Though I am unworthy,
I serve the Almighty.
With the City begins the Kingdom,
where God's will is done - on earth as is in heaven -
where the Great King reigns supreme unmatched
with love, grace and truth.
I look forward to the Perpetual Sabbath
when we praise God and His Christ
at all times forever.
Amen.

- James Thomas Angelidis (2016)
- *The City of God…* Book 11, Chapter 1/ Book 14,

Chapter 28/ Book 22, Chapter 30.
- Psalm 51:17

The Act of Creating

Creating is one of humankind's most divine acts.
God created and we instinctively follow His example.
It sets us apart from animals
and makes us like Him.
Some people create families, businesses, buildings,
armies, art.
I created literature
and very little has brought me greater joy
and fulfillment.
For me it is a natural high like nothing else.
The power of artistic muse
is as euphoric as eros
and, like when in love,
the artist does not know where it is going to lead.
The process of creation
began with inspiration
aroused in me exaltation
with the goal of education
and edification.
It is unbridled imagination
stimulated by reflection
and is an exploration
for original work.
Writing is sculpting, molding, painting, illustrating
and composing.
It is searching for and finding words,
structuring sentence and

fashioning paragraphs.
It is a discipline and craft.
Some people's dreams are bigger than those of others.
Constantine created an empire that lasted
for over 1000 years.
I put words, ideas and theology on paper
to lead people to God.
Some may say it was done in vain,
as the Preacher said,
"Vanity of vanities! All is vanity."
But, it was my natural inclination from many years
of reading and learning,
to share what saved me.
We human beings are compelled and driven to create,
like God.
It is the divine part of us manifest.
And, that which we create in life
defines us in the end.

- James Thomas Angelidis (2017)

For Little Leiby

Little Leiby,
my little friend.
It was summer
and you finished a full day at day camp.
On your way home,
the unthinkable happened.
You were stolen from us,
killed by another,
by a monster in flesh and will.
You were tortured, desecrated, abominated,
dismembered.
A sacrilegious death,
in the temple of your soul,
like the Lord.
We mourn you, dear Leiby.
We mourn for your parents.
Your father's words -
humble, true and strong -
bring me to tears.
He spoke so well…

"Had my dear son Leiby lived he would have contributed so much good to the world. He was such a sensitive and kind soul. Now that his beautiful life was cut so short we should not allow the world to miss out. Our family wishes to establish the LEIBY KLETZKY MEMORIAL FUND to perpetuate the memory of our dear Leiby and to keep him alive in our hearts and minds. This fund would help anguished families in crisis and need, something that Leiby would have wanted to do had he been given more years of life."

In one day the memorial fund's website raised $61,581 (2 years income for the average man) from 1,365 supporters.

May your memory be eternal,
little Leiby,
my little friend.

- James Thomas Angelidis (2017)

The Child's Soul

No one chooses to be born.
A child enters the world
not knowing what is going on.
But, it is up to those who have come before the child
to make the world beautiful for him or her
and to save the child from the hell that exists.
Children are the innocent,
but they will grow and become the guilty
if we do not teach them about the good.
No one knows when his or her end will arrive,
but it will.
And we have to do as much good as possible
with our limited time.
Do it for yourself.
Do it for the children.
They are the most important people in the world.
They come first
because they are the most pure and vulnerable.
Then the women
because they are most attuned to the children's needs.
Men come last,
but the men who help the women
who help the children
are next in line.

Children are the product of their parents
and the children's salvation begins

and is largely dependent on their parents.
Baptism into the Christian faith is the best beginning.
Outside of this is dangerous.
The world is a dark place
and is lost without Jesus and his teachings.
The children are the inheritors
of what their parents pass on to them.
Even if you were born a
Jew or Gentile,
Hindu, Taoist, Buddhist or Muslim,
Atheist or Agnostic,
give the children a chance to be saved
and teach them about God
and His Son Jesus the Christ
before time passes and it's too late.
They deserve it.
You owe it to them for bringing them into the world.
Your children's souls' destinies
could be contingent on it.
How is a child to learn about Jesus
if we do not teach him or her?
Otherwise, we contribute to their ignorance
and possible demise.
Introduce Scripture to the children.
It is the Word of God.
Go to church on Sunday.
It is the house of God.
Both are important.
Going to church is as important
as going to school and work.

The Orthodox Church
is the most direct means to Salvation.
I know because the prayers of its saints saved me.
However, there is also truth
in the other Christian denominations.
They have value, too.
They know about Jesus, as well.

Teach your children about God and Jesus
before they become lost,
lingering with despair
in the shadow of death.
After the opportunity for baptism,
the next crucial phase is the age of choosing
when they take on full responsibility
for their own actions
and they are no longer the innocent.
If they fail to choose Jesus Christ
they will inherit the sins of their forebearers
and the sins of Adam and Eve remain.

For those lingering now
who question the goodness of Salvation:
I have lived an active life
and found that it is more fun to do good
than to do bad.
Striving for purity is a challenge
with inexpressible rewards.
Everyday try to be better than the day before.
The fruits of good deeds are sweeter

than any and every sin.
Sin is fleeting and ultimately unfulfilling.
I know it and deep inside, you know it, too.
Take on the challenge to do good
and you will attain immortality
in God's Supreme Love.

- James Thomas Angelidis (2017)

DRAWINGS

Budding, 2002

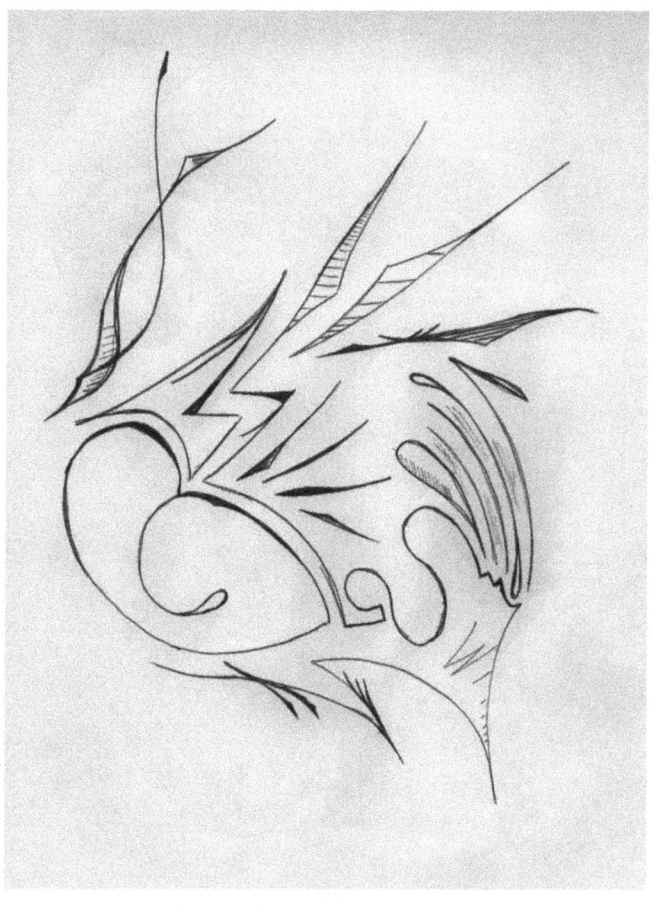

A Maddening Birth, 2002

In the Eye of the Storm, 2003

Anno Domini, 2016

The Good Shepherd King, 2016

PHOTOGRAPHS

Author Photo by
Eddie Manso

First Book Signing, 2015, Photo by
Eddie Manso

EVALUATIONS

[*In the Name of Salvation*]

IN THE SPIRIT OF TRUTH: IDENTIFYING MY THREE THEOLOGICAL TREATISES IN CHURCH TRADITION

JAMES THOMAS ANGELIDIS

First published on www.jtangelidis.com.
Original Copyright 2017 James Thomas Angelidis.
All rights reserved.
(Edited 5-26-2019)

    I see myself in Jesus Christ's words when he said, "every scribe who has been trained for the kingdom of heaven is like a householder who brings out of his treasure what is new and what is old" (Matthew 13:52). The Lord's cited saying is not a riddle to be wrestled with or parable to be pondered; rather, it is a metaphor that reveals a truth about theological treasures, a metaphor that elucidates, a metaphor that is as clear as water ready for drinking.
    I cherish the Church Fathers and Patristic literature and not only learned theology from them but have imitated their writing style and goals with

my three theological treatises in the positive apologetics manner. Apologetics writing is a defense:

> Typically these consisted of what are called negative apologetics, wherein a writer takes up a series of challenges to Christian belief, and shows them to lack the power that their proponents think they have.
> We also sometimes see positive apologetics, an argument that attempts to provide its audience with some fresh positive reasons for belief, intended to convince others who are not yet convinced of the truth of the Christian faith (Mathewes, *The Great Courses, The City of God, Guidebook*, 87).

My book - *In the Name of Salvation: Three Theological Treatises* - is a positive apologetics work.

Saint Augustine of Hippo is my dearest friend and his *The City of God* is the second most important book I have ever read - preceded only by the Holy Bible. Augustine showed us with his words the earthly City of Man and the heavenly City of God like no one else before. It was not dictated to him by anyone before him. His work is unprecedented. He observed it, dug deep into Scripture and revealed to us eternal latent truths. Like no one before, he illuminated to everyone after him the nature of the cosmos with his Scriptural insights. Truly, he brought out of his treasure what is new and what is old. I have carried on that tradition with my three theological treatises.

Church Fathers, like Augustine, saw truths in ancient Greek philosophy, particularly that of Plato. I see truths in Taoist and Hindu philosophy/theology. After my first university degree, at age 22, I immersed myself in the six great world religions' scriptures. I wrote about this intense two-year period in my book *Writings* in my article "A Theological Memoir." From this period, I began to see Christian truths in Taoist and Hindu philosophy/theology. Henry David Thoreau - one of America's best - wrote, "That age will be rich indeed when those relics which we call Classics, and the still older and more than classic but even less known Scriptures of the nations, shall have still further accumulated, when the Vaticans shall be filled with Vedas and Zendavestas and Bibles, with Homers and Dantes and Shakespeares, and all the centuries to come shall have successively deposited their trophies in the forum of the world. By such a pile we may hope to scale heaven at last (Thoreau, *Walden, Reading*). I - James Thomas Angelidis - am the product and fruit of this now realized prophesied era. Like never before, today, an individual can study the world religions' scriptures and witness common truths among them. All that is needed are discipline and desire.

In the 20th century, the Catholic Church spoke about a theology called "Hierarchy of Truths" to initiate Christian ecumenism and interfaith dialogue.

The Hierarchy of Truths Theology is very real and applicable to Christianity, religion, philosophy and humanity. God - the Great Sower - planted seeds across the world, seeds that took root and grew in the world's religions. Truths can be found in them all; however, what is said about the Jews is true - they were the Chosen People, they were God's Vineyard (Isaiah 5:1-7). For from them grew the True Vine - God's Son Jesus the Christ (Psalm 80:8-19) (John 15:1-17). I am just trying to be one of our Lord's branches and bear fruit for him because I love him so much. I believe my work can help serve God and the world in the economy of Salvation.

God, Jesus and Christian theology are eternal, limitless and unbound. They are so big that much can escape articulation until brought to attention. We see this in "Homoousios" and "Theotokos" theology which developed and blossomed after Jesus. They were unprecedented formulations, but are theologically appropriate. In this way, the theology in my treatises is similar.

The most traditional, parochial and conservative Saint Vincent of Lerins taught us in his *Commonitorium* that "theologians should say things newly without saying new things" (Guarino, *Vincent of Lerins*, 86). My work is a new presentation of traditional theology. There is no new theology in my treatises; rather, an affirmation of old theology presented in a new way (said newly). The deposit is guarded.

- The "Supreme Transformation" theology is based on Saint Melito of Sardis's "analogy" or "preliminary sketch" theology - his prefiguring theology - as it appears in his *On Pascha*.

- The "Agape into Eternity" theology is based on the Trisagion Prayers theology that many Orthodox Christians, like me, pray every morning and every night.

- The "Messiah Jesus" theology is based on Jewish prophetic theology as it appears in the Old Testament.

I spell this out to reassure readers that the theology in my work is not fabricated or an invention and that it is, in fact, within the tradition of the One Holy Catholic and Apostolic Church.

There is nothing new about God or Jesus's natures or the means to Salvation in my three theological treatises. They are observations that are authentic, honest, insightful and true. They illuminate, enlighten, elucidate, unfold, uncover, unearth, disclose, reveal. They are the result of the Holy Spirit's Agape in me. I was compelled to write out of agape for God and neighbor. They are authentic scholarly Scriptural insights. They are progressive explanatory clarifications and are supplementations that add further fullness to Christian theology. *In the Name of Salvation* is meant to save people and unite people with Almighty God by means of traditional theology in a fresh way.

My three theological treatises are not lies, not transgressions, not trespassings, not fabrications, not inventions, not novelties, not adulterations, not corruptions, not distortions, not perversions.

My book *In the Name of Salvation* is a part of the prophecy told to Daniel: "those who are wise shall shine like the brightness of the firmament; and those who turn many to righteousness, like the stars for ever and ever. 4 But you, Daniel, shut up the words, and seal the book, until the time of the end. Many shall run to and fro, and knowledge shall increase" (Daniel 12:3-4). Yes, indeed, knowledge shall increase.

So, I conclude and tell you to not turn away from my works because of the hardness of your hearts. And, do not fear. Open your hearts with the Spirit of Truth. Allow the Spirit of Truth to guide you and you will see truth in my works.

[*In the Name of Salvation*]

WORKS CITED
(in order referenced)

THE SUPREME TRANSFORMATION - WATER INTO WINE

- *Bible*, Revised Standard Version (RSV).
- Lao Tzu. *Tao Te Ching: The Definitive Edition* (trans. by Jonathan Star). New York: Tarcher/Putnam, 2001.
- Lao-Tzu. *Tao Te Ching* (trans. by Stephen Addiss and Stanley Lombardo). Indianapolis: Hackett Publishing Company, 1993.
- Lao Tsu. *Tao Te Ching* (trans. by Gia-Fu Feng and Jane English). New York: Vintage Books, 1989.
- Lao Tzu. *Tao Teh Ching* (trans. by John C.H. Wu). Boston: Shambhala Publications, 1990.
- *World Book Encyclopedia 1966*, "Wine." Chicago: Field Enterprises Educational Corporation, 1965.
- Melito of Sardis. *On Pascha* (trans. by Alistair Stewart-Sykes). Crestwood: St Vladimir's Seminary Press, 2001.

- Toussaint, Stanley D. "The Significance of the First Sign in John's Gospel." *Bibliotheca Sacra*, Jan-Mar 1977: 49-51.

AGAPE INTO ETERNITY
- *Bible*, Revised Standard Version (RSV).
- *Upanishads* (trans. Swami Prabhavananda and Frederick Manchester). New York: Signet Classic, 2002.
- *Bhagavad-Gita* (trans. Swami Prabhavananda and Christopher Isherwood). New York: Signet Classic, 2002.
- Antiochian Orthodox Christian Archdiocese of North America. *A Pocket Prayer Book for Orthodox Christians*. Englewood: Antiochian Orthodox Christian Archdiocese, 1956.
- Kreeft, Peter. *The God Who Loves You*. San Francisco: Ignatius Press, 2004.
- *Nicene Creed*. Greek Orthodox Archdiocese of America.

THE MESSIAH JESUS
- *Bible*, Revised Standard Version (RSV).
- Jennings, Peter. *ABC News Presents The Search for Jesus [DVD]*. ABC News Productions, 2000.

Not cited - though a bibliographical reference:
- Briggs, Charles Augustus. *Messianic Prophecy*. New York: Charles Scribner's Sons, 1886.

IN THE SPIRIT OF TRUTH
- *Bible*, Revised Standard Version (RSV).
- Mathewes, Charles. "Books That Matter: The City of God." *The Great Courses* DVD Course with Guidebook. Chantilly: The Teaching Company, 2016.
- Augustine [Saint]. *The City of God* (ed. and trans. by Marcus Dods). New York: The Modern Library, 1993.
- Angelidis, James Thomas. *Writings*. www.jtangelidis.com: James Thomas Angelidis, 2016; 2017.
- Thoreau, Henry David. *Walden*. New York: Signet Classic, 1942.
- Guarino, Thomas G. *Vincent of Lérins and the Development of Christian Doctrine*. Grand Rapids: Baker Academic, 2013.

[Drawing]

ANNO DOMINI EXPLAINED

JAMES THOMAS ANGELIDIS

First published on www.jtangelidis.com.
Original Copyright 2017 James Thomas Angelidis.
All rights reserved.
(11-9-2017)
- Format edited for *Anthology* -

The following is from my book - *In the Name of Salvation: Three Theological Treatises*, p.88:

Jesus applied Old Testament imagery to his teachings and also used it to illustrate his role as the Messiah. In the Old Testament, Israel is described as God's Vine:

> Psalm 80:8 (RSV)
> Prayer for Israel's Restoration
> To the choirmaster: according to Lilies. A Testimony of Asaph. A Psalm.

8 Thou didst bring a vine out of Egypt [when the Jews were slaves];
thou didst drive out the nations and plant it.
9 Thou didst clear the ground for it;
it took deep root and filled the land.
10 The mountains were covered with its shade,
the mighty cedars with its branches;
11 it sent out its branches to the sea,
and its shoots to the River.
12 Why then hast thou broken down its walls,
so that all who pass along the way pluck its fruit?
13 The boar from the forest ravages it,
and all that move in the field feed on it.
14 Turn again, O God of hosts!
Look down from heaven, and see;
have regard for this vine,
15 the stock which thy right hand planted.[b]
16 They have burned it with fire, they have cut it down;
may they perish at the rebuke of thy countenance!
17 But let thy hand be upon the man of thy right hand,
the son of man whom thou hast made strong for thyself!
18 Then we will never turn back from thee;
give us life, and we will call on thy name!

19 Restore us, O LORD God of hosts!
let thy face shine, that we may be saved!

Jesus identifies himself as the above son of man who sits at the right hand of God. He calls himself the True Vine with his faithful as the branches that bear fruit and that God is the Vinedresser:

> John 15:1 (RSV)
> <u>Jesus the True Vine</u>
> 15 "I am the true vine, and my Father is the vinedresser. 2 Every branch of mine that bears no fruit, he takes away, and every branch that does bear fruit he prunes, that it may bear more fruit. 3 You are already made clean by the word which I have spoken to you. 4 Abide in me, and I in you. As the branch cannot bear fruit by itself, unless it abides in the vine, neither can you, unless you abide in me. 5 I am the vine, you are the branches. He who abides in me, and I in him, he it is that bears much fruit, for apart from me you can do nothing. 6 If a man does not abide in me, he is cast forth as a branch and withers; and the branches are gathered, thrown into the fire and burned. 7 If you abide in me, and my words abide in you, ask whatever you will, and it shall be done for you. 8 By this my Father is glorified, that you bear much fruit, and so prove to be my disciples. 9 As the Father has

loved me, so have I loved you; abide in my love. 10 If you keep my commandments, you will abide in my love, just as I have kept my Father's commandments and abide in his love. 11 These things I have spoken to you, that my joy may be in you, and that your joy may be full. 12 "This is my commandment, that you love one another as I have loved you. 13 Greater love has no man than this, that a man lay down his life for his friends. 14 You are my friends if you do what I command you. 15 No longer do I call you servants,[a] for the servant[b] does not know what his master is doing; but I have called you friends, for all that I have heard from my Father I have made known to you. 16 You did not choose me, but I chose you and appointed you that you should go and bear fruit and that your fruit should abide; so that whatever you ask the Father in my name, he may give it to you. 17 This I command you, to love one another.

* * *

<u>Specific Branches in My Drawing that Bear Fruit</u>:
First Group:
- Peter (of the 12 Apostles)
- James (of the 12 Apostles)
- John (of the 12 Apostles)
- Andrew (of the 12 Apostles)

- Philip (of the 12 Apostles)
- Bartholomew (of the 12 Apostles)
- Thomas (of the 12 Apostles)
- Matthew (of the 12 Apostles)
- James (of the 12 Apostles)
- Thaddaeus (of the 12 Apostles)
- Simon (of the 12 Apostles)
- Matthias (of the 12 Apostles)
- Paul (Apostle to the Gentiles)

Second Group:
- Augustine of Hippo (Church Father)
- John Chrysostom (Church Father)
- Basil of Caesarea (Church Father)
- Gregory of Nazianzus (Church Father)

Last Group:
- Nektarios of Pentapolis (19th century Orthodox Saint)
- Therese of Lisieux (19th century Catholic Saint)

"Anno Domini" Meaning:
- Anno Domini - abbreviated as AD - is Latin for "in the year of the Lord." This is sometimes dubbed the Common Era. The time before this is referred to as BC, which is the abbreviation for "before Christ." This document was written in the year AD 2017.

Angels:

- "For an angel of peace, a faithful guide, a guardian of our souls and bodies, let us ask the Lord" (The Divine Liturgy of Saint John Chrysostom).
- "Encompass us with thy holy Angels, that guided and guarded by them, we may attain to the unity of the faith and to the knowledge of thine unapproachable glory, for thou art blessed unto ages of ages. Amen" (Antiochian Orthodox Christian Archdiocese of North America, Evening Prayers, Prayer of the Hours).

[Drawing]

THE GOOD SHEPHERD KING EXPLAINED

JAMES THOMAS ANGELIDIS

First published on www.jtangelidis.com.
Original Copyright 2017 James Thomas Angelidis.
All rights reserved.
(9-29-2017)
- Format edited for *Anthology* -

Introduction:
"The Good Shepherd King" is an original drawing that accurately captures the way I see the world with Jesus Christ as the central most important figure. This image has been clear in my mind's eye for many years, but I did not draw it until 2016. The illustration is Scripturally sound and it teaches many truths about the world and the Christian faith. The drawing illustrates the following Scriptural teachings…

In Matthew 25:31-46 (RSV), we are taught about The Judgment of the Nations:

"When the Son of man comes in his glory, and all the angels with him, then he will sit on his glorious throne. 32 Before him will be gathered all the nations, and he will separate them one from another as a shepherd separates the sheep from the goats, 33 and he will place the sheep at his right hand, but the goats at the left. 34 Then the King will say to those at his right hand, 'Come, O blessed of my Father, inherit the kingdom prepared for you from the foundation of the world; 35 for I was hungry and you gave me food, I was thirsty and you gave me drink, I was a stranger and you welcomed me, 36 I was naked and you clothed me, I was sick and you visited me, I was in prison and you came to me.' 37 Then the righteous will answer him, 'Lord, when did we see thee hungry and feed thee, or thirsty and give thee drink? 38 And when did we see thee a stranger and welcome thee, or naked and clothe thee? 39 And when did we see thee sick or in prison and visit thee?' 40 And the King will answer them, 'Truly, I say to you, as you did it to one of the least of these my brethren, you did it to me.' 41 Then he will say to those at his left hand, 'Depart from me, you cursed, into the eternal fire prepared for the devil and his angels; 42 for I was hungry and you gave me no food, I was thirsty and you gave me no drink, 43 I was a stranger and you did not welcome me, naked and you did not clothe me, sick and in prison and you did not visit me.' 44 Then they also will answer, 'Lord, when did we see thee hungry or thirsty or a stranger or naked or sick or in prison, and did not minister to thee?' 45 Then he will answer them, 'Truly, I say to you, as you did it not to one of the least of these, you did it not to me.' 46 And they will go away into eternal punishment, but the righteous into eternal life."

<u>In Psalm 23 (RSV), we are taught about The Divine Shepherd:</u>
A Psalm of David.
The Lord is my shepherd, I shall not want;
2 he makes me lie down in green pastures.
He leads me beside still waters;[a]
3 he restores my soul.[b]
He leads me in paths of righteousness[c]
for his name's sake.
4 Even though I walk through the valley of the shadow of death,[d]
I fear no evil;
for thou art with me;
thy rod and thy staff,
they comfort me.
5 Thou preparest a table before me
in the presence of my enemies;
thou anointest my head with oil,
my cup overflows.
6 Surely[e] goodness and mercy[f] shall follow me
all the days of my life;
and I shall dwell in the house of the Lord
for ever.[g]

<u>In John 10:1-18 (RSV), we are taught about Jesus the Good Shepherd:</u>
"Truly, truly, I say to you, he who does not enter the sheepfold by the door but climbs in by another way, that man is a thief and a robber; 2 but he who enters by the door is the shepherd of the sheep. 3 To him the gatekeeper opens; the sheep hear his voice, and he calls his own sheep by name and leads them out. 4 When he has brought out all his own, he goes before them, and the sheep follow him, for they know his voice. 5 A stranger they will not follow, but they will flee from him, for they do not know the voice of strangers." 6 This figure Jesus used with them, but they did not understand what he was saying to them. 7 So Jesus again said to them, "Truly, truly, I say to you, I am the door of the sheep. 8 All who came before me are thieves and robbers; but the sheep did not heed them. 9 I am the door; if any one enters by me, he will be saved, and will go in and out and find pasture. 10 The thief comes only to steal and kill and destroy; I came that they may have life, and have it abundantly. 11 I am the good shepherd. The good shepherd lays down his life for the sheep. 12 He who is a hireling and not a shepherd, whose own the sheep are not, sees the wolf coming and leaves the sheep and flees; and the wolf snatches them and scatters them. 13 He flees because he is a hireling and cares nothing for the sheep. 14 I am the good shepherd; I know my own and my own know me, 15 as the Father knows me and I know the Father; and I lay down my

life for the sheep. 16 And I have other sheep, that are not of this fold; I must bring them also, and they will heed my voice. So there shall be one flock, one shepherd. 17 For this reason the Father loves me, because I lay down my life, that I may take it again. 18 No one takes it from me, but I lay it down of my own accord. I have power to lay it down, and I have power to take it again; this charge I have received from my Father."

<ins>In Matthew 7:13-14 (RSV), we are taught about The Narrow Gate:</ins>
"Enter by the narrow gate; for the gate is wide and the way is easy,[a] that leads to destruction, and those who enter by it are many. 14 For the gate is narrow and the way is hard, that leads to life, and those who find it are few.

<ins>In John 14:6 (RSV), we are taught about Jesus the Way to the Father:</ins>
Jesus said to him, "I am the way, and the truth, and the life; no one comes to the Father, but by me.

<ins>Christian Faith Symbols that Adorn the King's Crown and Identify His Kingdom:</ins>
- Ichthys (aka the "Jesus Fish")
- Chi-Rho (as used by Saint Constantine the Great)
- Alpha and Omega (from Revelation 21, The New Heaven and the New Earth).

Angels:
- "For an angel of peace, a faithful guide, a guardian of our souls and bodies, let us ask the Lord" (The Divine Liturgy of Saint John Chrysostom).
- "Encompass us with thy holy Angels, that guided and guarded by them, we may attain to the unity of the faith and to the knowledge of thine unapproachable glory, for thou art blessed unto ages of ages. Amen" (Antiochian Orthodox Christian Archdiocese of North America, Evening Prayers, Prayer of the Hours).

Conclusion:
At the time of death, we will each have to confront the Cross. And how we react will be a testimony to our eternal fates. The Cross represents Jesus's crucifixion and agape love for us. He is Salvation and if we can weep - like the saints - for the Good Shepherd King - with an agape love lived life - we, too, will be saved and enter His Kingdom and Paradise.

Detail from *The Good Shepherd King*

www.ingramcontent.com/pod-product-compliance
Lightning Source LLC
Chambersburg PA
CBHW070713160426
43192CB00009B/1173